PENGUIN BOOKS

THE RIGHT JOB

Robert O. Snelling, Sr., is Chairman of the Board of Snelling and Snelling, one of the world's largest networks of franchised temporary and permanent employment services, with more than three hundred offices worldwide. In forty years this system has helped over ten million job seekers find the career of their choice.

His previous books include *The Opportunity Explosion*, a best-seller, and *Jobs: What They Are, Where They Are, What They Pay*, coauthored with his wife, Anne M. Snelling, who serves as the company's Vice President of Administration. Robert Snelling was appointed to the 1986 White House Conference on Small Business and served on the U.S. Labor Department's Special Advisory Committee on Employment and Unemployment. He was appointed in 1992 by the President to the National Commission on Employment Policy.

Bob and Anne Snelling have five children, nine grandchildren and live in Dallas, Texas.

THE
RIGHT
JOB

How to Get the Job That's Right for You

REVISED EDITION

Robert O. Snelling, Sr.

PENGUIN BOOKS

PENGUIN BOOKS
Published by the Penguin Group
Penguin Books USA Inc., 375 Hudson Street,
New York, New York 10014, U.S.A.
Penguin Books Ltd, 27 Wrights Lane,
London W8 5TZ, England
Penguin Books Australia Ltd, Ringwood,
Victoria, Australia
Penguin Books Canada Ltd, 10 Alcorn Avenue,
Toronto, Ontario, Canada M4V 3B2
Penguin Books (N.Z.) Ltd, 182–190 Wairau Road,
Auckland 10, New Zealand

Penguin Books Ltd, Registered Offices:
Harmondsworth, Middlesex, England

First published in the United States of America in simultaneous hardcover
and paperback editions by Viking Penguin Inc. 1987
This revised edition published in Penguin Books 1993

1 3 5 7 9 10 8 6 4 2

Grateful acknowledgment is made for permission to reprint the following
copyrighted material:
   Excerpt from "Ac-cent-tchu-ate the Positive" by Harold Arlen & Johnny
Mercer. © 1944 Harwin Music Co. © renewed 1972 Harwin Music Co.
International copyright secured. All rights reserved. Used by permission.

LIBRARY OF CONGRESS CATALOGING IN PUBLICATION DATA
Snelling, Robert O.
The right job.
1. Job hunting. I. Title.
HF5382.7.S64   1987   650.1′4   86-91506
ISBN 0 14 01.7823 6 (revised edition)

Printed in the United States of America
Set in New Baskerville
Designed by Kathryn Parise

To Solomon,
who was inspired by God to write in Proverbs 12:11
"Hard work means prosperity; only a fool idles away his time."

Acknowledgments

My gratitude to:

My wife, Anne, and our very successful children—Bob and Carol, Rick and Sherri, Rusty and Leigh, Bob and Linda, and Krista and Lee, who for years have had to listen to all of the advice in this book on a daily basis.

Our staff, Vi Stettler, Paul Burgdorf, and Ginger Stephens, who helped with research, typed, proofread, and agonized with me when great thoughts had to be cut.

Len Corwen, who researched, wrote, and helped update parts of the book.

Irv Settel, my agent, for his faith in me and his creative ideas.

Our many temporary and permanent Snelling Personnel Services franchisees, managers, recruiters, and Professional Employment Counsellors who encouraged and helped us.

Those tough but willing-to-listen editors who did a great deal more than correct punctuation and syntax. We love them all!

Contents

1 UNDERSTANDING JOB-MARKET DYNAMICS   I

Jobs Galore   3
Who Would Hire Me?   12
Moves Make the Difference   15
Women in the Job Market   17
The Work That Women Do   18
Earnings: A Product of Supply and Demand   20
Moving Up   21
Coping in a Changing World   24
Widen Your Knowledge   27
Success Is in Your Hands   28

2 KNOW YOURSELF   29

What Do You Want out of Life?   30
Out of the Frying Pan   32
Look at Your Life-style   35
Look at the Human Equation   40
Where Do You Want to Live?   42
Involve Your Spouse in All Your Decisions   43
Personal Motivation   45

3 ARE YOU PREPARED?   49

Mental Preparation   53
Family Matters   54

Do You Fear a Job Change?   55
What's Your Attitude?   56
Grade Yourself   58
Are You Physically Prepared?   59
Relating to Others   61
Abilities and Interests   62
Skills   63
What Are Your Credentials?   66
What Do You Do Best?   69

4 MAPPING YOUR JOB CAMPAIGN   **71**

Plan, Then Proceed   72
Count Your Blessings   74
Don't Quit Your Present Job   75
Be a Worker   75
Your Personal Job Plan   76
When to Job Hunt   77
Where the Jobs Are   79
Networking   83
The "Hidden Job Market"   84
Creating Jobs   85
Answering Ads   86
A Direct-Mail Campaign   87
Using the Telephone   89
Personal Visits   96
Stay on Top of Your Job Search   97
Tax Breaks for Job Seekers   98

5 WRITING A WINNING RÉSUMÉ   **100**

Collecting the Data   101
Preparing Your Résumés   103
Seven Deadly Sins   114
Résumé Style   117
Résumé Services   119
Résumé Samples   120
Cover Letters   122

6 USING AN EMPLOYMENT SERVICE 134

Professional Employment Services 135
Services Provided 136
What to Expect from a Professional Employment Counsellor 138
The Personal Interview 140
Choosing Employment Services 144
Pros and Cons 150
Guarantees 153
Other Employment Services 154

7 INTERVIEW STRATEGIES AND SALARY NEGOTIATIONS 161

Preinterview Preparation 161
The Interview 168
After the Interview 182
If You Didn't Get the Offer 184
When You Do Get the Offer 185
Salary Negotiations 187
Would You Hire You? 190
Seven Surefire Job Clinchers 190

8 LIVING HAPPILY EVER AFTER 192

"Who's on First?" 192
Working with Your Boss 194
Getting Ahead: Three Proven Steps for Raises and Promotions 195
Getting a Raise 201
Your Happiness Quotient 202
The Job Outlook for Tomorrow 205
Services Will Flourish 206
Science and Technology 207
A Bright Future 207

9 A BUSINESS OF YOUR OWN 209

Starting a New Business 211
Purchasing an Existing Business 214
Business Brokers 216
Franchising 217

Capital: Where and How to Get It   220
Have You Got What It Takes?   222

SUGGESTED FURTHER READING   **225**

SOURCES OF INFORMATION   **227**

INDEX   **237**

THE
RIGHT
JOB

1

Understanding Job-Market Dynamics

The right job can provide the greatest of life's rewards. Your self-esteem, your economic well-being, your happiness, and the happiness of your family are all tied to being in the right job. Yet, with over 7 percent of the work force changing jobs every month, only some of you are happily moving ahead. Some are marking time. Many are still unhappily searching for the right job.

Before you can find the right job, you must understand the job market and job-market dynamics.

The first point, and perhaps the most important, is that there *are* jobs available, at all levels, from file clerk to company president. Just consider these facts. By the year 2000, according to the U.S. Department of Labor, industry will need over 1 million additional clerks. That's a 30 percent increase. "Who cares?" you ask. "Who wants to be a clerk?" But wait a minute. With all those clerks, industry will also need over 200,000 clerical supervisors and managers, a 21 percent increase over today's numbers. And you can guess what I'm going to say next: Someone has to supervise the supervisors. Somebody has to be the top salesperson, whether in soap or salad dressing, automobiles or amplifiers.

Someone has to design the next can opener, house, high-speed train, shopping center, business plan, filing system, or software breakthrough. Someone, moreover, has to run the department, division, plant, or even the whole company. One of these jobs might be filled by you.

In the next ten years, programmers' positions will increase by over 70 percent, and systems analysts' positions, the next step up the ladder, will grow by over 76 percent. We're looking for another 425,000 secretaries; 150,000 computer operators; 71,000 bank tellers; over 2 million sales workers; and 175,000 accountants and auditors.

It's true, of course, that some job categories will dip during the same decade. The need for stenographers, for instance, will drop by 28 percent and central telephone operators by 30 percent. But what difference does that make? Most of these jobs will still be there. So many new opportunities are opening up, in any event, that displaced employees will be able to find even better jobs than the ones they're leaving.

"Official" unemployment statistics may paint a dismal picture. Stories may circulate about people out of work for long periods, unable to find jobs of any kind. You may even have heard that far-reaching social and technological changes will put many people out of work forever.

For instance, they say that typists will show a decline of 14 percent. Yet you can look at these figures another way. Even with a drop in the need for typists, there will still be almost a million typists' jobs available. A job as a typist now carries different titles; word processors, computer operators, and PC pros and specialists, now found in virtually every major company with an automated office, are typists with upgraded tasks and wages.

You can find job success. You can get a better job, double your income, move ahead more rapidly, live where you want to live, do things that you have only dreamed of doing. But you must dare to believe that you can. You must take the steps we show you. The beaten path is for beaten people. Follow us and learn how the winners break new ground.

Jobs Galore

Do you want a job? You can find one.

There is a job, and a future, waiting for you, as long as you really want to work. There are opportunities galore, as long as you make the effort to seek them out. There are tested ways to success in the job market: This book will show you those ways.

You may be seeking your very first job. Or you may be, for the moment, between jobs. Perhaps you have a job you would like to leave, or you are interested in exploring a new career field. Maybe you are reentering the job market after a long time. Or it may be that you're doing very well at your present job but would like to move onward and upward at a faster pace. Whatever your current situation, there is not only a job out there for you but a career opportunity.

You may be in the deep South, in a Midwestern suburb, or in a plush office in the heart of Manhattan. You may want to consider moving—and we'll talk about relocation later in this book —but, be assured, there is a job for you. All over this country, jobs are going begging for salespeople, computer operators, secretaries, engineers, accountants, paralegals, word processors, medical technicians, managers, and more.

First, however, let's get into a positive frame of mind for job hunting by dispelling the negative myths you may have heard from the gloom-and-doomers all around us:

- Myth 1: Population growth and automation mean cutthroat competition for available jobs.
- Myth 2: New jobs, where they exist, will all be either highly technological or no-growth entry level.
- Myth 3: You've got to be young, white, male, and well educated to land a good job.

Not one of these myths is true. Let's examine them one at a time.

Myth 1: Population growth and automation mean cutthroat competition for available jobs.

It's been argued, loud and long, that our growing population must inevitably reduce our standard of living, as more and more people call on fewer and fewer resources. Yet it can also be shown that population growth creates economic opportunities. With the increased demand created by more people, new business opportunities open up, says noted economist Julian L. Simon of the University of Illinois. With new and expanded businesses, more jobs are created.

Look at this situation in personal terms: If you live in a community that is growing, with an influx of newcomers, there are bound to be increased job opportunities. If the newcomers are young adults with school-age children, those children will need clothing, love fast food, and want after-school and weekend entertainment. If the newcomers are of retirement age with plenty of leisure time, they will be interested in leisure-time activities. If you are imaginative and industrious, you'll find a way to tap these growing markets, either by creating a business of your own or by working for someone else who has done just that.

The key is meeting a need. Mary Kay Cosmetics began as one woman's idea twenty years ago. Today, still a relative newcomer among America's corporate giants, it provides jobs and career opportunities for hundreds of thousands of people. New ideas, and the people who implement those ideas, create new jobs and new job opportunities. Whether you generate a new idea or help to fulfill the ideas of others, you too can tap these opportunities.

America's core "smokestack" industries may be reducing in size, as steel plants and automobile manufacturers and others cut back on operations. If this is a continuing trend, then where are all the new jobs to be found? They are to be found with companies meeting a continuing consumer need. They are often to be found in companies providing services rather than goods. And they are to be found, in general, in smaller companies. Massive job growth is taking place in small firms, according to a Dun and Bradstreet survey, with most new employment opportunities in companies employing from one to nineteen workers. These are the small businesses seeing opportunities in population growth and technology shift and moving to meet those opportunities.

The number and variety of jobs in this country have increased at an unprecedented rate over the last decade. Every time the jobless rate drops in one section of the country or another, employers report difficulty in filling certain jobs.

Unemployment has been up in recent years, according to official government statistics. Yet the number of jobs in this country is expected to increase over the next ten years, in spite of a recession, increased population pressures from the baby boom, and continued loss of heavy-industry jobs.

In the next four to five years, as the number of high school and college graduates diminishes, employers will be fighting to attract them. This shortage inevitably means a future need for middle and top management people. The competition for good people will be fierce, and for outstanding people it will be almost unbelievable. If you want to work, and take some trouble to find the right job, you can benefit from this competition.

Myth 2: New jobs, where they exist, will all be either highly technological or no-growth entry level.

Persistent negative thinking about job hunting in the 1990s is found among men and women adopting a science-fiction viewpoint: the premise is that we have moved into such a high-tech state of affairs that there are no jobs left for ordinary mortals with less than advanced technological training. According to this thinking, you can't get a job unless you can work with robots or, at the very least, know four computer languages. This is not so! Not only have most of the new jobs of the last few years been created in small and medium-sized businesses, says management expert Peter Drucker, but practically all the jobs are in low-tech or no-tech fields.

What's hot right now? Service jobs of all kinds, from salespeople to secretaries, are showing great demand. Service jobs in new and growing industries, from financial services to health services, are growing especially rapidly. What's going to be hot in the near future? According to forecaster Marvin Cetron in an interview in *Success* magazine, there will be an even greater demand for telephone salespeople, social workers to work with the elderly, energy conservation specialists, emergency medical technicians, specialists to work with the handicapped, respiratory therapists, and industrial hygiene technicians, to name a few.

How could this affect you? If you're smart, you'll look for job opportunities in fields that are growing to meet the changing economic scene. The deregulation of financial industries, for example, will prompt a great and growing need for workers at all levels to create, market, and service new competitive financial products. Or you might look to businesses growing to meet changing life-style needs. Our national fervor for keeping fit has spawned health clubs, weight loss and nutrition centers, and a lively market for exercise garments. Entrepreneurs and those who work for them are winners in today's job war. You can be among the winners. Just don't limit your thinking.

Secretarial jobs, for example, are sometimes considered entry level and dead end. Yet not only are skilled executive secretaries in great demand, but when they also include the responsibilities of administrative officers, secretarial positions are a great spot for learning about the internal workings of a company and a great launching pad for other jobs. Of the twenty-five executives whose careers are profiled in the book *The Managerial Woman*, twenty-three started out as secretaries. One example is Carol Taber, now publisher of *Working Woman* magazine.

Sales jobs, by and large, don't require a college degree or special training. If you have what it takes for a career in sales, opportunities abound. Look, for example, at a job selling insurance or at a job as an industrial sales representative. Think about a job selling products to consumers or a job selling services to businesses.

The job market is constantly changing. On the way out: telephone installers, farm laborers, and railroad car repairers. On the way in: data processing machine mechanics, paralegal personnel, computer programmers and operators, physical therapists, financial service workers, employment interviewers, fast-food restaurant workers, childcare workers, and nurses. Still think you need extensive education? Some of these workers-in-demand will need special training, it's true, but what about these up-and-coming jobs, all offering good pay: airline reservations agent, computer operator (despite the technological sound, many computer operators have only on-the-job training), mail carrier, or bus or truck driver? Twenty occupations will account for 40 percent of the new jobs during the next decade, according to the U.S. Department of Labor, Bureau of Labor Statistics, and only two of these occupations (accounting and secondary teaching) will require a college degree. These statistics could make you think twice about spending $75,000 or so on a college education. You could take this money, start or buy a business, and wind up providing jobs to other people.

Yes, jobs are lost to technology. But jobs are also gained. High-technology occupations will grow 83 percent by the year 2005, according to the U.S. Department of Labor. Most of these new jobs in high-tech industries will require no more than a high school diploma. Look at the growth area of communications. The telephone and telephone workers are now just one small element in this wide-ranging technological revolution. With telephone calls bounced by satellite, businesses linked by computers and mail transmitted electronically, the opportunities are virtually endless. The same can be said of a whole host of other fields. Look at entertainment. Who would have dreamed a few short years ago of a job selling video cassette recorders or producing community news for cable TV?

Today there are over 17,500 job definitions listed in the government's *Dictionary of Occupational Titles*. They range from abalone diver to Zyglo inspector. What's a "Zyglo," you ask? I didn't know either. So I looked it up. A Zyglo is a trade name for a penetrating fluorescent solution used to detect defects at or near the surface of nonmagnetic ferrous metals. (It's one job category that probably doesn't offer opportunities for many job seekers!)

Despite this extensive listing of job classifications, most people are aware of only a relative handful, thereby missing out on possibly productive opportunities. To expand your own mental horizons, just think about all that's involved in putting a box of cornflakes on your breakfast table. Trying to trace that everyday box of cornflakes to its beginnings will take you on a world journey: to the pulpwood forests of Canada, the sugarcane fields of South America, oil wells in the Middle East, the grain fields of the Midwest, and the skyscrapers of New York City. It's like picking up a peanut only to find an elephant holding the peanut, backed by a whole line of elephants strung out trunk to tail.

You might say, "Oh, my cornflakes started on a farm in Iowa." No, they didn't. The trail goes back much farther than that. Consider the tractor that the farmer in Iowa used. That tractor may be made from steel produced in a mill in Pittsburgh, which in turn got its ore from mines in Minnesota. Then there are the mining equipment, the ore ships, and the trains to carry the ore to Pittsburgh. The tractor itself includes parts of glass, copper, rubber, cork, and plastic, parts manufactured in many places.

The box that contains your cornflakes was made from paperboard made from trees; the trees were planted, then harvested, and trucks, saws, mills, and equipment played a role in making that paperboard. The box carries messages that had to be printed; here we have another set of equipment and—the point of this whole story—another set of workers. Along the entire path that your cornflakes travel to your table, in fact, are thousands and thousands of jobs. They range from planting the seed to selling the tractor, from baking the cornflakes and packaging the cereal to transporting it from manufacturer to wholesaler to retailer to customer. And don't forget the advertising copy—writers and artists who make you want to buy that particular brand of cornflakes, the bankers who loaned money to the manufacturers, the companies who insure the people and the equipment and the buildings. Just think of all the job opportunities along the path of a box of cornflakes! At least one of those jobs, entry level or above, could be right for you. And every one of those jobs, entry level or not, has growth potential. It all depends on what you make of opportunity.

Just because your skills are no longer in demand is no reason to head for the unemployment line or the welfare office. You can move ahead, today, into exciting new fields. All it takes is a little imagination, faith, and the willingness to work.

Every day we hear the frustrated cry of job seekers: "How can I get a job or get a start when every company I talk to wants someone with experience?" The problem in most cases is not the lack of experience. It is a lack of knowing how to set your goals, approach the job market, and land the job. We can show you thousands, no, hundreds of thousands, of résumés of individuals who jumped from one field to another, who moved into a position of higher responsibility and authority without ever having had one day's experience in that field or particular job.

If you stop for a moment and think about it, it just doesn't make sense to say that all the companies insist on experience. Anyone who has experience had to get it somewhere, and America's companies have done an absolutely fantastic job of hiring inexperienced people and teaching them to do the tasks that needed to be done to create the complex society in which we live today. It wasn't our government, it wasn't our schools or universities, as good as they are, it was American companies that took those neophytes and taught them their business and gave them the experience they needed to get the job done.

Here's an interesting example: An individual received his bachelor's degree in physics but couldn't find a job in that field, so he took a position as a high school mathematics teacher. Then, after two years of teaching calculus, algebra, trigonometry, and geometry, he became a programmer with a small steel-manufacturing firm. After three years there he was able to move to another company as a physicist, and then, interestingly enough, after three years on that job he moved to another firm as a senior engineer. There within a two-year period he moved into a group leader's job, and, at last report (the story isn't ended!), to a project manager's job. This individual has held four different positions, and not one of the positions provided the experience needed for the next job.

Companies do recognize personal skills and abilities and are willing to try people in positions they have never held before. If you are with a firm that, for one reason or another, has not recognized your abilities or has you pigeonholed, then you are going to have to consider, as these individuals did, moving to another firm offering that next step up the ladder.

With or without lengthy experience, with or without an advanced degree, with or without special training, there are more than enough jobs to go around. At Snelling, we have many more job openings than we can fill. And these are jobs of every kind: entry level, managerial, secretarial, sales, professional, and technical. We know you can find a job.

Myth 3: You've got to be young, white, male, and well educated to land a good job.

"They won't hire me; I'm too old." "I can't get a job; I'm black." "There's no way they'll hire a woman." Do you subscribe to this kind of defeatist thinking? Don't!

There are laws in this country that prevent discrimination on the grounds of age, race, and sex. More important, there are simply too many employers needing too many employees. These employers aren't going to cut off their noses to spite their faces; they're not going to diminish the pool of good workers by closing the doors on anyone. If you sincerely believe you can do the job, go after it. You stand as good a chance as anyone else.

Older women, for example, might think they have two strikes against them: They're "old," whatever that means, and they're female. Yet we know from experience that employers are delighted to hire mature women. Employers know that mature women, whose children are in school or on their own, are among the most stable, most dedicated of workers. The same is true of divorced women, of any age, who must support their families; they take their jobs very seriously and make very good employees. Employers know this. Women have to know it too and have the self-confidence it takes to go after the jobs they want.

Older men, especially those at upper salary levels and with long years at one company, sometimes have difficulty finding a new position. Yet here too many employers are delighted to recognize the value of experience. The older worker may have to take a cut in pay to get started in a new field, but that willingness to adapt can pay off handsomely in the long run.

You say you're handicapped because you don't have a college degree? Nonsense! Look at the man we placed at a hamburger franchise. He didn't have a college degree—he didn't even start college—but his natural abilities shone through. It wasn't long before he was named night manager, then day manager, then, after some time, he ran twelve hamburger stands. Not bad for a man with "no" education!

You've given up because you can't work full-time, and part-time jobs are impossible to find? It may take a little more effort on your part, a little more imagination, but employers need people so badly today that they have become increasingly flexible. There are now more part-time job opportunities, even shared-time opportunities, where two workers handle a single job.

Our files at Snelling are full of inspirational stories of workers who thought they were handicapped in their job searches because they were older or female or part of a minority group, until we showed them differently. When a New Jersey company needed a mail clerk, for example, they didn't care about the mail clerk's age, but they did want someone who could also repair machinery; the company was delighted with the retired postal worker sent along by our Morristown office. At the other end of the United States, in another familiar scenario, a woman who had spent twenty-six years as a homemaker approached one of our California offices for placement. She couldn't type, but our Professional Employment Counsellor asked if she had handled the household budget, gave her a math test to confirm her ability, and placed her as a cashier in a drugstore.

Even those who start out without a command of the English language can, if they're willing to work hard (a prerequisite for any job!), find a job and move ahead. Look at the Taiwanese immigrant who came here at the age of twenty-one, not speaking a word of English. He pumped gasoline for two dollars an hour, worked fourteen hours a day, saved his money, learned English, and enrolled at Syracuse University to study metallurgy. When we met, during the course of an airplane trip, he was twenty-nine years old, working for IBM, and on his way to address a business seminar in Florida.

The opportunities, in short, are out there. But you've got to be willing to grab opportunity when it comes your way. It may come with a lower paycheck than you'd like to have, but if it offers advancement, look at that job as a foot on the ladder of success. It may come with a different title than you thought you wanted, but you have to learn to look beyond job titles to what a job really entails. It may come in a different field, but willingness to try that new field may mean success. It may mean moving, and it may mean that you'll have to work extra hard.

If you don't want to move—after all, you have roots in your community—tell yourself that you must look at new frontiers, wherever they may be, in order to get the job you want (or sometimes to get any job). You say that you have to have the "right" job or no job at all? Maybe you need to redefine what the "right" job is. We have placed industrial equipment salespeople who make better money than many engineers we've placed. We know restaurant counter workers who have learned the business the hard way, bought roadside fast-food franchises, and are building fine businesses while making a good income. You say you don't want to work that hard? While Abraham Lincoln's story of laboring by day and studying law by firelight at night may sound amusingly old-fashioned to too many people today, that's a spirit that survives in the best of us. How many jobs did Lincoln take that he didn't like in order to get where he wanted to go? How many times was he a miserable failure at everything he tried until finally he landed the biggest job in the country? Don't laugh. Following Lincoln's example still pays off.

We can't all work at our ideal jobs. Most people probably don't. But untold thousands adjust to the unwanted job to keep afloat while planning a change to a more congenial way of life. If they didn't, our civilization would collapse. You may not, the first time out, find a perfect job. But you can find a job. It may mean that you will have to move to another part of the United States. It does mean that you have to be willing to do any honest work you can do, no matter how hard. And it means that you will accept the going minimum wage for that kind of work—not forever, but to get started.

The Bill of Rights offers no protection to the ego. It gives us the freedom to pursue happiness. It doesn't guarantee that society will bring you a neatly wrapped package of happiness and drop it in your lap. You've got to do your own pursuing.

Who Would Hire Me?

As job seekers, it's easy to get wrapped up in our immediate needs. An important part of job-market dynamics, however, is understanding employer needs. Lest we forget, these are the people who pay our salaries. These are the people who borrow the money to invest, to make business grow, to provide jobs for us. If we keep employers and their needs uppermost in our minds when thinking about what makes the job market tick, then we will be a long way toward finding the career opportunity we want.

That career opportunity may be in a large company or a small one. It may be through an advertised job or in a position the employer didn't even recognize until you came along. It may be with someone who demands training and experience or with someone eager to have you and willing to provide the training you need. Employers want people, are begging for people, and are even willing to create jobs for the right people. In one such case, a woman came to us who had run the office of a court officer who was getting ready to retire. We sent her to a company providing court reporters. That company wasn't actively looking for employees, but we knew they were growing and could use a good person. Sure enough, the applicant was hired for an administrative position at a good $3,000 over her last salary. Good employment services can tap this hidden job market. We'll be teaching you how to do the same thing for yourself.

Over 80 percent of all jobs fall into this "hidden" job market. That means that they are not advertised in the newspaper, they are not listed with an employment service, there's no Help Wanted sign in the window, but the jobs are there and can be tapped. Sometimes they're right within the company you're already working for. A prime example of this is Lee Iacocca, Chrysler's dynamic president. He was a graduate engineer but realized, soon after joining the Ford Motor Company, that he wanted to move to a marketing or sales position, that he wanted to work with people instead of with machinery, and that he wanted to be where the action was. Did Ford make this switch easy for him? No, they thought he was crazy. But they did let him go, on his own, to look throughout Ford for a sales job. He traveled all over the country to find one, and finally wound up in Chester, Pennsylvania, working at a low-level desk job in fleet sales. The point here is that this job was not advertised, not even throughout Ford Motor Company; Iacocca literally had to create the job on his own and talk someone into hiring him for the job he had created.

Big companies can provide opportunity. They can also stifle growth in more ways than one and be what we call big company burial grounds. Lee Iacocca didn't let himself get buried at Ford. When he later took over the helm at Chrysler Corporation, he unearthed a lot of outstanding people who had been buried. How does this burial happen? It's a form of corporate hardening of the arteries, a system for maintaining the status quo. It happens when people stagnate, when they become comfortable in the jobs they hold and expect those beneath them to stay comfortable too. People who won't let themselves be buried are the ones who make the most of opportunity for themselves and who create opportunity for you. When they move on, up, and out, their jobs open up for you.

We've often seen this happen. We placed hundreds of graduating electrical engineers with a large electronics firm. Within six months, some of those engineers came back to us looking for another job. When we asked them why, they told us that they had been there for six months, were pulling down paychecks, but they didn't have an office or a staff or enough work to do. That's almost akin to being buried before you're dead. If you understand this and carry the knowledge with you when you're looking at jobs, you can compare job opportunities and make sure that you don't wind up in one of these nifty little cemetery plots.

Small businesses provide another form of opportunity, along with a special kind of risk. If you have read the Dun and Bradstreet figures on bankruptcy, you might be afraid to join any kind of start-up operation. Fifty percent of all restaurants fail within their first year; 90 percent fail within five years. Other types of new businesses have similarly dismal failure rates. Nonetheless, the kind of experience you can get working for a small company, even if it later goes out of business, can never be duplicated in ten years of working for a large company. In a small company you get to do a little bit of everything. You get invaluable experience. You learn how to work in an environment that is tight with a buck. And you learn to produce under pressure. It's great experience. And, of course, not all new companies fail. Just think where you'd be today if you'd hooked your wagon to the star of Apple Computer when it was new and unknown.

Small companies, according to the Small Business Administration, can take credit for adding almost a million new jobs to the nation's economy over a two-year span. Small businesses are the leading force of job creation, during times of both economic recession and economic recovery; they employ almost half of the nation's private sector, nonfarm workers. More than half a million new businesses, most of them small, are started every year. Many small businesses, of course, are limited to the owner and perhaps an employee or two. But 40 percent of small businesses, according to the Heller-Roper Small Business Barometer, expect to add to their payrolls in the near future.

You might think about owning your own business. If you do, the last chapter in this book is a bonus section just for you. When it comes to starting a business, as that chapter will describe in detail, you may think in terms of buying a franchise or starting a business of your own. But there's another choice. Be alert to job-market dynamics and you may find yourself being propositioned in an interview. What we mean is that the individual who owns the business and is interviewing you for a job may be subtly telling you that if you work hard, learn the business, and take an interest in it, then the owner might just be willing to sell it to you in four or five years. The key to this is that many people who want to sell their businesses cannot find someone to make an outright cash purchase, so they look for someone who will pay some cash down and pay the rest out of the business's earnings. Their greatest fear in this situation is that the new owner won't know how to run the business properly, will run it into the ground, and they will never get the payout. But they would have a great deal more confidence in someone like you, someone who has worked for them for a few years and learned the business inside out. Be alert to these opportunities, because such an owner may be willing to sell you the business with a very small down payment. If this happens to you, and if you can seize the challenge and make the most of it, it will be a win-win situation for everyone.

Moves Make the Difference

Many examples of successful job seeking, as you've probably noticed, involve people moving from job to job. Now, there's nothing wrong with starting out in a good company, staying there, forging your career, and moving ahead with that company;

there's nothing wrong with this path so long as you are moving ahead and meeting your career goals. But if you find yourself bottlenecked, pigeonholed, or just simply overlooked when promotions roll around, then you must consider making a move. In some cases you'll look at a lateral move. In some cases it may even be a demotion in either position or pay that lets you start up the ladder again somewhere else, in a new company or even in a new field. You must be willing to consider these various options if you are seeking greater career rewards.

An example that comes vividly to mind is one of my own close friends who had worked in management for a major oil company since graduating from college as a chemical engineer. Another division wanted him, but because of company policy requiring the permission of his present manager, he could not take the job. To him, it was a dilemma and a frustrating experience because his future was at stake. To us, it was a simple problem of logistics. We took him out of his firm and placed him with another firm for one year in an excellent job. He could have stayed on and moved ahead with that firm in fact, but that was not his objective. He wanted to return to his old firm but in the new division, coming in from outside. The ploy worked perfectly; today he is president of that division.

Sometimes it is necessary to move to another firm and stay there. After seven years with a major corporation, an employee realized that the company either did not see his potential or did not feel that he was qualified for management. He moved to a new firm and within four years was promoted to plant manager. Today he is director of manufacturing of a $70 million division employing more than 450 people; he earns over $75,000 plus bonuses and stock options.

There is a great difference between job hopping and "career pathing." The man in the above example had to move to another company in order to fulfill his own career objectives. Sometimes a move is necessary in order to fulfill an employer's needs. Companies looking for programmers, for instance, want people with experience in several companies and on varied equipment; this brings new insight to their problems and gives them more for their money. Eventually, of course, moving from job to job reaches a point of diminishing returns. Before then, though, it increases your skills and experience and abilities so that you are prepared to move upward. Later on we'll discuss in greater depth the pros and cons of moving and show you how to make an intelligent decision when confronted with a choice. This is especially necessary when a recruiter calls to tell you about a great job waiting for you. If you have done your homework in advance, developed your own career objectives, and thought about moving in terms of those objectives, then you'll be ready to respond.

Women in the Job Market

Now hold on there, men, don't skip this section. It has serious but positive implications for your future. There's no doubt that the increase in the number of working women is altering our national economy and having a tremendous effect on the job market. Over half of all women now hold paying jobs. By the year 2000, when the U.S. Department of Labor expects three out of every five women to be working outside the home, these women will represent fully two-thirds of the growth in the overall labor market.

This surge of women into the workplace is perhaps the single most outstanding phenomenon of this century, as significant as the industrial revolution. Women have always worked, of course, usually at least as hard as their husbands. But that work has seldom been paid. If you look back to when we were an agrarian society, you'll find that women (and children too) carried a full load right alongside the men of the family. They tended animals, grew vegetables, made the family's clothes, tended the children, and worked in the fields. Men and women and children worked without wages side by side to sustain the family unit. The industrial revolution, which redefined work as something that was performed for wages outside the home, changed the picture insofar as women were concerned. Since women had to make a choice between earning wages and caring for their families at home, some women began to stay home. Many women, often because of financial need (the same reason many of today's women hold jobs), went into factories alongside their husbands and, often, their children.

Women have always worked, and large numbers of women have always worked outside the home. But rising affluence made it possible for many men to support their families with a single salary while their wives remained at home raising children. Women did enter the labor force in the thousands during World War II, but when men returned from the war and were once again available to fill those jobs, the women returned to their homes.

Today the world has changed once again. Many women want to work for fulfillment, for the same rewards that men receive. Many women, and their families, simply need the money that working brings. According to the U.S. Department of Labor, a rising standard of living combined with inflation is the greatest motivation for women to work outside their homes. A wife's additional income frequently provides not only extra money for vacations, luxuries, and children's education, it also frequently makes it possible for the family to maintain a middle-class standard of living. Our high divorce rate means that many women must work to support themselves and their children. The death rate among older men, combined with inadequate retirement income, has sent many older women back to the job market as well.

The Work That Women Do

Not only do more women work, more women work at an ever-wider variety of jobs. In 1880, 86.3 percent of all women workers were employed in just ten occupations, including domestic workers, dressmakers, agricultural workers, cotton- and woolen-mill machine operators, teachers, and restaurant and hotel workers. Today, while slightly over half of all women workers are still employed in twenty traditional "women's occupations," including teacher, nurse, and beautician, there are some women working in almost every occupation. Women repair telephones, install machinery, fly airplanes, provide medical care, and manage businesses.

We still hear a great deal about women being relegated to jobs as secretaries, teachers, and nurses. We also hear that even when women occupy traditional male jobs and even when women move into management their salaries are often below those of men. In part this is due to discrimination. In part it is because an ever-upward career path is short-circuited by time out to raise a family or by the expectation that a woman would give up her job to follow her husband on his corporate moves. Today many women continue their careers while raising their children, and men may follow their wives' career relocations. Today too employers recognize that women are committed to careers. With this recognition, women are moving into management and into high salary brackets in a wide range of occupations. Our own firm has found that women make outstanding Professional Employment Counsellors; they also make top-notch managers and owners of our franchises across the country.

Women may continue to have an in-and-out pattern of participation in the labor force, with time off to care for children. But with a trend toward later marriage and later childbearing, young women are increasingly likely to start career building before taking time off. They are also likely to take less time off. Their mothers, meanwhile, who may have been at home for some years, are more and more likely to reenter the labor force.

If you are one of these reentering women, you may feel that you have nothing to offer an employer. You may feel that no employer could find anything useful in someone who's been conversing with seven-year-olds, baking brownies for the Cub Scouts, and coping with ring-around-the-collar. You would be wrong. Look at it this way. If you've been successfully running a four- or five- or six-person household, you must be well organized and skilled as an administrator. If you've been getting children and husband to pitch in and do what needs to be done, you're also skilled as a negotiator, talented in the vital area of interpersonal communication. (We placed one former housewife with a national catalogue company in a newly created position as public relations coordinator, based solely on her skills in communication.)

Look at yourself as family budget maker and bookkeeper. Identify yourself as a mediator and settler of conflicts. Recognize that homemaking involves planning, scheduling, expediting, and decision making, all of which are useful skills in the job marketplace.

Then look beyond your home. Have you been involved in your community, running church or civic or political affairs? If you've been a fund-raiser for the PTA, you've learned how to approach people for money. If you've been treasurer for the Girl Scouts, you've kept books and been fiscally accountable. If you've organized a church fair, you've run a business enterprise. Don't belittle these things that you've done on the home front. They're all important to your community. And, more important in your job search, they've all helped to develop the skills and talents you can bring to an employer.

Women, young and old, are definitely moving ahead on the job front. What does this mean to you men? It means that you will face more competition from women for the opportunities you are seeking. It also means that, if you are smart, you will hire capable women and learn to work with and for women. Working together, both men and women can move forward.

Earnings: A Product of Supply and Demand

What kind of money can you expect to earn? A lot depends on the profession you select. If money is your sole object (the right job will offer many other satisfactions as well), then pick yourself a job in a high-growth field and just let the normal, natural growth of the field move you up into management and into the salary, perks, and benefits that accompany a management job. The field of computer maintenance and repair is a good example. By the year 2000 we are going to need more than 250,000 of these people. If you start in that field right now, do a good job, and show just a little bit of initiative, you will quickly be moved into management, ready to train and supervise all those new people who will be hired. We know one young man who went to school to study computer technology and repair and was hired before graduation. He was sent to the company's headquarters before he could even pick up his diploma. As soon as he was trained, he was sent into the field as a supervisor of four technicians. The same thing can happen to you—if you pick the right field.

If you don't look ahead to projected demand, it may be a

different story. If you decide to enter the field of drafting, for instance, you should know in advance that your climb up the career ladder is likely to be slow, regardless of your abilities, because the growth rate in drafting over the next decade is going to be less than 2 percent. In banking and insurance, by contrast, credit clerks will increase by 54 percent; in medicine, medical assistants will grow by almost 70 percent; and again, in computers, programmers will grow by over 75 percent, and computer operators by 76 percent.

By and large, salaries are related to the economic equation of supply and demand. Where employers need workers, the demand is great. Where there aren't enough workers to fill the demand, the supply is limited. If you are one of those workers, you will be in demand. It's very simple.

Of course there are exceptions to every rule. A company situated where living and commuting costs are high may pay higher salaries than one where living is relatively inexpensive and commuting is easy. A company in a high-premium area where people want to live and work can pay lower salaries and still attract good people. Competitive skills affect your wages. Unions can affect them too. As you move into the job market, for the first time or as a repeater, an understanding of job-market dynamics will be very useful.

Moving Up

Is the road to America's executive suites open to all? Is a superior education a deciding factor? Will hard work and long hours guarantee success? Or is knowing the right people the key to reaching the top?

To get the answers to these questions, we conducted a study of applicants who answered an advertisement placed by a major corporation in a national newspaper. The title of the position was chief executive officer, and the salary offered was $250,000 a year. The results revealed some intriguing facts. If there was one characteristic evident throughout the more than six hundred résumés received through the advertisement, it was the diversity of education, experience, and background. In a large number of cases, the candidate's field of study bore little or no relation to the kind of job they currently held. Several who had worked themselves up to high-level positions had only a high school education.

Thirty-eight percent of the respondents were presidents or CEOs. The rest were executive vice presidents, vice presidents, general managers, or directors. Here is the breakdown.

President or CEO	38%
Executive VP	33%
Manager or director	23%
Self-employed	6%

What fields did the CEOs come from?

Finance	26%
Operations	25%
Sales & marketing	21%
Engineering & technical	10%
Manufacturing	10%
Law	8%

It's not surprising that with today's corporate emphasis on the bottom line, those with financial backgrounds led the pack, with operations and sales and marketing a close second and third.

In evaluating the work records of all the candidates, we discovered that 74 percent of them changed jobs frequently as they moved up the ladder, and 27 percent changed careers at least once.

What role did education play? We found that the candidates' degrees and choice of studies ran the gamut. Here are the statistics.

Accounting & finance	19%
Business administration	18%
Marketing	16%

Engineering & technical	14%
Liberal arts	14%
Law	8%
Economics	7%
Communications	4%

About 27 percent earned an MBA or a master's, and many held more than one degree. Some attended college without graduating, and a few went no further than high school.

What brought these people to the zenith of their careers? Where did they start? When did they change direction? How many jobs did they have, and how did they know where to look?

You can be sure of one thing: Companies are continually on the lookout for top managers, leaders who never stop learning, who are willing to accept new challenges and turn obstacles into opportunities, and who have the motivation and the drive to reach new heights. The people you are going to read about here grabbed the opportunities dropped at their feet, eagerly took on added responsibility, and accomplished great things. Education varied broadly. Degrees included finance, English, economics, accounting, computer science, engineering, marketing, history, business administration, law. What they all had in common was the ability to recognize opportunity, the willingness to accept challenges, and the determination to overcome obstacles.

For example, here is the work history of an individual who received a degree in journalism, spent a year in law school, and then wound up in Vietnam for two years. Hardly an auspicious beginning for a career. Upon his discharge, without experience or contacts, he took the first job he could find with a large, well-known brokerage firm. He stayed for two years, just long enough to decide that he wanted to make a career in finance. Hoping to broaden his experience and using the knowledge he gained, he obtained a job with a large bank and found himself in their import and export department, where he spent the next four years learning and doing.

Then came a major shift. Using his training in finance and banking, he joined a world-class engineering and construction company, part of a huge, multinational holding company, as its assistant treasurer. His ability and dedication to his work brought him to the attention of another division, a manufacturing company, which appointed him assistant treasurer. Two years later he was tapped to become vice president and treasurer responsible for acquisitions. A short time after that he wound up as assistant treasurer of the holding company itself, earning in excess of $200,000 per year. Not bad for a man with an undistinguished education who got off to a sputtering start.

Coping in a Changing World

According to Alvin Toffler, the prophetic author of *Future Shock*, the world is not only changing, but it is changing at an increasingly faster tempo. This trend toward accelerating change is no more evident than in the area of an individual's life's work. Change is occurring so fast that it's hard to predict where the opportunities in your field will be, or whether you will even have a field five or ten years from now. There is no such thing as job security anymore. Traditionally a career followed a more or less fixed path, in which a person had a single occupation and moved up through periodic promotions and salary increases. This was often accomplished under the auspices of a lone employer, or at most two or three. Employee loyalty plus a paternal attitude on the part of the employer, for better or worse, was the norm.

Today company loyalty no longer motivates upwardly mobile people to stay on the job. This change in workplace ethics is due in part to the explosion in new technologies and the accelerated expansion of business, resulting in the proliferation of new industries and new job opportunities. Employers' attitudes toward their work force have also changed. Mergers, buyouts, and the global control of commerce loosened the traditional bond between most employers and employees. This means that you can no longer afford to sit still and wait for opportunities to come to you. You have to search them out on your own. The next two cases prove that it is not necessary to stay with the same job or even the same industry to reach the top.

The first, after receiving his MBA, started out in food sales for a Fortune 500 company. After four years he switched to a large consumer products company as a sales manager. Two years later, realizing that he had reached a plateau and would have to move out to move up, he went to work for a leading consulting firm, which brought him into contact with his next employer, a large manufacturing company. Within two years he was promoted to group vice president, and three years later, at age forty-five, he was made president and CEO of the firm, earning $250,000 plus.

Here's another example of someone who made several sharp turns in his career before he hit the jackpot. His BA was in pre-law. He then ran a family business for five years, which he sold in order to provide his parents with financial security.

After returning to college for his MBA, he was hired by a major oil company as a financial analyst. After five years he rose to the position of senior financial analyst. From there he moved to a lighting manufacturing company as manager of planning and was promoted to vice president and controller. He was recruited away by a manufacturer of retail store fixtures, where he is now earning $220,000 as a vice president and chief operating officer at the ripe old age of forty.

Now let's look at some who made the grade by staying in their own fields. The first has a BS in communications, and a master's in economics. He landed his first job as sales and marketing trainee for one of the top three auto makers, advancing in nine years to assistant sales manager. Then at thirty-five, when the last thing you think a man wants to do is to go back to school, he received his MBA. He moved into field sales, becoming zone manager for another major auto firm. His third job was vice president of business planning for a truck manufacturer and from there to vice president of sales and marketing for a man-ufacturer of automotive parts. He is now president and CEO of that firm.

You can see he cut his eyeteeth from the bottom up in the automotive business, switching to trucks when the opportunity presented itself. He moved from the sales and marketing end of the business to the president's office.

Another applicant decided that the best way to join the ranks of top corporate managers was to get a job with a Fortune 100 company and work her way up. She did just that. With a liberal arts degree under her belt, she went to work for one of America's largest manufacturers of office equipment as a sales representative—a good entry-level spot for someone without a professional degree. She applied herself to her job diligently and was ultimately promoted to marketing consultant at the firm's headquarters. From there it was a series of jumps to district manager, sales manager, and finally vice president of operations. She set her sights and hit her target.

For those who think it's necessary to work twenty or thirty years on the job before reaching the top rung of the corporate ladder, consider these next fast trackers.

After receiving a BS in accounting, this applicant joined a Big 8 accounting firm. After five years he realized that he had reached a plateau with his employer, and he switched to a bank, where he worked his way up to vice president, financial manager, and from there to senior vice president and financial controller. His professional reputation brought him to the attention of a major savings institution, where at thirty-seven he is paid a handsome $185,000 as a senior vice president.

Another who made his mark before he was forty had a degree in business administration. He made four company changes along the way, holding jobs such as manager in training, business development officer, sales manager, vice president of marketing, regional vice president, and senior operations manager. It took him only fourteen years to become president and chief executive officer of a major trucking firm.

There was one particularly intriguing résumé of a man who received his degree from a theological seminary and began his career as a minister. After substantially increasing the membership of his congregation, he decided that he wanted to use his education and abilities in more secular activities, and he founded a consulting firm providing management development and human resources services to major corporations.

After five years, during which he built a solid reputation as a consultant, he was recruited by a major national nonprofit health organization to be its director of human resources.

This is yet another demonstration that it is not necessary to remain in a particular field because of your education or experience, and that you can change the direction of your career several times.

Widen Your Knowledge

A question that is frequently asked by young people in college or just entering the job market is, Who is in greater demand, the generalist or the specialist? Specialization can be an advantage as long as you're making progress and your employer is making profits. But your career can come to a dead stop if you do not have some education or skills in another occupation. It may not be necessary to change employers, but you should be prepared to change jobs within your company. Traditionally most corporate presidents have come up through the ranks of sales and marketing. More and more CEOs are now coming in from other areas. With the diversity of today's global economy, it's wise to broaden your education and training as much as possible. Finance majors should take marketing courses, business majors should not ignore journalism or communications courses, and science and engineering students should avail themselves of as many liberal arts courses as possible. For those out of school, further education is available through adult education courses in just about every community.

Increased flexibility gives you options when you reach a plateau in your career and there seems to be no place to go. A key ingredient for moving up in the corporate world is to assume responsibility for your own career. No one can do it for you, and you can't pass the buck by blaming your boss, your co-workers, or the economy.

For example, here is the case of one applicant who made it to the top by keeping her options open. She first took her BS in public relations. She then earned an MBA in marketing with a minor in finance, and then a PhD in communications. Talk about diversification! She obtained her first job as a press assistant for a university. Later she took a position with a financial services company, where she rose in a few years to become an assistant vice president of its securities trading department. When the company relocated to another state, she moved to a marketing company as media marketing manager. She was recruited by an executive search firm representing a major computer manufacturer and was ultimately hired as a senior vice president and director of administration. She attributes her success to her ability to wear several hats while moving up the ladder.

According to Christine Fara, Director of Career Services and Cooperative Education of Manhattan College in Riverdale, New York, today's workers will probably change jobs five times before they are forty and change careers three times before they retire.

Success Is in Your Hands

Who says opportunity is not there? The case histories of people who made it to the top show that there are many roads to the hallowed halls. Some appeared to be in the right place at the right time. Others set specific goals and held to them regardless of setbacks along the way.

The candidates we surveyed shared certain common traits. They were result and goal oriented. They took advantage of opportunities within their own companies, but they also recognized when it was time to move on. They had the courage to take risks. And finally, they had an unwavering will to succeed.

2

Know Yourself

Before you can know what you're after, you have to know where you are in terms of what really matters to you. To you, and not to anyone else. One young man who came to us for placement insisted that his most important goal was to make money. After we explored the subject for a while, it turned out that he was saying this because he thought he'd come across as a go-getter; after all, "everyone" expects money-making to be a primary goal. In fact this particular young man didn't really want to make a million dollars—not if it meant working long hours away from his wife and children. His personal needs and values actually differed from what he imagined were basic prerequisites for success. If ever he were to take a high-pressure job (which might or might not lead to that million dollars), he would make both himself and his family miserable.

Goal setting and success are extremely personal things. You may go along for a while with goals imposed by others, but you'll be much better off in the long run if you take some time for yourself and determine your own goals. What do you want out of life?

Arthur Treacher, the late English actor who portrayed the impeccable butler in many films, started his career as a London barrister, following his father. But there was one problem:

Treacher hated every moment of it. He decided instead that he really wanted to be an actor and work in the theater. The only job he could get was as a dancer in a chorus line, a job he accepted to the accompaniment of his family's wails of anguish. Yet that job was only the beginning. Once he found his niche, his personally chosen career, he was extremely happy and successful.

You can't begin to develop an effective job-search strategy if you don't know what you want or take the time to discover what's really important to you. Too many people do what their families expect. Too many drift through life just taking what comes, without deciding what they really want and mapping a plan to go after it. Don't you be a drifter. Rev up your engines instead, identify what you want, set your course for your goals, and get moving.

Otherwise you'll be like the Mexican youngster encountered by an American tourist. He was selling oranges one morning in a village marketplace when the thirsty tourist offered to buy his entire stock of six oranges. He would sell her only three. "Why won't you sell me the other three?" she asked. "What will I do in the afternoon?" he replied. That boy didn't know one of the secrets of life, the secret we're sharing with you: If you haven't made plans, then you are compelled to tread water while others race ahead toward their goals.

The difference lies between having a job and looking for the right job, between standing still and finding a job that's a step forward on a carefully planned career path. Before you think about what you will do in the afternoon, before you begin to spell out your career goals and develop a career strategy, study this section, determine what's important to you, evaluate your preparation and experience, and assess your skills and abilities.

What Do You Want out of Life?

Success means different things to different people. Each individual defines "the right job" differently. It all depends on what you want out of life. Some people get lucky and just fall into a perfect job. Some people happen to be in the right place at the right time. But most of the people we know who get the right jobs are people who look for those jobs, fight for them, strive for them, and plan for them. These are the people who always make sure they know exactly where they are and exactly where they're going. For these career-oriented people, each job is a step on the way to the next position. These are the people who seize opportunity and make the right place and the right time happen.

An article in the *Wall Street Journal* described such a man. Douglas Ivester was depicted as a person with "modest academic credentials, a short résumé and a reputation of subdued but solid competence." Some of his colleagues even regarded him as "lackluster." Yet, in a move that surprised many, Coca-Cola named the thirty-seven-year-old Ivester its chief financial officer.

How did he get there? He planned it carefully, from start to finish. After graduating with honors and a degree in accounting from the University of Georgia, he joined the big accounting firm of Ernst & Whinney. He got on the team that audited Coke, and when he became that team's chief, Coke hired him away. Once on board, Ivester made the most of his opportunities as Coke kept loading on the work to see what he was made of. Satisfied that he could leap ahead to the top, Coke gave him a top rung as chief financial officer.

Companies like Coke are continually looking for chiefs, for people who are willing and able to accept the challenges, opportunities, and problems that come with top positions. Do you want to be a chief?

The office may be out of sight, but it's seldom out of mind for the men and women at the top. In a survey of thirteen thousand corporate executives who subscribe to *The Hideaway Report*, Harper Associates found that while on vacation, 72 percent of these executives check in periodically by phone to see how things are going. Almost all the executives (93 percent) need a full week to unwind.

If you aspire to a chief's position, you must do some deliberate career planning. Before you do, however, before you risk a nervous breakdown or a bleeding ulcer on your way to the top, take a good look inside yourself and make sure that you are indeed the one person out of a hundred who really wants to make it to the top.

The point is this: Not everyone wants to make a million dollars!

You may be chuckling to yourself and saying, "Well, that's not me because I sure want to make a million." Let me tell you what we have found: Most people are not willing to pay the price to make that million dollars. They are not willing to take the required risks and gambles. They are also often not willing to put in the time.

We have a vivid example of this right here at Snelling among our hundreds of franchisees. Although these franchisees have the opportunity to make virtually any amount of money they want, most find a certain level of earnings, which we call their comfort level, and stop there. This happens even though some of them sit in the middle of tremendous job markets, with plenty of opportunities for growth. In such situations some won't hire even one more Professional Employment Consultant; others won't open another office, even though they have the capital and the expertise. They are happy and satisfied with a certain level of earnings and responsibility, content to make $50,000 or $100,000 a year. Others making $250,000 a year, meanwhile, are unhappy because they want more responsibility, greater opportunity, and higher earnings.

Where do you fit in? Is your heart set on being a leader? Or will you be content with being a follower? All companies need followers, and not just in menial jobs. Many jobs with responsibility and authority exist, but they are simply not at the very top of the heap, not the jobs that pull in enormous salaries tied to enormous headaches. The people who hold these lesser jobs enjoy them, by and large, are good at what they do, and are happy to do it.

Out of the Frying Pan

If your immediate goal includes a change of jobs, you are not alone. While some people stay in the same job for five, fifteen, or even thirty years, 7 percent of the work force changes jobs every month. There is nothing inherently wrong with making a move. The problem is that many people make the wrong move for the wrong reasons and, on balance, do nothing to improve their situation.

Look at these two examples and the contrast they illustrate. We placed a woman in a new job, a lateral move with no increase in salary or responsibility, because there was a personality conflict between her and her boss. Just one month later that boss was promoted and moved, within the company, to another location. All her former co-workers raved about the new boss the company had hired, but she couldn't reverse her steps. She had moved, and she stayed moved. In another situation, a young chemical engineer started out as a process engineer with two industrial giants, first RCA and then Alcoa. After a while, however, he felt stuck, unable to advance. So he moved to a much smaller firm and started as a manager in charge of fabrication; within four years he was supervising 125 employees. He took one small step backward, in a carefully planned career move, and several giant steps ahead.

Before you make a move, do a full and complete review of your present situation and your possible alternatives. In evaluating your present position, try to look ahead. When is your next review, and what is the possibility of a raise? Is a bonus in the offing? What is the possibility of a promotion? Might you be moved to another location, or might your boss be moved, leaving the next rung open for you?

I remember too well the salesman who had been with his company for five years but, like the woman referred to earlier, simply couldn't get along with his sales manager. Finally, in frustration, he resigned. Within six months his former sales manager had left the company and taken three other salesmen with him. The company had to go outside to find a new sales manager, and our friend realized too late that he could have had that job.

It can be difficult to guess other people's career moves, to know that your boss is going to leave, but you should do your best to make your own moves in terms of your own long-range career planning. Don't make a lateral move out of boredom. An example of this is two young mechanical engineers who sought my help some years ago. One was with Hunter Springs in Pennsylvania, selling a variety of springs, from the barely visible to railroad-car size. The other was with U.S. Electric Motors, selling variable drive motors. The first was burned out and unhappy in his job, so I placed him with U.S. Electric Motors. Two days later, the second was in my office, and you know where he wound up. Yep, Hunter Springs. I performed a service and gave each of these clients what he wanted, but if they really had taken time to think, to assess their long-range goals, they might have found that the grass was really green enough where they were.

Nonetheless, it's important to be happy about what we do. We spend eight hours a day at work, sometimes more, and we need to know that we are being productive. Look at the example of Peter M. Dawkins, who made a midlife career move that enhanced both his productivity and his income. When Peter Dawkins played college football for Army, he was named All-American and awarded a Heisman Trophy. When he graduated, he went to Oxford as a Rhodes Scholar and later earned both a master's and a doctoral degree in public affairs from Princeton. As an officer in Vietnam, he won two Bronze Stars. In 1981 he became the army's youngest general. True to form, for a man who does everything exceedingly well, he appeared to be rising toward chief of staff. But then Peter Dawkins decided, as he put it in an interview, that "the opportunity cost of [becoming] the chief of staff was too high." He quit the army and accepted an offer to run the public finance department at the investment banking firm of Lehman Brothers Kuhn Loeb. When American Express purchased Lehman Brothers only six months later, he made a tidy $1.5 million profit. Not bad timing for a midcourse correction!

You can't count on winding up with $1.5 million when you change jobs, but you can count on positive results from well-planned job moves. The following three job switches, all handled by one of our Dallas offices, show the good things that can come from moving onward and upward. One woman had been a real estate agent for several years. She was in her thirties, had a college education, and could type. She was placed as a legal secretary, where she feels much more fulfilled and sees a career opportunity opening before her. The second woman had been a secretary, then became a waitress for the sake of increased earning potential; tired of the irregular hours, she came to us. She was placed as a bookkeeper, making more money than she had as a secretary. The third woman, a longtime secretary, created her own opportunities. Fed up with being a secretary, she took accounting courses at night and was quickly placed in the accounting field.

One of the reasons that many people who are eager to move on stay locked in place is a counteroffer by the present employer. You may be familiar with the script: Tell your boss you're leaving for a better job and he offers you a salary increase to stay. If this happens to you, don't stay. Follow through on your original intent and leave. Here's why: The vast majority of people who accept a counteroffer and stay on are not there a year later. The company may have really wanted to keep them, it may have matched or beaten the outside offer, but the simple truth is that none of us likes to be blackmailed, and that's the way the employer, consciously or unconsciously, feels when this happens.

The boss who makes a counteroffer has absolutely nothing to lose and everything to gain. That large salary increase is going to be spread out over the next year in small weekly or monthly amounts. He may find your replacement long before he finishes paying you the annual increase. You had him over a barrel when you announced you were leaving. He had no one to replace you at the time, the work had to be done, clients had to be satisfied, his bosses had to be satisfied, so he turned on the charm and kept you. When we discuss salary negotiations and how to get a raise, you will find that threatening to leave is not a recommended technique.

If you want a new job because you are unhappy in your present job, that reason for leaving is not going to go away just because you get a raise. So analyze your circumstances carefully and then make your decisions. If you really want to stay, pull out all the stops to get what you want in the way of a raise, promotion, change in location, and so forth. We will show you how to do so in a later chapter. If you really want to leave, don't fall for a counteroffer. Accept that new job, and move on with a free spirit.

Look at Your Life-style

John Houseman, the legendary actor who played Professor Kingsfield on "The Paper Chase" and the grandfather on "Silver Spoons," when asked about his success, replied, "It's simple. I enjoy what I do every day and I would recommend to anyone to keep looking until they find what they enjoy doing; then they will still be going strong, like I am, when they are eighty."

What do you think you want out of life? Happiness? A sense of self-worth? Financial success? The chance to be creative?

Do you feel that you're achieving these things now? Are you happy most of the time, or tense and nervous? Are you satisfied with the way you're using your skills and talents, or do you think you could make better use of them in another way? Do you feel respected, or are you unhappy with your self-image? Are you, by and large, proud of yourself and your accomplishments, or do you feel that there is considerable room for improvement?

You may find it hard to answer these questions. Here are two self-tests that will help. The first, a general self-analysis, consists of two exercises developed by Dr. Sidney Simon of the University of Massachusetts.

1. As a long-term exercise, keep a "values journal" for a few weeks or months, making periodic entries as something seems worth noting. The entries might be the high or low points of your day. They might concern your own private thoughts or some interaction with other people. Then, after you've kept the journal for a while, review it to see if you find a pattern. See if you can then answer these questions:

- How do I, on an average day, generally spend my time?
- What are five or ten things that really interest me?
- What conflicts or problems do I have with my life? Which ones did I create for myself, and which ones stemmed from outside factors?
- What short-range and long-range goals can I identify? What, ultimately, do I want to accomplish?

2. As a short-term exercise, something you can do right now, write down two dozen things you like to do. Big things or little, it doesn't matter. Do you like to stroll by the river? Nap? Read? Tinker with your car or your computer? Play a

musical instrument? Teach Bible studies? Solve a physical or mental challenge? Write them down.

Now code your list: Put *A* next to the things you like to do alone and *P* next to those best enjoyed with other people. Put *S* next to those that may be spontaneous and *PA* next to those that must be planned ahead. Place an asterisk next to those you do very often and an *X* next to those you hardly do at all. Use a dollar sign to mark the activities that cost money and a zero to note those that are free. Finish up by numbering in order of preference the five activities that mean the most to you, and next to each item list the advantages, pleasures, goals, benefits, or satisfactions you gain from the activity. Review your coded list when you've completed it. What have you learned about yourself?

Another self-test involves a look at yourself in relation to people, data, and things. One of the most important things to sort out before you start your job search—whether you are searching for the first time or in the midst of a long and fruitful career—is whether you are happiest working with people, with data, or with things. You may never have stopped to think about it, but most people are clearly happiest if the bulk of work time is spent in one of these categories. It doesn't mean that you can't overlap or that you can't find a job combining various qualities at various times; but your most productive route to job satisfaction will probably lie along one of these three paths.

Just look, for example, at the shy young woman who thought that she'd be best off in a quiet, removed-from-people kind of job. She believed library work would be good, or some kind of clerical job where she wouldn't have too much contact with people. But our trained counsellor, after spending some time with her, detected a spark of something that said "This woman is good with people!" Sure enough, we placed her in a project team, requiring close work with other people, and she did beautifully.

What are your preferences? The following checklists should help you to get beneath the surface and see what your real preferences are. (We're not interested now in what your mother always told you you'd be good at, or what some favorite school-teacher said; we're interested in the real you.)

People: Do you like to spend your days with others, working as a team? On a scale of one to ten, with one denoting your primary preference, how do you rank the following activities in your personal scheme of values?

(1–10)

- Providing a sympathetic ear to friends   _____
- Helping groups make decisions and solve problems   _____
- Generating enthusiasm for a project you've developed   _____
- Persuading others that your ideas are right   _____
- Providing other people with information or assistance   _____
- Teaching or supervising task performance   _____
- Helping people who need help   _____
- Amusing or entertaining an informal audience   _____

Data: Do you like abstract concepts? Rate the following activities:

(1–10)

- Gathering and sorting information   _____
- Analyzing information to figure out a logical course of action   _____
- Assessing facts and recombining them to form new knowledge   _____
- Developing systematic approaches   _____
- Organizing things in a logical manner   _____
- Arranging and coordinating data for other people to apply   _____

- Observing facts or figures to sort out
differences and similarities   _____

Things: Where the data lover deals with the abstract, the thing
lover values the concrete. How do you feel about and rate

(1–10)

- Operating and controlling machinery   _____
- Doing precision work with your hands   _____
- Using tools to manipulate objects   _____
- Driving heavy machinery   _____
- Fine-tuning delicate instruments   _____

Where do you stand? If you derive real pleasure from helping
others, then you may find most satisfaction in a job working
closely with people. The shy young woman we talked about earlier, who thought she should work alone, actually valued inter-
acting with others and persuading them to accept her ideas; that's
what convinced us that she'd make a good team worker. If you
are challenged by numbers, or by the mentally demanding task
of compiling information, you may be better off looking at jobs
to stimulate that part of you. And if you are happiest working
with your hands, recognize this and look for jobs that will allow
you do so.

There are other factors to consider too:

- Do you prefer to work indoors or out, in a structured
environment or a more flexible one?

- Do you need to see a tangible result of your work, some
physical product? Your efforts might result in a sturdy new
chimney on an old house or a multipage report detailing
new production techniques or in a new sales record, but
they may also result in the success of a team effort and no
immediately visible outcome where you can indicate what
you've done.

- Do you like to work on your own, setting your own goals, or do you function best as part of a team, working alongside other people, with your duties defined by others?

- Do you like to take responsibility, make decisions for yourself and for others, or would you rather be an essential cog in a smoothly running machine, doing what you're told?

- Do you need variety in what you do, or are you happiest with the same defined task day after day?

- Are you competitive, doing your best when you are measuring your achievements against others, or are you content to perform your own job, doing the best you can without worrying about what others are doing?

- Do you have physical stamina, so that you can work long hours without fatigue? Do you prefer a nine-to-five job, without much physical or mental stress?

- Do you value creativity of expression, or do you want security above challenge, stability over variety?

There are no right or wrong answers to such questions. The world offers a great many jobs, and a great many jobs that are right for you. There's no point in misinterpreting your own values and looking in the wrong direction, for the wrong job, for the wrong reasons. Sort out what's important to you, and start your "right job" search from there.

Look at the Human Equation

When it is time to look at the human element of your job-search formula, you need to be alone, with time to reflect and to meditate. Go out and sit on the beach. Go sit under a tree somewhere. Get yourself away from all interruptions, from the family, friends, TV, and telephone, which will break your train of concentration. This is the time for some real soul-searching. When you ask yourself questions like, What kind of a life do I want with my family? you need to have uninterrupted time to listen to your innermost feelings.

Like the young man mentioned at the beginning of this chapter, you may decide to put family relationships ahead of making a million dollars, or you may decide that you can do more for your family by working long and hard to get ahead. That's a choice you have to make, but you should deliberately make the choice, not drift into it by indecision. Remember, not making a decision is making one by default. If you stay in your present job because you can't make up your mind to leave when you know you should in order to get ahead, you've really made a decision (albeit a lazy one) to stay put. You can see then that decision making takes place via inaction as well as by way of action.

If you want a job that will let you spend time with your spouse and children, you can find one. You can be available to help the kids with their homework; get involved in community activities; attend school plays, sports, and other functions; and work with the PTA. Chances are, though, that such a job may limit your opportunities to advance. That's okay as long as it's what you want and you know what you want. If this turns out not to be what you want, you may wind up taking out your frustrations on that same spouse and children.

If, on the other hand, you decide on an all-out effort to get ahead, you will have to be prepared to travel, work nights and weekends, bring work home from the office, and so on. As a result, family life and family relationships may suffer.

Managers do their best work before and after normal working hours, according to a poll by human-resource consultants Goodrich & Sherwood of two hundred top managers at leading companies. Prebusiness hours are favored by 46 percent of the managers, while 22 percent say they work best after other employees have left for the day. Over 70 percent work at home on weekends, while 88 percent work at home in the evenings. Their average work week totals sixty-five hours. Are you—and your family—prepared for this?

If not, you may be able to find an understanding employer and strike a happy medium. At one time in our company we were working our area vice presidents very hard. Travel was up to 80 percent of their time, with most of them away from home every night. We had divorces, job turnover, poor productivity, and an identifiable lack of results. We reduced travel to a maximum of 40 percent. Turnover is virtually gone, production is at an all-time high, and results are gratifying in every respect. The human equation must be taken into account, and you should do so at the very beginning of your job campaign.

Where Do You Want to Live?

You can't decide on what's important to you in your life and in your work without looking at where you live and where you'd like to live. Do you thrive in the stimulation of a big city—an urban environment with its hustle and bustle, its cultural attractions for your leisure time—or do you dislike the noise, crowds, and dirt and worry about possible violence? Perhaps you want to raise your family in a small town, where you and your children can enjoy the outdoors and a quieter life. Or maybe you'd find the quiet life stultifying and dull. An article in the *Wall Street Journal* described the unhappy plight of managerial employees transferred to company headquarters in suburban areas who were pleased with the promotion but displeased with what they considered a one-horse town. The locale was fine for folks bringing up children; it was severely limiting for young or older singles and for two-earner families where the manager's spouse couldn't find an appropriate job in small-town surroundings.

Climate is a consideration too. You might enjoy the changing seasons, the shift from hot to cold, the colorful leaves of autumn and the snow of winter. Or you might prefer to leave all that behind, all the heavy clothing and heating bills, and settle in an area with mild temperatures and year-round sunshine.

The choice of where you live may be tied in with the choice of what you do. If you work with people—if you are a teacher or a nurse, for example, or work in sales—you can work just about anywhere that people live. If you develop a specialized skill or throw in your lot with a specific industry, however, you may find your location determined by your employer. New York City is the heart of the advertising and financial world, while we think of Detroit in connection with automobiles, Pittsburgh for steel, and so on.

Perhaps the choice won't be your own. Many large companies, in order to both train and test the mettle of their up-and-coming young executives, move them on a regular basis. In the jargon of these aspiring movers and shakers, in fact, IBM stands for I've Been Moved. It has not been uncommon for managers to move eight times in ten years as they move up the executive ladder, although the rising cost of such moves combined with many families' increasing reluctance to keep moving has slowed this pace somewhat.

If you're just starting out and choosing a career path, or if you're making a midlife change, give a lot of thought to the question of location—not only where you'd like to live but what kind of living options you'll have with various kinds of jobs and various kinds of companies. You and your family may have strong preferences, and you should try to honor those preferences. But don't lock yourself in. Jobless managers, according to the *Wall Street Journal*, are more willing to move, to take new jobs out of state, than used to be the case. But why wait for unemployment? Willingness to move makes any job hunt easier.

Whether you're just starting out or making a major midcourse correction, the world is your oyster, but it won't be if you limit your mobility by the path you select.

Involve Your Spouse in All Your Decisions

Few things can wreck a marriage faster than one partner making assumptions about what the other thinks or feels. If you are to have a meaningful conversation with your spouse concerning your career plans, you should first ask yourself what you think your spouse wants. Do this in terms of all the questions that you have just asked yourself. Where would your spouse like to live? What kind of participation in family life does your spouse expect of you? Do you think your spouse wants to be married to a "very important person"? How would traveling affect your relationship? With one out of every two marriages ending on the rocks, you must consider the effect of each career decision on your spouse. If you don't, if you make unilateral decisions, you may find yourself working sixty to eighty hours a week to support two families, an ex-spouse and children and a new spouse and children. Don't laugh! It happens every day.

You may assume that your spouse wants you to work endless hours, if that's what it takes to provide material luxuries. In fact your spouse may much prefer your time and attention. Similarly you may assume that your spouse wants to live in the town where he grew up or the city where she went to school. Your spouse may in fact have entirely different ideas. You won't know unless you talk it over.

We can't emphasize enough how important it is for married persons to make major decisions in consultation with their spouse. The days are long since gone when a breadwinner could come home and announce, "We're moving." Yes, you must first think through what you want, what's personally important to you. But if your marriage means anything to you, don't act on your findings unless and until you work them through with your spouse.

Decision making works best when you communicate openly with each other, when you say what you mean and mean what you say. Don't offer to take a low-key job, to spend more time with the kids, if doing so will only make you miserable. Instead explain why you feel you must take a particular job or follow a particular career path. But listen to your spouse's reasoning too. Maybe it wouldn't hurt your career to slow down for a year or two while the children are at a particularly vulnerable age. Then again, maybe it would. But evaluate all the factors, including the quality of your family life, before you make a decision.

Decisions made jointly, by the way, don't always mean total agreement. You may at times agree. But you may at other times find it necessary to accommodate each other's wishes on certain issues, compromise, or simply give in on occasion. Different solutions may suit different issues. When it comes to where to live, for instance, it doesn't have to be an either-or situation: I have a job opportunity in Florida, but you want to stay in Massachusetts, so we'll live in Florida. Try brainstorming instead. This is a tested technique in which you suggest every possible alternative solution before evaluating or making judgments on any one.

When you brainstorm, one idea leads to another and you may well find yourselves with a realistic solution that otherwise would never have occurred to you. In the case of the couple with a job offer in Florida and family ties in Massachusetts, the solution was a move to Florida and buy a house large enough for extended family visits.

To brainstorm, listen to each other's ideas, all ideas, and don't rule out anything, no matter how preposterous it may seem. Write down all the ideas as they come along. Then, when you've run out of ideas (you'll have a lot more than you thought you would), evaluate the list. Each of you write down all the items on the list in order of your personal preference. Drop the ones you both agree to drop. Then measure the remaining alternatives in terms of their pluses and minuses—and in terms of what is important to you, to you alone and to you as a couple. Look at the consequences of each decision, at what will really happen if you do one thing or another. If you still can't agree, try one more step. Take each other's role and give your partner's arguments for a particular move. See how persuasive you can be—and see if you change your own mind. If not, you'll at least be better able to understand your partner. And you may still reach a third decision, one that will please you both.

Personal Motivation

A lot of things go into job satisfaction. Money is one factor. Where you live and the people you work with are others. But further things to consider are ego gratification and responsibilities related to performing the job. How important is it to you to hold an "important" job? Do you need the status of being recognized on the streets of your town or in professional or trade associations? Do you want to be elected to office in your hometown, in your church, in the PTA? We all know that different jobs have different benefits. Some jobs provide outstandingly high pay for a lot of hard work, but there is little visibility. Other jobs provide moderately good pay and a high level of visibility, which some people call glamour. You must consider what you need in the way of ego gratification.

Some people hate business travel, preferring to be home with spouse and children. Others love the stimulation of new places and new people and look for a job entailing days and weeks on the road. Still others don't particularly like travel but recognize that it's a necessary part of getting ahead. Where do you stand? If you're just starting out, reentering the job market, or switching fields, keep it in mind as you develop your job campaign, because the amount of travel you'll have to do depends to a large extent on the job field you select. If you are in sales, accounting, buying, or management consulting, you may be on the road a lot. But how much you travel as you move along in your career will also vary. In some fields, such as sales, you may travel less as you advance; in others, such as management, you may have to travel more as you supervise more people in more locations. Decide now, before you map your job search, whether you think you'll want to travel and, if so, how much.

In Pete Dawkins's case, cited earlier, he must now spend as much as half his time on the road, meeting with elected and appointed officials all over the country. Would that be exciting to you, or just too much?

A good way to get a handle on your personal motivation is to daydream. Close your eyes and think about your fantasy job. If you could have anything in the world in the way of work, what would it be? Where would you choose to do the job? How would you structure your day? Perhaps you'd choose a retail sales career in a medium-sized city in the Southwest, because you like the one-on-one contact of retailing, find a not-too-big city just right, and enjoy a warm climate. Perhaps you'd also choose to work mornings and evenings, keeping the afternoons free for personal pursuits. Or perhaps you'd choose an entirely different scenario to suit your fantasy. Whatever your dream job, identifying it may help you move toward it.

Robert L. Page is a good example of a man who turned fantasy into reality. No longer merely dreaming about independence, he has parlayed his spare time interest in china, crystal, and flatware into a successful business, something he has always wanted to do.

Page was a certified public accountant working for the State of North Carolina as an auditor when he decided to go into business as a supplier of active, inactive, and obsolete china. He named his firm Replacements, Ltd., and his first office was his bedroom in his home; the company's warehouse was his attic.

Today the company that grew out of Page's passion for china, crystal, and flatware has 104,000 square feet of office and ware-house space and employs 145 full-time staffers who fill orders for Replacements' ever-growing list of 600,000 customers.

Know thyself, says the sage. Right. Know what you want, and you are well on the way to knowing yourself. Do what you enjoy doing, and you are well on the way to success.

Some time ago, speaking at an awards dinner of the American Academy of Achievement, I was asked by some of the outstanding students in attendance just exactly what I, as a career counsellor, believed they should take home with them. Was it inspiration? Was it dedication? Was it determination?

Before asking me these questions, the students had heard from the achievers on the platform, including people like the Wallaces, who founded the *Reader's Digest* and made it the most widely circulated magazine in the world; the father of strobe-light pho-tography; the first man to have set foot on both the north and the south pole; the father of the atom bomb; and the man who invented the pacemaker battery to snatch heart attack victims back from the brink of eternity. The students had made brief addresses too, giving us their reactions to meeting with such people. Some told how enthusiastic they were, how excited, and how they were now going out to seek fame and fortune.

I replied to their questions: "If you start out with these goals in mind, you may or may not succeed, but the message you seem to have gotten is not what these people came here to tell you. Evidently you have not listened closely. If you had, you would have discerned that these people went out to seek not fame or fortune but happiness. They sought a career that they would enjoy, that they were itching to get at, that would fulfill them.

"By finding the work of their lives," I told the students, "the work that made them enthusiastic, that gripped their interest, that kept them working long after others had quit, they found the key to success. It took long years of great effort and dogged determination to solve the problems they chose to face. Then came success—through love of work."

Try to discover what you want to do. Investigate, dig, probe, see the things and the tasks you are happiest at. Once you have that—and believe me, it's a blessed thing to have—once you are working at your kind of work, you will leap out of bed in the morning before the alarm goes off, eager to get at it. You'll be so eager that you sometimes won't want to stop for breakfast, looking forward to the day's challenges, bursting with ideas and what you want to accomplish that day. You will even hate to go home at night when quitting time comes, because you are enjoying your work so much. And if you find yourself waking up in the middle of the night, not worrying over problems but finding solutions that allow you to leap ahead to new worlds to conquer, then you will have found happiness.

Do not go forth seeking fame and fortune alone. Go forth seeking happiness in what you do; the rest will follow. Success loves a happy worker.

3

Are You Prepared?

Before you can find the right job, you have to be prepared. You have to know what's important to you, what you want to do, and what you do best. You have to evaluate your preparation and take well-thought-out steps to boost your performance and improve your skills, if that's what it takes to be successful in your job hunt. You also have to have the right attitude. "The power of positive thinking" is far from idle talk.

Perhaps you've looked at superachievers and decided that they have something you'll never have. Not so! Don't be defeatist! The qualities that lead to success are qualities you can adopt. You just have to know what they are, then move toward integrating them into your own life.

The first step—identifying the qualities of success—is easy. After sixteen years of interviews with more than fifteen hundred successful people, psychologist Charles Garfield has identified ten key traits that the "extraordinarily talented" possess. These are all traits that can be learned. As you read the list, think about your own characteristics and which ones you could acquire to help you move ahead. According to Garfield, peak performers

- Like to take control
- Have a purpose in life

- Train and use those around them
- Solve problems rather than place blame
- Formulate plans to accomplish their goals
- Base their self-confidence on their past successes
- Rehearse future events mentally, with a positive outcome
- Are concerned with quality performance, not just quantity
- Take risks after determining what the consequences will be
- Don't get trapped in a comfortable stage of life very long

The next step, integrating these traits into your own life, takes a little more effort. But you can do it. Just focus on one trait at a time. Identify your own past successes, for example, so that you can be confident about the future. Learn to solve problems rather than placing blame on others and absolving yourself of responsibility. Rehearse future events mentally, or in role-playing with a spouse or friend, so that you can predict a favorable outcome. Decide to take a risk, perhaps to move to a different city in quest of the right job, after evaluating and weighing the possible consequences.

Two items on Garfield's list, formulating plans and taking risks in pursuit of those plans, have always been keys to successful career development. Look at businessman Jon M. Huntsman, as described in the *Nation's Business* article "A Plan for All Seasons."

"When I was a boy, I wanted to be a builder of American businesses," Huntsman says. "I analyzed where I could get the best background to solidify my goal in learning business." With this goal in mind, Huntsman methodically designed his career and took whatever risks he felt were necessary to implement the plan.

He began with four years at the Wharton School of the University of Pennsylvania and two more in the U.S. Navy. With this background, Huntsman set out to find a medium-sized business in a basic industry with $30 to $50 million a year in sales. He joined a major egg producer as a trainee and within five years had become the executive vice president of Olson Farms of Los Angeles. Experiments in producing the best egg cartons introduced Huntsman to polystyrene, an oil derivative. The experiments also led, ultimately, to a merger with Dow Chemical Company, and, at age thirty, Huntsman was named president of the new subsidiary. He stayed in that job for three years, then felt it was time to leave that comfort zone and move on—another calculated risk based on his lifetime game plan. "After almost a decade in this type of industry," he says, "I felt comfortable knowing how to run a business. I felt it was time to move out on my own."

Government work, not business, attracted him first. After two key jobs in Washington, in the Department of Health, Education, and Welfare and the White House, Huntsman moved on again. His new container enterprise was so profitable that it was bought out for $34 million. Now a wealthy man, Huntsman did not stop for any victory celebrations but continued to devote considerable time to his church while he formed Huntsman Chemical Corporation, a polystyrene manufacturer. As chairman, president, and owner, he continues on course, taking risks whenever prudence dictates.

You may read Jon Huntsman's story and think it totally irrelevant to your own job plans. You are not going to be a company president, you may think, or head your own corporation. But Huntsman's story, whatever your personal job goals, is relevant. It carries the message of preparedness. You have to decide what you want and make your plans accordingly.

Remember too that there is planning and there is implementation. One is no good without the other. If Jon Huntsman had planned to be a business leader and done nothing to implement those plans, the plans would really have been idle dreams. You can say you're going to prepare yourself for a move, and then not make that move. Or you can actually do it. Some people, in short, do full-scale job-search preparation and then follow through. Others pay lip service to preparation but actually do very little.

The job seekers I like to see are those who are prepared and who will follow through. One good example is the man or woman who takes advantage (literally) of an employer policy permitting attendance at important industry or professional seminars. These savvy employees realize that attendance at such courses adds immeasurably to their résumés while also adding to concrete knowledge and experience for the next job up the ladder. Another good example is the individual with a professionally written résumé and collateral materials showing business systems he or she may have designed, important projects supervised, patents obtained or worked on, and articles published.

Unfortunately (although fortunately for them), such people stand out in any crowd of job seekers. Most people who come to us are woefully unprepared. They don't attend seminars, if given the opportunity, because it's too much trouble or because they think they're leaving anyway, so why should they bother. Their résumés are homemade, poorly reproduced, and fall far short of the professional image they are attempting to project. Some are unprepared in other ways. Some men actually start looking for a career change without even mentioning it to their wives, for instance, much less carrying on the kind of family discussion that should precede a major move. Then they wonder why there is conflict at home, which puts strain on the job search as well as the marriage when the spouse finds out what's going on.

You may think all of this is unnecessary, that the right job is a matter of happenstance. Perhaps you're willing to accept yourself as you are and keep plodding along at the same kind of job you've been doing. But we've repeatedly seen clients who are determined to improve both their job and their interpersonal skills move into positions far beyond their wildest dreams. Why should you set your sights low? Why should you settle for just any job when you can have the job of your dreams? You too can do better than you think.

We are facing a shortage in this country of middle management people; in the next few years this shortage is going to do nothing but get worse. Employers will be scouting for capable people. They are going to have to take people just because they have reason to believe—with no solid evidence—that those people can do a particular job. They will hire them, put them in it, and try them out. You can be one of these people—even if you never pictured yourself as a manager, supervisor, executive, leader— if you do something about preparing yourself both mentally and physically, if you develop the proper attitude, and if you acquire the proper credentials.

Mental Preparation

When it comes to mental preparedness, you want to psych yourself for the job search and for the new job itself. We've talked a bit, and we will talk more, about gearing up for the job search. Now what about the job itself? Are you mentally prepared for the right job? Are you mentally prepared for change and for the difference that change will bring about in your life-style? It may mean moving to a new location. It may mean doing a different type of work. It may mean taking a step backward in order to take two giant steps forward, taking a cut in pay for now while you build for the future. Look at the machinist who came to us wanting to leave that field and to sell machine tools or machine-cutting oils. He was upset when we pointed out that his machinist wages were much higher than the base salary for that type of salesman and that it would take some time to build up both his client list and his earnings. Once he was able to clear this mental hurdle, however, he moved on and became a very successful machine-tool salesman. Not everyone is willing to make such sacrifices. Not everyone has such a clear sense of the path to success.

Your new job may entail greater responsibility. This may mean longer hours. It may mean travel. It may mean the tension that comes with working with a new team, with supervising others, or being supervised by a new boss. It may mean uprooting your family, asking your spouse to find a new job in another city, and taking your children out of a familiar school and away from their friends. You have to decide—and only you can decide—whether all this is worth it to you.

Nineteen years ago Peter A. Magowan was a recent graduate of Johns Hopkins University. Today, in his forties, he is chief executive officer of Safeway Stores, and he is proving to be one of the most innovative and aggressive leaders in the retail food business. How did he get there?

Magowan's ideas were not out of textbooks. He learned creative retailing in the marketplace when he began at the bottom as assistant store manager at a Safeway store in the nation's capital. After serving as a store manager, still in Washington, he moved up to district manager in Houston, then to retail operations manager in Phoenix, to division manager in Tulsa, to head of international operations in Toronto, and then on to manager of the company's western region in San Francisco. All this moving and seasoning led eventually to the right job for Pete Magowan. When he moved to corporate headquarters in Oakland, he was fully trained and ready to become the chief executive officer of Safeway.

Family Matters

As you gear yourself up for your job quest, be sure to involve your family and to see to their mental readiness. Your job search, especially if a major life change is involved, must be a team effort. A dramatic example of this is the thirty-six-year-old who decided to become a physician. He was married, had two children, and was holding down an extremely fine position in the industrial relations department of a large national firm. Which areas of mental preparation did he need to go through? Not one of the above or even some of the above, but all of the above. He was giving up his steady income and the status of his job. His family had to move. His wife had to go back to work, and the children sought after-school jobs, all to help support the family while Dad went back to school. This family survived the years of belt-tightening because they were pulling together. Because they were mentally prepared, they were excited and enthusiastic about the challenge, willing to sacrifice in order to help him reach his goal. He became a doctor, while giving a tremendous object lesson to his children at the same time—that you are never too old to change careers, to try something new, or to do something that you have always wanted to do.

This is where the answers to those questions on what's important to you come into play. If you really do your homework on what's most important, and if you include your spouse and children, you will be mentally prepared for the new career step or job change you are about to undertake.

Do You Fear a Job Change?

The manager-turned-doctor just described made a carefully planned move from one field to another. Other people would like to make such a change but are afraid, literally terrified, to move. Still others stay put in an unsatisfying job then suddenly up and leave.

Quitting your job in a fit of anger is like throwing a car into gear and taking off at top speed before you know where the wheels are pointed. Yet thousands of men and women commit this irrational act of rebellion every day without thought for the consequences to them, their family, or their future. It is living proof that age has nothing to do with maturity. Some people are mature at eighteen, others at twenty-eight, and some never. Quitting a job is too serious a move to make lightly.

But just because you shouldn't quit your job in a fit of anger doesn't mean that you shouldn't quit it at all, that you should remain immovably stuck in the same old rut. If your job isn't right for you, it doesn't matter if it's a "good" job, the kind of job your dad always told you to hang on to. If it isn't right for you, it's time to move out. It's usually best to job hunt while you have a job, to operate from a position of strength. But if you must leave, if circumstances make it impossible to stay, then do it. The average term of unemployment is only eighteen weeks, and that's among people with the cushion of unemployment compensation. Fully 40 percent of the people who leave their jobs, of their own volition or not, are back at work within a week.

Many people stay in a rut out of fear. We call it the fear of the dark at the top of the stairs. When asked why they don't get up and get moving, they can't answer. It's a deep and abiding fear of the unknown. They "what-if" themselves to death. "What if my present employer finds out I'm looking and fires me?" If that happens, you can collect unemployment compensation and look for a better job on a full-time basis. "What if the new company doesn't like me and lets me go?" Not likely, but if it should happen, simply remember that you landed that job and you can land another one. "What if I have to move?" If necessary, you'll move, along with lots and lots of other people who want to get ahead. "What if the job is worse than the one I have?" If you really do move to a worse job, then your own judgment may be at fault. If you truly couldn't tell until you were on the job, then set out and look again.

All of these what-ifs and a dozen more lead back to a basic insecurity, a fear of the unknown. Sure, it's easier to stay with the familiar, even if you don't much like the familiar. But think of the options you have if you're willing to take a little bit of risk. Changing jobs may be the best thing you ever do for your own satisfaction and peace of mind, for your family, for your future. Commit yourself, work on mental preparedness, and head for the top of the stairs.

What's Your Attitude?

Preparation for a better job includes developing the right mental attitude, it includes being physically fit, and it includes educational, employment, and life experiences. Of these—and they are all important—mental attitude may be the most crucial.

A few years ago we conducted a seminar for some of our franchisees at the Holiday Inn Headquarters Training Facility outside Memphis. As we were about to enter the building, we noticed a large plaque on the walk with these words set into it: Attitude Is Everything. Class of 1983. That Class of 1983 had recognized what we have known for a long time. Attitude *is* everything. Take two groups of people, give them the same training, and the group with a positive attitude will consistently outproduce the other group. It happens every time.

Employers know this. A poll of businessmen in Madison, Wisconsin, revealed that student attitudes were considered more important by employers than any vocational skills that might be brought to the marketplace. What are those attitudes? The three stressed by most employers were attitudes toward authority, cooperation, and reliability. This particular poll may have been taken about students, but the attitudes in question are vital in employees—especially in those seeking to be employees—in any age group.

Young people frequently have a problem both getting and holding jobs because they have the wrong attitude. The average firm now loses 50 percent of its college recruits within five years, a 300 percent increase since 1960. This high turnover stems partially from an unreasonable expectation on the part of these young people that every job must be perfect; they have to learn, as older people must, that every job is a learning experience, that a time may come to move on but that in the meantime it's important to stick it out, to do their best, and to learn all they can. The turnover among high school and college graduates alike may also stem in part from an unwillingness to conform, to recognize authority. This rebelliousness shows up in a supersensitivity to individual "rights." We hear it all the time: "He can't tell me to do that." "The nerve of that Mr. Wilson, coming down on me like that just for being half an hour late." "If he tells me that one more time, I'm going to quit." "For what they're paying me, I don't have to put up with this." When it comes to the bottom line, rebelliousness just has no place in a business environment. Yet recent graduates, according to a Conference Board study,* often find it difficult to take orders, to recognize that there's nothing subservient about following instructions. What's more, as one utility company executive puts it, "We still have a basic problem convincing the high school graduates that there is an ethic of responsibility in the workplace that requires that you show up for work. It's that simple."

When employers complain about workers over age forty, as some do, it's also not age but attitude that they perceive as the problem. The attitude in this case is not rebelliousness or non-conformity but rigidity and inflexibility. Employers don't want to hear "We tried that at the last company I worked for; it didn't work," "It's never been done before," "I always say, if it ain't broke, don't fix it," "We're going to look like fools if we try this," "Let's appoint a committee to study this before we try it." An attitude of "I don't want to change; I can't possibly try anything

---

* Conference Board is a New York City–based independent business research organization.

new" is not an attitude that endears employees to employers.

Attitude is everything, not only on the job but in your search for a job. Where do you stand? Are you respectful of authority yet willing to say no when no is the right thing to say? Are you cooperative, working well with managers, subordinates, and peers? Are you reliable, so that employers can count on you to get an assigned job done? Are you flexible and willing to tackle new projects, willing to listen to new ideas, willing to think of reasons why something should be done rather than why it should not? Do you say, "Let's give it all we've got," instead of, "Well, all right, if we must"? All of these traits count more than you can imagine. So do enthusiasm and an eagerness to get to work and get the job done.

Grade Yourself

What's your attitude? How does it come across to other people? If you and I were facing each other across my desk right now, how do you think I would rate you as a job holder? As a job seeker? As the right person for the right job?

Are you as good as, maybe, you think you are? Think twice. Are you as bad as, in the doldrums, you might decide you are? I doubt it. Neither cockiness nor self-doubt are winners in the job-seeking game.

At Snelling we have a system of grading applicants. We agree with the fellow who says all people are created equal, but some are more equal than others. When we score job hunters for their placement potential, we rate them as E+, E, or E−. The top rating, E+, means that you are exceptional among job seekers, much better than average, head and shoulders above the crowd. The middle rating, E, means that you are good, but not great, just average, normal, regular, everyday American. And E− means that we'll put you to work, all right, but you do have some definite drawbacks.

This rating, based on our impression of your appearance, manner, and attitude, goes on your application along with your experience, attributes, education, abilities, and skills. Don't get the impression that we're looking solely for cheerleaders, for potential employees with pizzazz. Such people have their place, of course, but so do job applicants with a little less sparkle but with solid attributes and measurable self-confidence. The amount of sparkle required depends on the particular job. Appearance and attitude, however, are important for every job.

Let me show you what I mean. Two attractive young women, both seeking office positions, came to our offices one day. One, a graduate of an expensive college, had traveled and studied in Europe. The other, a high school graduate with average grades, was right out of school. In my score book, the better-educated applicant got an E, or average, rating. The high school graduate an E +. Why? Well, the college graduate spoke beautifully, carried herself well, was firm in requiring a top starting salary, was independent in her manner, and hurried the interview. The high school graduate earned her E + with warmth and enthusiasm and by showing her eagerness to get started on any good job with growth possibilities. The cool and collected college graduate gave me the impression that she was marking time in seeking a job and would move on to something better as soon as she could. The enthusiastic high school graduate convinced me, just by her manner, that she would be the kind of employee an employer dreams about.

Does this seem like a superficial judgment? It isn't. It is used in assessing $400-a-week secretaries and $75,000-a-year executives. As you evaluate your own readiness for the job search, remember that your outward attitude is the thing that people see first. Let it bespeak the best that is inside. Let your attitude help you take a giant step toward the right job.

Are You Physically Prepared?

Did you ever wake up one day and say, "Hey, this house needs a paint job"? You must have realized that it wasn't a sudden change at all, even though it seemed like a revelation, but that the paint had changed so gradually from bright to dingy that you didn't see the change as it took place. You may have noticed the same thing in your office if you started out when the office was new and everything was bright and shining. Then all of a sudden—only, of course, it really isn't all of a sudden—there are stains on the carpet and on the furniture, frayed upholstery, smudges on the walls. You may in fact not notice it, because the change has been so gradual, but anyone walking in from outside spots the shabbiness immediately.

The same is true of you and your physical condition. You look in the mirror every morning as you shave or apply your makeup, and you never really notice day-to-day changes. If you've been sick for a while, or if you've just marked a major birthday, you may become aware of your physical condition. Otherwise you probably never notice drooping skin, sloping shoulders, and an extra inch or two around the midsection. An outsider, however, either a stranger or someone who hadn't seen you in a number of years, would clearly see that this is not a bright, alert go-getter, not someone worthy of that great job you really do deserve.

If you approach the job hunt in this less-than-perfect condition, you'll be like the unfortunately all-too-typical applicant who approached us looking pasty-faced and washed out, with circles under his eyes and a defeatist attitude. "I'm here," his manner seemed to say, "but you won't be able to find a job for me." After our Professional Employment Counsellor talked to this applicant like a Dutch uncle, he got plenty of rest and lost the circles under his eyes; he also changed from what looked like bowling clothes to a business suit. His improved appearance plus a more optimistic frame of mind let us quickly and easily place him in a job far superior to any that he had held before.

If you're in the market for the right job, you've got to bring the right person to that job search. That means that you've got to take care of yourself, keep yourself in fighting trim. You've got to eat properly, dress properly, exercise, and keep yourself in good health. When was the last time you had a physical checkup? We're not out to make either doctors or labs wealthy, but we do know that if you take care of your body, your body will then take care of you. Studies have shown that improper diet does more than bulge the waistline; it can actually diminish your mental capacity.

One of the ways for you to be prepared mentally is to make sure that everything is physically in good working order. One woman who came to us, for instance—and this is admittedly an extreme story, but it does make an important point—was so irascible that she argued with the receptionist, then argued over every one of the interviewer's questions. Most employment services would probably have sent her packing, but our counsellor felt that there was something wrong and asked the woman about her physical health. The counsellor found that the woman had not been to her doctor in years and encouraged her to make a visit. She was back a few days later, a changed woman. She had been on diuretics in an effort to control her weight, and, as a result, a severe lack of potassium had totally altered her personality. Now she was cheerful, buoyant, positively ebullient, and looking forward to a new challenge. We had no trouble placing her in a top-notch job.

You may not need such a drastic change, but you may well need—as many of us do—to lose some weight, get enough sleep, and eat well-balanced meals. You may have to see a dentist and have some needed work done, visit a hair stylist (whether you're a man or a woman) for a becoming new look, buy some new clothes, the right clothes to go with the job that you're after. Whether you need minor corrections or a drastic overhaul, you'll find that paying attention to these physical details will also do wonders for your mental outlook. Take care of yourself, in other words, and you'll be hitting home runs.

Relating to Others

If you're going to function well in a business environment, if you're going to do anything other than work alone in a garret as a starving artist (and you may well starve if you stay in the attic; even artists have to sell their work), you've got to interact with other people. The way you interact and the ways you choose to get along have a great impact on finding the right job in the first place and staying in that job and moving ahead in the second place.

To get along in the real world, you've got to get along with all sorts of people. Start with the interviewer in the personnel office (we'll talk about managing your job interview in another chapter), then just think about all the others whose paths you'll cross: co-workers and superiors and, if you're in management, subordinates; clients and customers and suppliers. To get along with all of these people and to work well with them (it doesn't matter at all whether or not you could ever be friends), you may have to make some adjustments in the way you operate. You may have to learn to take instructions cheerfully or to give them pleasantly. You may have to master the art of negotiating, of managing conflict. You can take a course in human relationships, or you can study or practice on your own. Just remember, you're on a quest for the right job. Finding that job makes it all worthwhile.

Abilities and Interests

You may have natural ability in some area but not much interest in pursuing that area. Or you may have a lot of interest in some area that you're really not much good at. Fortunately for most people, however, our abilities and interests do tend to go hand in hand. We enjoy what we're good at and are good at what we enjoy. Rate your abilities and interests, on a scale of one to five, in the following areas:

I am social. I like talking to people, being with people, and prefer work that lets me do so.
My ability level is   1   2   3   4   5
My interest level is   1   2   3   4   5

I am ambitious. I enjoy competition and the rewards of coming in first. I like to influence other people, and I relish receiving recognition for my efforts.
My ability level is   1   2   3   4   5
My interest level is   1   2   3   4   5

I am creative. I enjoy music, painting, photography, and/or writing, and I don't mind working alone.

My ability level is   1 2 3 4 5
My interest level is   1 2 3 4 5

I am well organized. I enjoy detail work and do all my work in a precise, orderly manner.
My ability level is   1 2 3 4 5
My interest level is   1 2 3 4 5

You may have known your ability/interest configuration in general, but measuring this way will give you a clearer picture. Use this picture, along with the result of the self-evaluation in the preceding chapter, as you assess your specific skills.

First, however, do one more exercise: Sketch a "work pie" for yourself. Dr. Sidney Simon describes a work pie as a large circle representing the hours you spend on the job, either the job you have now or a hypothetical sought-after job. Slice your work pie, drawing lines on the circle, to show how much of your on-the-job time is creative, interesting, dull but important, and busy work (dull and relatively unimportant). Then decide how you would prefer, given a choice, to spend your workday. Will your skills allow you to do so?

Skills

What is a skill? According to Dr. Howard Figler, former director of counseling at Dickinson College in Pennsylvania, a skill is any one of a wide variety of attributes representing "your strengths, your key abilities, the characteristics that give you your greatest potency, the ways in which you tend to be most successful when dealing with problems, tasks, and other life experiences." Skills, therefore, can include an almost innumerable array of talents. Dr. Figler lists about one hundred skills, ranging alphabetically from administering programs to writing for publication, and including (to name just a few) arranging social functions, assembling apparatus, dispensing information, operating equipment, sketching charts or diagrams, supervising others. There are even some things on this list that you might not consider skills but that a trained career counsellor does; among them are confronting other people, enduring long hours, persuading others, and tolerating interruptions.

As you assess your skills, try to use a career counselor's perspective. Look at your skills in three distinct categories:

   1. *Adaptive skills* are self-management skills, the kinds of skills you exhibit in coping with the world. These skills may seem to be character traits, but they can be learned. Examples include assertiveness, cooperation, diplomacy, resourcefulness, and versatility. These skills are important in the performance of any job.

   2. *Functional skills* are transferable skills. They are the skills, such as analytical ability or organizational talent, that help determine whether you are best at dealing with people, data, or things, as discussed in the previous chapter. Some functional skills you might try to sharpen, because they can be used by almost any employer, are budget management, supervising, speaking, writing, negotiating, teaching, organizing, and coordinating.

   3. *Work content skills* are related to a particular job, although they are transferable to similar jobs. These skills, learned either on the job or through specific training or education, include such things as computer operation, purchasing, or selling.

Some people rely on aptitude tests to assess their skills. Aptitude tests can be useful, especially if you're just starting out and are unsure what skills you have and should develop. Aptitude tests can also be useful if you are unhappy in your job, are considering reentering the job market after some years away, or have to decide about a promotion or transfer offered by your current employer. But aptitude tests, if they are used at all, should be only one of many tools used to help give you direction. They should never lock you into a given direction (as they do in some other countries but, thank God, not here) or make you unwilling to entertain new job possibilities. Aptitude tests measure broad aptitudes, not specific skills. They look at such things as the ability

to reason, think ahead, manipulate objects, see spatial relationships, observe accurately, and produce ideas. The results suggest,
and *only* suggest, that you might be best off entering journalism,
for example, or sales or engineering. They don't suggest what
particular job you might pursue within the broad work category.
They don't rule out other broad categories. And they don't, as
noted, assess your specific skills.

You don't have to spend money on aptitude tests. You can
assess your own skills. You can also learn how to make the most
of your skills, transfer them from one job situation to another,
even turn skills that seem negative into positive ones. For example, one woman we interviewed was candid about what she
saw as a failing: her tendency to be very outspoken, saying exactly
what she thought even when it was inappropriate. We pointed
out to her that this trait could be very useful in certain jobs, and
we placed her in a collection agency, where she dealt with people
slow in repaying loans. Another client saw himself as dull and
methodical, unwilling to cope with change. A potential employer
saw this client as careful and systematic, paying careful attention
to detail.

Do you have skills that you make the mistake of seeing as faults?
Perhaps you're overly loud, in your own estimation, resented by
others because you dominate a group; perhaps we might see this
characteristic putting you in the forefront for a position as tour
leader or group organizer. Maybe you've been criticized as nosy,
always poking into other people's affairs, but maybe this same
trait would suit you for a job as a reporter or a social worker. Or
maybe you think you're just plain slow, while an employer might
value your patience in approaching difficult tasks. Almost every
skill can be judged in more than one light; it's up to you to put
your own skills into a positive light and treat them as useful tools
in finding and keeping the right job.

Skills can also be acquired and, once acquired, used in more
than one job situation. If you take a course and learn bookkeep-
ing, for example, you might find that you've acquired skills useful
in a number of ways. You might be able to work with numbers
in another job or handle all kinds of detail or be methodical in
tackling problems. All of these skills suit a bookkeeper; they are
also useful in many other occupations.

Similarly, if you express yourself well orally or in writing, you have a skill that can be used in many occupations. If you think clearly and can evaluate alternative solutions, you will be valuable to many employers. If you can do research or get along well with other people or develop ideas and persuade others of their merit, you definitely have a marketable skill. A good employment counsellor can help you pinpoint that skill and apply it to the right job.

So try to view your own skills with both a narrow-focus and a wide-angle lens. Look at what you can do now, and what you can learn to do, in terms of the job you have, jobs you know about, and new jobs you may just be ready to tackle.

What Are Your Credentials?

You have a storehouse of education and experience, the things you've learned in the classroom and on the job and (maybe more important) by living. But what have you done, consciously, to advance your abilities, to improve your skills, to suit yourself for the right job, to convince a potential employer that you are suited? Have you gone back to school to study speed reading or salesmanship or computer programming? Have you taken correspondence-school courses or taken advantage of on- or off-the-job employee seminars?

Most job holders seem to feel that once they've gotten their basic education, that's it; there's no need to do more. Then they sit and wonder why they don't move ahead or why they get turned down for advancement. The answer, of course, is continuing education. This can be accomplished in many ways. Some people simply keep on working until they save up enough money to go back to school full-time. Sometimes it takes some family help or a part-time job or scholarship aid. But these are dedicated students, more dedicated than they would be if they stayed in school for endless years. A few years in the work force provides new motivation to enter technical college, start college, complete college, or go on with an advanced degree. A few years in the work force lets you set a direction for education, decide what you really want to learn, and get a lot more out of it.

Other people take a different tack. Instead of putting their careers on hold temporarily while they resume education, they do both at once. They keep moving ahead on the job while absorbing the information that will ready them for a bigger and better job. Many of these smart folk take advantage of company tuition-reimbursement programs, to learn at little cost. Others, whose employers may not offer such programs, take advantage of tax deductions for job-related education. In order to be deductible on your federal income tax return, educational costs must be incurred to maintain or improve your skills for a job you already hold or another job in the same field. (If you take courses that will let you switch fields or get you off the unemployment rolls, the costs, regrettably, are not deductible.)

Some people need training or retraining before they can find a new job. Many women, especially those who have been homemakers for many years, need training both for specific skills and to build self-confidence. If you're in this position, or if you're a young adult of either gender with inadequate skills, consider a training program sponsored by government, industry, or an educational institution.

Or do your own training. It's possible, if you're motivated. One of our California clients, for example, wanted to leave retail sales for a clerical position because of a varicose vein problem. Our Professional Employment Counsellor, after testing her math skills, suggested that she take an accounting course. She studied and read for the course while recuperating from her vein surgery, and when she was ready, we placed her in the business office of an auto dealership.

Don't tell yourself that you don't have time to keep on learning. And don't tell yourself that school is boring, that you're not interested in academic subjects, and that they wouldn't do you any good anyway. You may not in fact have the time to enroll for a fully scheduled semester or year, but can't you find the time to take a single course? You may not be interested in theoretical knowledge, but have you considered all the other helpful courses that are available, courses in stress management or computer literacy, running seminars or marketing? Have you even looked at the broad array of courses offered in your own hometown during evenings and weekends by local adult education programs, community colleges, YWCAs and YMCAs, and libraries and recreation centers? Have you examined the catalogues of correspondence schools or considered self-learning tapes? The knowledge you can glean this way may not give you a college degree, but it will provide you with know-how you can apply in the world of work. What's more, the very fact that you have taken this initiative and sought this extra learning increases your credibility to employers and potential employers. When I see a résumé noting ongoing education, I'm impressed.

But it doesn't take formal education or even informal but organized education to make an impression. What it does take is an evident zest for learning. One of the greatest ways to prepare yourself for virtually any job, in short, is by reading, and reading wisely. What about simply taking the time to read on your own, to broaden your horizons through a program of independent study? Read books and periodicals on sales techniques, for example, or on personnel management or accounting. Study materials on time management or stress reduction or getting along with others. Enjoy current best-sellers along with classics in fiction and nonfiction. Your local library can help you map out a course and select the appropriate reading materials in any field you choose. Or you can do it yourself. What about reading business magazines in your own and related fields, for example, to keep abreast of ongoing developments? What about newspapers and news magazines to keep informed of what's going on in the world? An old but true adage goes, You can't lead if you don't read!

All of this reading may even lead you to writing, and writing about your field in trade journals and general magazines can bring you to the attention of prospective employers. An engineer who admitted that he was just a so-so engineer wrote six different papers and got them published, thereby landing himself a management slot with another firm; it turned out that he was a better manager than engineer, and his career is still in full swing.

You should also consider belonging to business and trade associations and civic and service organizations so that you keep involved with your peers and in your community. Not only does networking itself mean personal contacts that can lead to jobs, but you may be able to use—and display to good advantage—

your organizational or financial and technical skills. A sales-woman found that the outstanding job she did in coordinating a local political campaign brought her to the attention of top executives in her company; she wound up with a regional sales manager's job.

All this studying and reading and community involvement may not seem directly job-related, but both the engineer and the sales-woman just cited found very direct job benefits. As you conduct your search for a better job, you'll see just how much difference it can make to many employers to have knowledgeable and well-informed employees. This is particularly true as you move up into more important and better-paying positions.

The lesson to be learned is that you are never "prepared," never finished developing and growing as a human being, if you want to be interesting to yourself and to others, and if you want to continue to move ahead.

What Do You Do Best?

A full evaluation of your potential as a prospective employee for a better job involves looking at your personality, the way you get along with others, your abilities and interests, and the skills you've mastered. Take a look at yourself—a long, hard look—and decide where you are and what you have to offer in each of these areas. Then decide if making a change will help you in finding the right job.

We talked a little about personality at the very beginning of this chapter. Have you looked at your own personality and at how it might look to a prospective employer?

You may be warm or cold or in between, outgoing or quiet or some of both, optimistic or pessimistic, stable or flighty, and so on. It would take another book to measure personality traits in depth. But you can look at your own traits, as they affect your work, and decide whether or not it's worth trying to make a change. Even if you don't want to go so far as to change your basic personality, you can alter your image, the way you appear to the outside world.

In changing your image, of course, you may find that you have gone a long way toward actually changing your inner self. The great psychologist William James said, "Action seems to follow feeling, but really action and feeling go together; and by regulating the action, which is the more direct control of the will, we can indirectly regulate the feeling, which is not."

He gave an example. If a person is not spontaneously cheerful, a way to become so "is to sit up cheerfully and to act and speak as if cheerfulness were already there. If such conduct does not make you feel cheerful, nothing else on that occasion can." He added that to feel brave we should "act as if we were brave, use all of our will to that end, and a courage-fit will very likely replace the fit of fear." Or, as you may remember from *The King and I*, you can "whistle a happy tune" and overcome feelings of fear.

You may ask what difference it makes if your ulcers make you act like a regular s.o.b. in the office but you happen to be the most proficient technician on the payroll? My dear top-technician friend, it can make a world of difference. There is a wealth of evidence to prove that the foremost reason people lose their jobs is not lack of skill but inability to get along with other people. If you are in this boat because of personality traits you should be able to mask, it certainly makes sense to change.

What great talent is lost when an athlete cannot get along with his teammates, the media, or the fans. We have all wondered why a home-run king feels obliged to pout or give an obscene gesture to his public. Has the pressure gotten to him, made his head too big? Or did the megabucks blur his vision of where they were coming from? It is sad to see great talent wasted by pro sports stars who fade prematurely because they can't get along with their fans, and sadder still to see ordinary working men and women never rise to their potential (or who rise and then fade fast) because they simply can't get along with others.

4

Mapping Your Job Campaign

At Snelling we call the job search all-out war. This is what we mean: Instead of going about the job search the way most people do—sending out a few résumés, answering a few ads, visiting a few companies over a period of several weeks or months, and then, with luck, securing a couple of interviews and just maybe a job offer—we urge our clients to make the job search a full-time plus overtime effort. The amount of time you can actually put in is, of course, tempered by whether or not you are currently working, but the message is the same. Your attitude and, as much as possible, your time commitment to the job search have to be all-out dedication, all-out war. At least if you're to get the right job, the one you're after.

If you follow our advice, therefore, you will put a good fourteen hours a day into your job search. With the help of this book, you will become extremely well organized, and you will work harder than you may ever have worked before. Every evening you will plan the next day's activities. You will write letters, send résumés, research companies, read ads, and contact individuals who can help. When you visit companies, you'll arrange your time so that you can hit one right after the other, getting to see four, five, even six companies a day. Some of these visits may be prearranged appointments. Some may be cold calls. Either way, you will be as well prepared as it's possible to be, so that you will make a good impression. If you do all this, concentrating your efforts within a two-week period, you should find yourself with four to seven job offers, all of them good and all of them in line with your chosen career path. Then you'll be able to choose among them, deciding which one best fits your long-range career plans.

Why take this approach? Well, think about this: The last thing in the world you want to do is get a good offer from a good employer and then put him off while you beat the bushes to see if there isn't something just a little bit better. When you are faced with a "bare" job offer, one of two things is bound to happen. You will feel, rightly or wrongly, that there must be a better job just around the corner, or you will give in to the pressing need for a job and be tempted to accept. The problem is, you have nothing to weigh it against. If you put on the hard-hitting campaign we recommend, concentrating all your efforts in a two- to three-week period, you'll wind up with simultaneous job offers. Then you'll be able to pick the very best one possible.

Our eldest daughter moved to another state and put this plan into action after she graduated in accounting. Within ten days she had five job offers, all with good companies, at annual salaries ranging from $17,500 to $22,500. She took not the highest salary offer but the job she felt was best for her. By putting this strategy into play she had a choice, and she was working two weeks after hitting town.

You may think that, perhaps because you have separation pay or unemployment compensation, your job war should be an extended two-month campaign. We're telling you instead, from our long experience, make it a fourteen-day blitz. Here's how.

Plan, Then Proceed

Success in any endeavor demands a plan. Don't you plan your yearly vacation? Don't you know where you're going, how you'll get there, what you'll see and do, and how much it all will cost?

You bet you do. Yet if I ask you if you've planned your career, you'll probably say no. Chances are you've moved from school into a job and from one job to another without a coherent, long-range plan. Well, just as that's not the ticket to a very successful vacation, it's certainly not the ticket to the kind of career you want and deserve.

It has been our experience, not at all surprisingly, that the most successful people in the job search are those dedicated to a plan. You may have heard the joke that goes, "Mister, can you tell me how to get to Carnegie Hall?" The one-word, but oh-so-true reply is, simply, "Practice." Johnny Carson's goal was to make it big in show biz, so he practiced and practiced and he made it. He continued practicing until he retired, just to make it look easy. But most people take the path of least resistance. They don't practice, don't map out a career plan or a job-search strategy. Instead they drift from one job to another and one false start to another. Do it our way. Map your campaign strategy from the start and keep at your quest until you succeed. And you *will* succeed.

There is an almost legendary story of a man who drifted in and out of greatness because he never had a career plan. Rufus Porter was a remarkable, natural genius who drifted from one thing to another and never settled on anything. Hang on, it's a long narrative.

Rufus Porter had no formal education after the age of twelve. But he could make all sorts of mechanisms, he could play the fife and violin, and he enjoyed writing poetry. In need of a vocation, he apprenticed to a house painter and graduated to painting sleighs. He beat the drum for soldiers, taught this "art" to others, and then wrote a book about it. He taught school, made wind-operated gristmills, then went into portrait painting. He took up the camera, went into landscape painting, and invented a cord-making machine. As an inventor, in fact, he was prolific, producing a wonderful clock, a steam carriage, a washing machine, a signal telegraph, and a fire alarm. When he was offered an interest in a newspaper, he decided to become an editor. He converted it into a scientific paper, then lost interest as his fascination with electroplating took hold. In New York he later wrote a prospectus for a new paper, which he called the *Scientific Amer-*

ican. Recognize the name? Today, of course, it's a recognized magazine with a worldwide audience. But Rufus Porter didn't stick around to see it happen. A desire for change again swept over him, and he left his publication to others while he occupied himself with inventions and moved from place to place until the end of his life.

Count Your Blessings

Before you get started on your job search, do some soul-searching. All right, you're unhappy in your present job. There's no opportunity to move ahead, there's no opportunity to use your skills and ability, you're not using the education and training you have, your boss is a real stinker, the working conditions are rotten, the costs of commuting are killing you, raises are few and far between. Your TV set is broken and you can't afford to get it fixed, your car needs a valve job and you can't afford that either, and, to top it all off, you just got your paycheck and in it is a pink slip. You don't even have a job anymore. Boy, do you have problems. No, as a matter of fact, you don't. Remember the fellow who complained and complained because he had no shoes? He stopped complaining when he met a man who had no feet.

You may think that you have problems. No matter how bad your job situation, your problems don't hold a candle to some real problems we can name. Look at our nation's problems: drug addiction, alcoholism and crime; unmanageable debt, spiraling federal deficits, and a lack of capital for housing and industry; a deteriorating educational system and "graduates" without basic skills; family fragmentation and its impact on children; depression and suicide; threats, both economic and military, from other nations; a lack of pride and patriotism in this great nation of ours.

You should count your blessings. Take an inventory. Here are a few to get you started: You are in good health; you're either young and energetic or older and wiser, with the benefit of experience. You've had a good upbringing and a solid education; you can read, write, spell, and understand; you've got a place to live and a car, a wonderful family, and some good friends; you've got common sense and some good skills. You can probably add to this list and keep right on going.

So what are we saying to you? "Get up off your duff and get moving. There are plenty of opportunities out there for you, there are all kinds of jobs, all kinds of career opportunities. So stop bellyaching, grousing, griping, and complaining. Put a smile on your face, a bounce in your step, and go out there and get it!" Our Constitution guarantees us the right to life, liberty, and the pursuit of happiness; well, you've got your life and liberty, now get busy pursuing your happiness.

Don't Quit Your Present Job

One important point needs to be emphasized right here: Don't quit your present job. Don't stop working during your campaign for a new job, not if you have any choice in the matter. While you are laying out your campaign plans, mapping your strategy—whether for a new career, a retrieved career, or a stepped-up career—don't let down in the job you have, and never say, "I quit," until you say, "I do," to that new job offer.

All of us have a tendency to take it easy, to do less and less work once we've decided to quit. That's natural. You might also think it's a good idea to leave your present job so you can devote that fourteen hours a day to the job search. Don't do either. Don't let up on your present job, and don't quit. Keep giving your best until the day you accept another job. This way you'll be running your job campaign from a position of strength. You'll look more attractive to a future employer, who won't have to ask why you have a blank on your employment history, and, not to be overlooked, you'll keep an income coming in. With an income, you can afford to be choosy about taking the right job. You won't be so hungry you'll take the first offer that comes along.

Be a Worker

If you are already unemployed, you have an opportunity to devote full time to your job search. But you may not be able to afford to for very long. In that case, you might have to take the next-to-best job, or virtually any job that is available, until you can land the one you really want. Take a night job and job hunt during the day, if you can. Or see if you can find a part-time job. Don't worry about working beneath your status. It won't hurt your work record. To have nothing on your work record is much more damaging. Flip hamburgers, if necessary, or bus tables in a restaurant. Do whatever you must do, and be proud of your work. A prospective employer will appreciate your efforts.

Your Personal Job Plan

A good way to develop your personal plan is to work backward, starting with your ultimate goal and moving back toward where you are now. Write down your final job goal—national sales manager, tax consultant, public relations director—whatever your actual goal may be. Then backtrack and figure out what job you must hold before that one—assistant sales manager, CPA, publicity writer, whatever. Then move on back down from there, through whatever steps you will have to take until you reach where you are right now. Thus:

7. president

6. vice president, sales

5. national sales manager

4. regional sales manager

3. district manager

2. outside sales representative

1. telephone sales correspondent

Once you've mapped your job sequence (and don't worry if you can't identify each step right now), think about what you'll have to do to attain each step. It may be additional education. It may be volunteer work in your community. It may be a part-time job. It may involve reading literature in your particular trade or profession. Whatever it is, you can do what's necessary and move toward your ultimate goal one step at a time.

A friend of mine who was just starting out on a new career at age forty-eight told me of the best advice he had received. A successful industrialist and self-made man invited him to lunch one day and told him, "Build your new life one brick at a time. Don't try to do it all in one flying leap, but take it step-by-step, patiently, and if you're determined to succeed you will." The man realized that disappointments would come, that progress would always be slower than hoped for, but that the steady, brick-by-brick progress would inevitably lead to the completed task and career fulfillment.

When to Job Hunt

Okay, we've told you to put in two solid weeks of fourteen-hour days in your all-out job hunt. Now we're going to tell you that some times are better than others when it comes to the job hunt. There are certain months, weeks, days, even hours when you improve your chances in the job market. If you're out of work and very much in need of a job, of course, you'll get on with your search no matter what. But if you have some choice in the matter, you'll benefit by what we've learned through our years of experience.

Let's take the time of year. A lot of people say that you shouldn't bother looking during the summer because employers are on vacation and things are just generally slower. Nonsense! Employers are always looking for good people, and summer is no exception. In fact, because many people wait until they get their vacation and then turn around and give notice, employers may need you even more in the summer months. Moreover, because other job seekers wait out the summer months, you won't have as much competition.

Other people have the same negative outlook about the month of December, waiting until after the holiday season to get serious about the job search. They figure that employers make staff changes in January. In fact good employers are on their toes all year round, making staff changes as necessary. Good employers hire in December to implement start-up plans in the new year. August and December may even be the best months for a job search, if you have a choice, just because so many other people think they aren't.

Summer and winter may even be the best times for another reason: The weather is likely to be awful. If you show the fortitude to be out there on your job search when you could fry an egg on the sidewalk or when the humidity is 150 percent, you're going to impress an employer. Or if you carry on with scheduled interviews during a blizzard, when other job applicants curl up in front of the fireplace, you're going to stand a very good chance of getting that super job. I remember one job seeker who did just that. Hank was second in line for an engineering job, he found out later, until he managed to make it to a scheduled interview by walking over a mile in a snowstorm that had paralyzed all transportation. When he walked in that door, covered with snow, he got the job on the spot.

Within each month, the first two weeks are the optimum time for job hunting. We place the most people in the first two weeks and find that hiring drops off in the third week and goes way down in the last week. It's as if employers tied up loose ends toward the end of the month, waiting until the new month to make a fresh start. So don't spin your wheels in nondecision-making time, if you can help it. Get going as close to the first of the month as you can.

The best days of the week are Monday, Tuesday, and Wednesday. Yes, that's when the competition is out in force, responding to all those weekend employment ads. But that doesn't matter. You want to reach that employer when he is in the hiring mode and in the hiring mood. And you'll know, after you finish this book, how to beat out the competition. However, we did tell you to put ten days back to back, so we'll recommend that you start your job search on Thursday and Friday. Use this practice time to see companies that you would consider your second choice. Then when you hit your first choice companies on Monday, Tuesday, and Wednesday, you will have gained some experience and confidence and be able to do a much better job.

When it comes to time of day, you'll have to schedule interviews at the employer's convenience. That may mean 8:00 a.m. for an employer who is at her desk at 7:30. It may mean 5:30 p.m. for the executive who stays at his desk until 7:00 and wants to interview after his staff has gone home. When you have a choice, however, aim for 9:30 to 11:00 a.m. and 1:30 to 3:30 p.m. This is prime time in most companies, the time when interviewers are less likely to be distracted by thoughts of lunch or closing time. Again, try to schedule your first-choice companies in these prime hours when you'll get the best hearing.

And, of course, it should go without saying that the best time to job hunt is when you are rested and looking and feeling your best. Don't come in to see us, as some job seekers do, with rings under your eyes from staying up too late partying or watching midnight movies. Don't choose your job-hunting days to run the marathon or to organize the church fair. Concentrate your energies on your job hunt during this period, and rev up those energies with proper diet, enough sleep, and modicum of exercise. Now you're ready for the job campaign.

Where the Jobs Are

One of the first and most important steps in any job campaign is locating prospective employers. You may think in terms of newspaper want ads, but if that's all you think of, you're needlessly and seriously restricting your thinking—and your job opportunities. Studies have shown that fewer than 20 percent of all job openings are advertised. Those advertised are usually the hard-to-fill jobs at either end of the spectrum: the highly experienced or the unskilled entry level. So look at newspaper ads, but look beyond these ads as well. Here's where to look.

Newspaper Ads

Scan newspaper ads as a starting point. Before you do so, identify your job skills and the job categories under which your skills will fit. Group jobs by their characteristics. If you're good at detail work, for example, you might look at listings under clerical titles, but you should also look at listings under administrative headings: administrative assistant, administrative secretary, office administrator, and so forth.

Then review the wants ads but not just on Sundays when most openings are listed. Some employers place their ads on Monday for lower rates, others use a three-time ad rate for Friday, Saturday, and Sunday, and still others run an ad the day they actually have the need. Don't overlook ads placed by employment services. One of our New Jersey offices placed an ad for a college graduate with good English and writing skills and some media experience. As a result of the ad, they successfully placed an employee with a publishing company, and the company was so pleased that it came back to our office six months later seeking another person with similar skills. While many employers place their own ads, many others build up a rapport with a Professional Employment Counsellor and take the counsellor's recommendation.

Don't restrict your reading to your local newspaper, unless your local paper is the *New York Times* or the *Los Angeles Times* or a comparable metropolitan daily. Read the ads in the most important newspaper in your geographical region. In the Northeast, that's the *New York Times* and the *Philadelphia Inquirer*; in the Midwest, the *Chicago Tribune* and the *Denver Post* are good bets; in the Southwest try the *Dallas Morning News*, and in the Southeast the *Atlanta Constitution*; on the West Coast there's the *Los Angeles Times* and the *San Francisco Examiner*. If you order these newspapers from out of town, by the way, be sure the classified advertising section is included, and don't overlook display ads in other sections of the newspaper, such as the business section. These sometimes feature the most interesting opportunities. For a national picture, especially if you're looking for a job with corporate America, be sure to see the *Wall Street Journal*, with its "Tuesday Job Mart" section and its special edition called "The Business Employment Weekly."

It's amazing what can be triggered by one small ad. A man with a growing retail watch business stood on the threshold of new opportunity when he moved to Chicago in 1887. But as his business grew, he found customers expected him to repair the watches he sold. He knew nothing about watch repair, so he placed an ad in the *Chicago Daily News*. The response changed retailing history, because it was Richard W. Sears who placed the ad and Alvah Curtis Roebuck who responded.

Don't overlook the possibility of placing your own "situation wanted" ad, highlighting your abilities and experience. One successful magazine writer I know got her start doing editorial research and writing part-time when, as a new mother, she placed an ad in her local newspaper. That was twenty years ago, and her career has been growing ever since—because she knew what she wanted and set out to get it.

Magazine Ads

While you're doing your homework by reading help-wanted advertisements, don't neglect magazines. Although most don't run classified ads listing jobs the way newspapers do, magazines—especially trade magazines aimed at a particular business or industry readership—do run notices of job openings. If you belong to any trade or professional association, that association's newsletter or magazine is a good bet here. The notices here may not find their way into newspaper help-wanted columns. Here too you may be able to place your own ads.

Another important thing to remember is that magazine ads touting a company and its products tell you a lot about job possibilities, even though they are not designed to do so. If you see a great many ads pushing one company's products or services, you know that the company is expanding aggressively and that the company probably has jobs to fill. As you survey job opportunities, such companies are good additions to your prospect list.

Corporate advertising and news about companies on the move can give you excellent leads to good jobs. A study of eight innovative companies done for *Fortune* reveals the spirit that runs deeply in the winners. "We want our people to focus on the up side" is the refrain heard over and over again. Employees at these eight companies—and at the kind of go-getter company you're looking for—are extraordinarily upbeat and believe they can change the world, or at least transform their companies. Aggressive companies like Apple Computer offered superb job opportunities; today's rising stars, whose names you'll find in corporate advertising as well as in magazine features, offer the same.

Two final thoughts about job ads, whether in newspapers or magazines: Go through back issues—if a company needed programmers or salespeople or engineers six months ago, it may still need some today, or at least you know the kind of people that company hires; companies advertise their hard-to-fill jobs, not every job they have available. If you feel your skills might fit in from what you see in their ads, put the company on your list of prospects.

Government

Don't overlook Uncle Sam and his state and local relatives as you do your job search. Opportunities range from architecture to zoology and everything in between. It takes a lot of people to make government function. You could be one of those people.

Some government jobs are civil service positions, which are offered through competitive examination; others are appointments, offered at the discretion of officeholders. You can find out about both kinds by getting in touch with agencies or departments of interest to you. If you are under age thirty-seven, in good health, and without real job skills, you might consider the armed services. Their training is superb and highly transferable to the private sector, if you choose to do so. Or you might stay on and make a career in the military.

Employment Services

Your campaign list should also include the private-sector employment services: professional employment services, employment agencies, placement services, recruiters, temporary help services, and the like. These resources can in fact play such an important role in your all-out job campaign that an entire chapter of this book is devoted to employment services—how to use and make the most of them. For now, just note that they belong in your campaign strategy. If you are collecting unemployment compensation or are unemployed through no fault of your own, the state-run employment services may also be helpful in your job search.

Networking

The first commandment for any unemployed job seeker is to tell everyone you know that you are in the market for a job. Tell them just what kind of job you are seeking. It's not just any job, remember, it's the special one that you've identified as furthering your long-term career plans.

The rise in networking—defined as a deliberate building of business contacts—is yielding sizable career benefits. People are exchanging everything from tips on job openings to advice on handling personnel problems. All across the country communication links have formed among co-workers, professional colleagues, college alumni, women's groups, and so on. These networks provide emotional support while you're seeking a better job. They also provide tips on where to find that better job. They help you overcome the isolation and frustration in working alone, so that you can get a faster start and outreach the competition. That's what happened to a woman working in what she considered a dead-end job with a large New York insurance company. Through meeting another employee of the same company, she learned of a job opening in that employee's department. She applied for and got the job, with a big boost in both salary and challenge.

If you already belong to a network, formal or informal, you're fortunate. Make use of it. If you don't already have a network, now is the time to start one, to reach out to everyone you know who might be bound by similar background or interests. You don't have to "know someone" to get a good job. In fact we believe that a successful job hunt depends nine-tenths on attitude, energy, and know-how. Nonetheless, the one-tenth that depends on human contact should not be overlooked. The more people who know you, and who know that you are in the market for a better job, the better the chance that a prospective employer will hear about you. The better the chance too that you will hear about a perfect job opening before it is advertised and made known to the public. This is not the time to be shy. This is the time to spread the word, through your wide network of friends and acquaintances, neighbors and colleagues, that you are actively engaged in a special job hunt.

Look at what happened in California, described by Mary Scott Welch in her valuable book *Networking*: Two women meet at a seminar and keep in touch thereafter. Two years later a newcomer to the area meets Woman A, who introduces her to Woman B. Woman B invites the newcomer to a network get-together, where she meets Woman C, who just happens to have a job available!

Tell your barber or your hairstylist about your quest for a job; he or she may just have heard about the perfect job opening, which was discussed by the last occupant of the chair in which you're sitting while you get your hair cut. That's exactly how Jeannie B. wound up happily selling ads for her suburban weekly paper. Tell your accountant, your lawyer, your dentist, and don't forget all your relatives. Tell your next-door neighbor; he or she may be, or may know of, an executive who can put you in touch with another executive who . . . Tell your co-workers and everyone at church, in the PTA, Lions, Rotary, in the local Democratic or Republican club or the Jaycees. Don't hide your light under a bushel. Spread the word! If you're employed while you conduct your job search, you will also want to spread the word. But do so judiciously, especially if you don't want word to get back to your current employer.

The "Hidden Job Market"

One of the reasons for telling everyone in sight about your job search is that many of the best jobs are never advertised, never made known in a formal way to the outside world. It's not that anyone is deliberately hiding job openings; that would be nonsense, because employers want jobs filled as soon as possible with the best available people and the minimum amount of fuss. But sometimes the minimum amount of fuss is achieved by hiring people who walk in off the street, hiring those recommended by present employees or by colleagues in other firms, using a recruiting service to find the right person, taking applicants referred by an employment service, or by interviewing people whose names are already catalogued in the personnel office's computer.

An employer may be thinking about replacing someone but is unable to let that person go without a replacement in hand. He's in the same boat you are, unwilling to give up your income until you have a new job lined up; he doesn't want to risk leaving an important job slot open. But when you appear on the scene, voilà, suddenly a job appears. That's called being in the right place at the right time.

These "hidden" jobs don't have to stay hidden. You can learn about many of them by spreading the word about your own job search. You'll be surprised how often you'll hear, "Oh, yes, now that you mention it, my department manager is looking for someone," or "You know, I remember hearing Joe say he could really use a capable assistant." You can also tap the hidden job market in a very productive way by creating your own job.

Creating Jobs

Over 40 percent of the people placed by the Snelling system are placed in jobs that were not even on file at the time the job seeker came to our office. While some of those jobs actually existed and were located by our Professional Employment Counsellors because of their company contacts, a great many were simply created. This means that even though an employer had no particular opening, no particular need for a new employee, the counsellor was able to present such an intriguing combination of skill, ability, and experience that the employer interviewed the person, made an offer, and actually created a job.

A young college graduate named Jim, for example, a computer science major but with no computer experience, came to our Morristown office. The counsellor knew that a local computer company, although it had no listed job openings, was interested in expanding into educational sales. The counsellor sent Jim on an exploratory interview, in which he demonstrated his knowledge of hardware and software and clinched a newly created job.

In another case, a law firm didn't have an opening listed with an employment service. They were not running ads. They were not really looking for a secretary and not at all interested in finding one. Yet when one of our offices told them about an outstanding legal secretary with five years of experience and the ability to use a word processor, they were smart enough to say, "Yes, send that individual over."

If the applicant is really good, the firm may well create a position. Why? Well, any smart manager knows that there will be a certain amount of staff turnover. The next time one of their legal secretaries leaves because of a spouse's job transfer, in just one common situation, the firm will already have a trained replacement on hand.

The same thing happens all the time with sales managers. A firm has no opening. It isn't running an ad. It hasn't listed a position with an employment service. But if an outstanding salesperson comes along, one with a background with this firm's products or experienced in calling on its customers, the smart sales manager will pause for a talk. Maybe there's a weak link in the sales-representative chain. Maybe there's a new territory ready and waiting to be carved out. When this experienced salesperson happens along, the weak link can be replaced, the new territory assigned.

Now that you've mapped your own career plan and identified where the jobs are, it's time to explore the strategies that can land you the job you want. Those strategies include answering ads, conducting a direct-mail campaign, using the telephone, and making personal visits. Each and every one is designed to sell you to potential employers.

Answering Ads

Many classified ads, even those claiming that "our employees know about this ad," use blind box numbers rather than telephone numbers. This means that you must respond in writing. For this purpose, you'll use your résumé (see the chapter on how to write a winning résumé) along with an individually drafted cover letter.

How can you write a targeted cover letter when you don't know the name or function of the company? Well, you simply have to take your cues from the ad itself. In some cases, such as "the region's no. 1 bakery," you may even be able to figure out just who the employer is by doing some simple research. Go to your local library and enlist the aid of the research librarian. These highly trained men and women will cheerfully ferret out information for you and direct you to additional sources. Find out the name of the largest bakery in the region and then check it out in business directories. What do they make? Where do they market their products? How many employees do they have? There's no surer way to impress a potential employer than with a broad knowledge of the company.

If the ad doesn't contain clues about the company itself, look at the information it does contain. What is the job description? Does it refer to a go-getter? Someone with an eye for detail? Someone with a proven track record in sales? Whatever the specifications, highlight your own ability or experience in that particular area right in the first paragraph of your cover letter. Catch the employer's attention, refer to your enclosed résumé, and conclude by asking them to call you for further information or to schedule an interview. If you are presently employed and don't want to take the chance, give the "day number" of a family member or friend who can relay a message to you. Also give your "night number."

One word of caution: If you're currently employed and answering blind ads, try not to apply to a subsidiary, division, or parent of your own company. It may not be easy to tell, especially these days as companies buy and sell each other, merge, and divest with great frequency, but do your homework. If you are not employed but are under a noncompete restriction, eliminate any companies that are off-limits. If you're not sure, tell the company; they will know whether or not they can consider you.

A Direct-Mail Campaign

You may have targeted a career specialty in which reading classified ads isn't going to be of much help. You may have to cast a wider net, rounding up potential employers through an aggressive direct-mail campaign. By "aggressive," I don't mean hitting the employers over the head. That won't make them come back for more. I do mean embarking on some serious research into desirable companies, then marketing yourself in a professional way via direct mail. This approach is strictly a numbers game, tantamount to being in the right place at the right time. Fifty or one hundred résumés just won't do the trick. If you are not prepared to send a minimum of five hundred, don't even waste your time and money.

The mailing piece itself will be your résumé, once again accompanied by an individually drafted letter. What's different now is that you're making up your own list of companies to receive that mailing piece.

There are many ways to put together your mailing list. First, however, you must decide two things: the type of firm you're looking for and the region in which you'd like to live. With these two facts in hand, you can set about creating your list. Here's where those research skills you learned in school will come in handy, along with the invaluable assistance, once again, of your local library's research specialist.

Start by using the telephone directory's Yellow Pages. If you want to stay with a firm close by, you can actually do this research at home, compiling a list of firms in your chosen field. If you want to canvass a broader geographic area, however, you can visit a central library, your county library perhaps, with Yellow Pages directories from a variety of cities.

Then look to specialized directories. Here is a list of some of the major ones. Their titles indicate the kind of information they contain. You can probably find most, if not all, of them at your local reference library.

College Placement Annual
Directory of Corporate Affiliations
Dun and Bradstreet Reference Book of Corporate Managers

The National Job Bank, a Comprehensive Guide to Major Employers in the U.S.
Standard and Poor's Register of Corporations

Dun's Million Dollar Directory	*Thomas Register of American*
Dun's Regional Directory	*Manufacturers*
Encyclopedia of Associations	*U.S. Industrial Directory*
Fortune Double 500 Directory	*Ward's Business Directory of U.S.*
Inc 500, America's Fastest Growing	*Public and Private Companies*
Private Companies	
Moody's Industrial Manual	

And the *Directory of Directories*, published by Gale Research Company, is itself a "buyer's guide" to nearly seven thousand major industrial, professional, and mercantile directories.

You can use these directories in several productive ways. First, you can target prospective employers for your direct-mail campaign. Second, you can often identify the individual executive to whom you should write; this usually won't be the human resources or personnel department but an executive in the department in which you'd like to land a job. These are the people who can create a job when none exists at the moment. Third, you can use the directories as a research source, learning facts and figures about each company before you have an interview.

Concentrate your activity! All mailings should be completed within the first week of the two-week period.

Using the Telephone

The telephone—if you use it wisely in your job campaign— can save countless hours of expensive travel, prevent valuable time being wasted in reception areas, and forestall daily job-hunting frustrations. The telephone can be used to open closed doors, create an interest in you where there was none before, and arrange timely interviews that fit into your schedule. You can and should use the telephone to answer ads, to arrange appointments for interviews, and to do market research. In each case you'll find it helpful to write out and rehearse your telephone approach before placing your call.

Answering Local Ads

When you respond to a local advertisement by telephone, your objectives are to

1. Set an appointment that fits into your schedule. You don't want to be rushing from one interview to another and having to drive clear across town in between.
2. Find out approximately how long the interview process will take so that you can gauge your time accordingly.
3. Obtain the full name and title of the person who will conduct the initial interview as well as the same for the person with hiring authority.

When you place your call in response to an ad, ask the person who answers for the full name and title of the person who is interviewing for the position. Then ask for the individual's assistant or secretary, so that you can make the appointment. You don't want to talk to the interviewer at this stage of the game, because you don't want to be screened out by a telephone preinterview. You want the chance to be interviewed in person, while the interviewer may welcome the opportunity to reduce the number of interviews that must be held. You may be tempted to conduct a preinterview on the telephone, to ask about salary, duties, working hours, and so forth, to save yourself a trip if they don't measure up. Resist the temptation. Line up the interview. You need experience in being interviewed, the opportunity to sell yourself, the chance to change their minds on salary, working hours, and the like. You can't accomplish these things on the phone.

When you do reach the assistant, proceed along the following lines:

"Good morning, my name is Roger Wilson, and I'd like to make an appointment with Mr. Adams for the opening you have for [the advertised position]. Three o'clock today would be good for me; may I come in then?"

After setting a time for the interview, don't hang up. Continue:

"Could you tell me approximately how long your initial interviewing process takes?"

Get the answer, but don't hang up yet. There's still some more information you need, and you want to try to get it.

"By the way, is Mr. Adams the person I would be working for?"

Or, if you realize from the title that Mr. Adams is in human resources or personnel and most likely would not be your supervisor, then ask:

"By the way, who will this position be reporting to?"

Now you can thank the person you've been talking to, hang up, and move on to your next call.

If you do find yourself talking to the person who will actually be conducting the interview and who may even be the hiring authority, impress him with your footwork, your professionalism, and your ability to handle yourself by using the following approach:

"Mr. Adams, good morning, this is Tom Dunlevy. I'd like to arrange an appointment to see you concerning the position of —————. Two-thirty would fit my schedule. Would that also be suitable with you, or would you prefer another time?"

If you follow this approach, you'll notice, you are not asking if you may have an interview. You are asking when you will be interviewed.

The response may be a lackadaisical "Come in anytime and fill out an application and someone will speak with you." If you get this kind of response, you should show your professionalism.

"Mr. Adams, I'm very interested in your fine firm and the position you offer, and I am most willing to complete your application. But I do have another appointment scheduled for three-thirty. If I get to your office by two o'clock to fill out the application, could we make a definite appointment for two-thirty?"

Whatever the interviewer's response, the secret is to be fully prepared. Have your approaches well thought out, anticipate as many responses as possible, and you won't appear flustered. Be professional, cool, collected, and in control. Learn from your mistakes.

If you can't avoid a telephone preinterview, and you are asked about your qualifications, be prepared with a concise but hard-sell response. It might sound something like this:

"Mr. Adams, I have had three years' experience on Hewlett Packard computers with Higgins and Forthright. I was fully responsible for all input, storage, and retrieval, and hired, trained, and supervised a staff of five. I'm dependable and hardworking, and I'm looking for a career position with a firm such as yours. Could we lock in that two-thirty appointment?"

Try to avoid being too specific in this initial telephone conversation. Keep away from dates, education, and anything that might throw a roadblock in your path. Always remember that you are selling your most important product: you. Always end the sales approach by asking for the sale. This usually precludes further questions and gets you what you want.

Answering Out-of-Town Ads

Answering ads long-distance is another kettle of fish. You will still be trying for the interview, and you will usually be looking for travel expenses. The company, naturally trying to keep costs to a minimum, will want a preinterview on the telephone and will probably ask you to mail your résumé. Your objective is to get the interview without sending the résumé. No matter how well written (we'll show you how to write your résumé in another chapter), a résumé cannot foresee all the qualifications that may be listed or the objections that may be raised in a personal face-to-face interview. Don't get us wrong. We are not trying to put square pegs into round holes. What we do know, though, is that job requisitions usually call for a Prince Philip when a fairly good polo player would do.

We have said before, and we will say again, that people hire people and they usually hire people they like, specifications or not. This is called the people principle. Put yourself in the ball-park for a particular job and if you hit it off with the interviewer, you'll probably get the job.

In this initial phone call, you have to sell yourself to get that interview. You have to deliver a thirty- to forty-five-second sales pitch, highlighting your strong points against the job description spelled out in the ad. You can expect some give and take, as the person on the other end of the telephone looks for reasons not to pay your way for an interview. But you have to emphasize your strong points, pound them home, and keep going for the interview.

Calling Cold

When no job has been advertised, and no positions (that you know of) are open, you can still use the telephone as a tool to sell yourself. Arranging appointments for interviews without ads, we've found, is duck soup. Once you get the hang of it you'll love it, find it fun, and enjoy the challenge. You'll also find it extremely productive.

Your first task, when no known position exists, is to uncover these unlisted jobs. Do your research. For starters, scan all the want ads, not just the ones in your chosen field. Companies that are advertising for a wide range of positions are on the move and could probably use your skills as well; they just haven't advertised for them yet. Companies who are running hard-hitting ad campaigns are also on the move, often expanding their operations. They may need people with many skills to manufacture, market, sell, and service their products. And remember, companies using personnel with your particular background are always experiencing employee turnover for a variety of reasons. For this reason alone, you should never take no for a final answer.

When you're calling cold, your telephone strategy is not all that different. What you need to do now is get the name. You might say, "Good morning, could you please help me? I'd like to talk to your comptroller. Could I have his name, please?" or "I'd like to talk to your sales manager, and, by the way, what is his name, please?" or "Could you give me the name of the head of your drafting department?"

If the person who answers the phone transfers you to someone else without responding to your question, hang up immediately and call back. Be nice. Use a drop of honey. Say something like this: "I seem to have gotten cut off before I got the name of your comptroller. May I have his name, please?" Go for the full name and the individual's extension number if you can, so that you will have it for future calls.

When you do get to the right extension, try to get directly through to the boss. An early-morning or lunchtime call will sometimes find Ms. Big at her desk, picking up her own phone in her secretary's absence; it's worth a try. But if you do get stopped in your tracks by a protective secretary, do the best you can. Be precise, be prepared, and be direct about what you want: "I'm a staff accountant and I just wanted to introduce myself to Ms. Big, for her future needs. Is she in?"

With this approach, you've done it all. You have identified yourself as not being a salesman trying to sell a computer or anything else. You've stated that you want only a moment. And you have overcome the objection that there are no job openings by stating in advance that you want to talk about future needs.

This approach won't always win, but you'll be surprised at how often you do get through. This type of call is a numbers game. You have identified several hundred companies that might have a spot for you, and you are trying to line up ten to fifteen interviews. Keep your eye on these numbers, and you won't be discouraged when you don't get through.

With practice, moreover, you'll develop refined techniques. If you simply can't get the secretary to put you through, for instance, ask for the best time to call, make a note of it, and call back then. If you're told that there are simply no openings, then ask for help: "Oh, thank you for telling me. But you could be a big help by allowing me a moment with Mr. Adams. I'm sure he has many friends in financial circles, and he might have heard of someone who can use my skills. Is he free for just a moment?"

When you do get through to Mr. Adams, don't waste his time. Hit him hard and fast with a thirty-second pitch; then ask for the sale:

"Mr. Adams, my name is Bob Walters. I'm a graduate of Penn State University with a BS in accounting, and I've spent the last three years with RCA in cost accounting. On their government contracts I was able to shave costs on the XT Three project by eight percent, which landed them a twenty-million-dollar contract. I used an IBM Three-sixty and supervised four accounting clerks. Now I'd like to move ahead, and I'd be interested in a career opportunity with your firm. I'd like to come in and talk to you. Will you have time this afternoon or would tomorrow be better for you?"

With luck, you'll land an interview. If you don't, go for other leads. Ask him if any of his colleagues might be in the market for someone with your skills; ask if other divisions or subsidiaries might be looking, get a name, any name, and call.

You can apply these telephone skills both close to home and far away. We know a topflight legal secretary with ten years' experience who wanted to work in a Southwestern state, in a midsize law firm, where she might be able to become an office manager within five to ten years. Her first step was to select specific cities and towns where she would like to live; for this research she contacted the chamber of commerce in several cities, read local newspapers, and so on. Her second step involved finding midsize law firms in the region; she found this information through the American Bar Association. Then she got on the phone, using the approach described earlier, to set up interviews.

You can do the same. Once you know where you want to work and in what kind of firm, do your research. Then make your calls. Get the name of the person who hires in your area of expertise. If asked why you want the person's name, always be honest; say, "Because I am seeking employment." If the person on the other end, trying to be helpful, responds, "Oh, there are no openings here," don't let that dissuade you. Just say that you would still like to talk to the responsible person because he or she may know, through colleagues in other firms, of openings elsewhere.

Once you get the name, if the person is busy, you can call back and briskly ask for the person by name. If the operator asks who is calling, simply say in your most professional voice, "This is Mrs. Barrett calling; is she available now?" You'll find that this approach usually works and you'll get through to your party. When you do get through, go right into your prepared and practiced script about yourself. It might go something like this: "Good morning, Mrs. Angus, this is Peg Barrett calling, I'm a legal secretary with ten years' experience. I worked with Quick, Brown and Fox and, for the last three years, was personal secretary to Mrs. Quick. I've done paralegal work, drafting docu-

ments and helping to prepare cases for trial. I'm also familiar
with the latest in word processing equipment. I'd like to talk to
you about opportunities in your firm. Would tomorrow at ten-
thirty be convenient, or would two be better for you?" That's if
the firm is local. Otherwise your last line might be "I'm making
a trip to your city next week to conduct some interviews; would
Tuesday at ten or Wednesday at eleven be better for you?"

Notice that you're not asking if the firm has any openings.
You're not asking whether or not she wants to see you. Instead
you're giving a choice as to when she will see you. What you're
trying to do, of course, is get your foot in the door, arrange a
personal interview so that you can convince the firm of your
merits, and perhaps create a job where one does not exist.

If you use this approach, you should have three or four interviews lined up in short order. Even if a specific job does not
result from this set of interviews, you will gain experience in
being interviewed. And you may come up with a recommendation to another firm that is hiring.

This approach can work for you whether you are in personnel
or purchasing, drafting or data processing, sales or service. Using
this approach, making cold calls but with foresight and planning,
can help you to be in the right place at the right time. We all
use the telephone, all the time, as part of our personal lives. Be
sure to use the telephone too as part of the all-out war in your
job campaign.

Personal Visits

All of these campaign strategies are building toward one end:
the personal visit. You want to show an interviewer, in person,
just how good you are. If you've done much shopping from
catalogues, you know that sometimes it works out well but all too
often it's disappointing. People prefer to buy, and most often do
buy, what they can see in person. Employers are no exception.
Making a personal visit can make all the difference in the world.
You won't be a faceless name, a résumé to be weeded out on any
flimsy pretext just because there are too many résumés. Instead
you'll be face-to-face, ready to overcome any objections there

might be, ready to find out what they're looking for, ready to show how you fit their need.

Long distance, as we've shown, is no exception either. If you've decided that it's time to relocate, if you're looking for a job in another part of the state or even of the country, it's probably well worth your while to pick yourself up and make the trip. If you're responding to an advertisement, you may be able to get a prospective employer to pay your way. If you're making cold calls, you'll have to pay your own way. But if you tell a prospective employer that you are coming to the area specifically for interviews, and if you offer a choice of dates within a period of a week or so, you stand an excellent chance of securing an interview. Do your research ahead of time, on both the area and the company, then go. Don't try to combine job hunting with a vacation. Show that you are serious, that you are committed, and, not at all incidentally, that you're willing to work hard at getting a job and harder still once you get the job you want.

Stay on Top of Your Job Search

Unless you possess a photographic memory, there is no way you will be able to remember the details of the activities involved in looking for a job. You will be answering ads, sending hundreds of résumés and letters to prospective employers, and making countless telephone calls. Hopefully this will result in your having many interviews.

Each interviewer will be evaluating you and making notes about your education, experience, personal characteristics, and career goals. You will give and receive information about job specifications, salaries, qualifications, dates, names, titles. It can take as many as four or five interviews to get hired. Unless you make accurate notes during and after each interview, you are almost certain to get into difficulty somewhere along the line.

To keep track of your daily activities, you can use any method that you are comfortable with. A good system is to set up a standard manila file folder for every employer contacted, whether you answer an ad, get a positive response from a résumé, register with a personnel agency, make a telephone call, or have an interview. Place copies of correspondence, records of calls, business cards, company literature, annual reports, and other pertinent information in the appropriate folder. Remember what we said about putting down your thoughts on a call or interview as soon as it has ended—along with details such as job requirements, salary and benefits information, and personal impressions so you will be prepared to follow up properly. Organize the files into two major categories, "Interviews" and "Leads," alphabetically by company name in each group for quick follow-up. When direct mailing five hundred to a thousand companies, you establish a folder only when you receive a positive response.

Using a methodical system to record and file job-search results will keep you on top of your campaign and provide you with an instant recall of facts.

Tax Breaks for Job Seekers

If cost is a worry, remember that as long as you are employed or recently unemployed and seeking work in the same general line that you're in, whether or not your job hunt is successful, most of your job-hunting expenses—travel, printing, postage (for résumés and cover letters), employment service charges, and so on—are tax deductible. Most regretfully, and for reasons that totally escape us, this does not apply if you're seeking your first job or have been out of the labor force for a long time or are changing fields. It would seem logical to us that the government would want people off the welfare and unemployment rolls and working and paying taxes instead. Moreover, if you meet IRS requirements, you may deduct (up to specified limits) certain costs of pre-move house-hunting trips, temporary lodging, moving household goods, selling and buying a place to live. Just be sure to get receipts and to keep careful records, in the form of a daily log or diary, of all your job-search expenses. The IRS may require documentation.

So that's it—your job campaign. It consists of developing your own personal campaign strategy for the career you want, then going after each rung on the career ladder via answering ads, conducting a direct-mail campaign, using employment services, using the telephone, and making personal visits. It means all-out effort for a concentrated span of time.

A good campaign strategy also means continuing to pay attention, monitoring your career progress even after you get this next job, and the one after that. Over forty years ago I began my own plan. We had one office then. At this writing we have over three hundred. I started as a Professional Employment Counsellor and receptionist-secretary substitute, moved to franchise sales, trainer, and office manager; thence to vice president, president, and now chairman.

You too should devise your personal career plan, then monitor it on a regular basis. Write down your goals and your plans to achieve those goals. Then see how you're doing.

Don't leave your lifetime career up to chance. Don't make your career a blind gamble with fate. You are in the game of making a living. Win or lose, while you live and breathe you can't get out of it. You must play the game. So why not give yourself at least an even break? Learn from our experience; let us coach you. Plan your moves. That's the way to win.

5

Writing a Winning Résumé

Nine out of ten people don't have the faintest idea how to prepare a résumé. I'm talking about a good résumé. And by this I mean one that really stops employers in their tracks as they plow through piles and piles of résumés. The résumé that throws the spotlight on one face in the crowd. The résumé that *sells*. Sells *you*.

A poorly prepared résumé is worse than none at all. It can bore or, worse yet, annoy the person who has to read it. A poor résumé gives a very poor first (and probably last) impression of the writer. And it invariably goes with the rest of the junk mail —straight into the wastebasket, often without a full reading. This is the fate of most résumés. It shouldn't be the fate of yours— and it won't be, if you follow this advice.

Your résumé presents your face to the employer, very often before you can do so in person. Writing a really good résumé, therefore, is worth more time and effort than most job hunters give it. It requires following a few simple rules and avoiding some common pitfalls. We'll tell you those rules and point out those pitfalls. If you follow my instructions and study the sample résumés at the end of this chapter, I guarantee that you will write a good résumé, that your résumé will get a fair reading, that it will be far and away better than the vast majority of other résumés.

To begin, it is my strong personal opinion that in most cases if the job you are after is worth a résumé at all, it is worth not one but two. The first will be a brief one- or two-pager to introduce you—a teaser, a come-on, a foot in the door. Its purpose is to get you an interview, to make you sound interesting enough so that the reader wants to know more, to see you in person, to question you. This is the résumé you mail, only when necessary, to open doors. The second résumé is an elaboration of this first one, describing your qualifications in greater depth. This is the one you will take with you to the interview and, possibly, leave behind.

The trick here is to say enough in the first résumé to really get across your full and true potential worth as a candidate for the kind of job offered, or that you are trying to ferret out, but at the same time to reserve enough ammunition to make your second résumé really impressive. The double-résumé treatment is designed as a one-two punch. You must make sure that you don't shoot the whole load the first time around.

This chapter will illustrate the differences between résumé number one, the introductory sales résumé, which is usually mailed, and résumé number two, the comprehensive or leave-behind résumé, which is usually presented in person. Don't flinch at the thought of preparing two résumés. The first is simply a condensed version of the second, so you'll want to prepare the comprehensive résumé first and then cut it down. The writing of both résumés, moreover, consists of two basic tasks: (1) getting organized and getting all the facts together, and (2) presenting those facts in a proper sales package.

Collecting the Data

Before you even start to write your résumé, collect all the information you will need. Enlist your family's help, if necessary, to dig through files, so that you'll have every fact, date, name, and so on firmly lined up before you begin. You may not include every piece of information on the résumé itself, but you will want the facts in your mind during the interview, so do the groundwork now. This is quite a task, we know, but if you do it properly, you'll never have to do it again. Once you produce a comprehensive résumé, you'll find it easy to keep up to date simply by adding current information.

Here's what you'll need on hand:

- The inventory of skills and abilities you developed after reading the earlier chapters. Rereading your self-evaluation will help you decide what kind of job you are seeking and what attributes best recommend you to a prospective employer.

- Your employment history, including the name and current address of each company, the precise dates you worked there, the jobs you held, and, to the best of your recollection, all your duties and responsibilities and accomplishments on those jobs. Go all the way back to part-time jobs you held during your school years, but include more detail (starting and ending earnings, fringe benefits, immediate supervisors, their titles, and their current telephone numbers) on just the last job or two.

- Your educational background, including degrees and courses of study and extracurricular activities. List seminars and professional/technical conferences that you've attended, tapes and books studied, anything at all that indicates preparation for the next phase of your career.

- Military service, including dates, rank, schooling, awards, medals, and actual experience.

- A list of any books or articles you have had published, talks and speeches you have given, conferences you have run, patents or copyrights you hold, foreign languages you speak and read and write, foreign travel you have undertaken either for business or pleasure.

- Community activities, including civic, religious, and political organizations. Name the groups—Lions, PTA, church board, chamber of commerce—and indicate any offices you held, committees you chaired, accomplishments you can name. While some of these will not be used in your résumé, the skills you learned may be. If you are no longer active, put down the dates that you were.

- High school and college activities and accomplishments: honor roll or honor society, school band, class offices, sports, ROTC, and so on. Even if these things seem like ancient history to you right now, even if they've been over-shadowed by more recent accomplishments that deserve a premier place on your résumé, you'll find that making the list is a tremendous ego-booster. If nothing else, you'll have a good, positive sense of yourself and your own self-worth when you set out on your interviews.

- Family history, if it is relevant, might be worth making a note of too. What jobs did your parents hold? Your grand-parents? Suppose you're asked in an interview why you chose the field of sales. Wouldn't it be nice to say, "Well, my dad earned his living as a salesman. He worked for the 3M Company in their electric tape division and became a regional sales manager for them. Before that, my granddad was in sales all his life and was one of the top salesmen with Campbell's Soup. All I have heard all my life is sales, sales, sales. I guess it's just born and bred in me. I like it and I'm making my career in that field." Sounds nice and spontaneous, doesn't it? Yet this kind of answer can be well thought out ahead of time if you do your homework and, of course, if you are actually following in the family foot-steps.

Preparing Your Résumés

Both the long and the short version of your résumé include the same information in the same sequence. The difference lies in the amount of detail. In this section we'll show you just what to include in each version; the sample résumés at the end of the chapter demonstrate exactly what we mean.

First, however, a word about tense. No, we don't mean the

tension you feel as you look for a job. We mean grammatical tense: Should your résumé be written in the first person ("I did thus-and-such") or the third person ("he or she did thus-and-so")? Obviously you are writing about yourself in your résumé so that the first person comes naturally. Equally obvious, if you stop to think about it, self-description—especially in the immodest terms of a résumé—seems self-serving. You want the reader of your résumé to see you as an experienced, accomplished person. You want that reader to see you as the perfect employee. You don't want that reader to sense that you're bragging about yourself. Whether you deliver your résumé yourself or via an employment service (and an employment service can be a perfect intermediary, just because it can brag about you), you'll want your résumé to make the right impression. All this is a long way of saying don't use "I" in your résumé. Don't use "he" or "she" either. Instead use action verbs to convey what you've done. Don't say, for example, "I am currently employed as a customer service representative; my duties are . . ." Instead try it this way. Under the heading "Customer Service Representative," list, "Recognized as senior problem solver and troubleshooter," followed on another line by "Designed and implemented all training programs for department," and so on. See the before and after résumés for illustration. And refer to the lists of action and self-descriptive words prepared by the Hope College Career Center.

Now that we've got the tense straight, here's what your résumé should include:

1. *Your name* should appear on the first line of every résumé. It need not be prefaced with "Name:" because the reader knows that this is your name (again, see the before and after résumés). If you choose, it may be preceded by "The Résumé of" or "The Confidential Résumé of."

Your name is followed by your objective. It is not, as you might expect, followed by your address and telephone number. Remember, we said that your résumé should be a hard-hitting sales piece. Look at some full-page advertisements in the nearest magazine. These are certainly hard-hitting sales pieces. Where do you see the company's address and phone number? Never at the top. It's always at the bottom of the ad. That's because the address has nothing to do with selling you the product or service or concept. Instead savvy advertisers hit you with a picture, a head-line, their name, something to grab your attention, and then, because now you're interested, you look at the bottom of the page to find the company's location.

If you put your address at the top, you may even lose out on an appealing job. Say the company has an opening in the Tucson office, and you live in Philadelphia. You may fit the job to a tee and be willing to get yourself to Tucson, at no expense to the company, because your husband's family lives there. Yet with your address right at the top, the interviewer may never read any further. The company doesn't want the expense of relocation so won't go to the expense of interviewing you. Sell them on your credentials first, before they see where you live, and you're more likely to have a shot at the job.

Now that I've got you convinced that your address belongs at the bottom of the résumé, let me emphasize that I mean the bottom, as far down on the page as possible (see examples). This way, if you use an employment service, the address line can be neatly removed, leaving your résumé intact. It's not that em-ployment services don't trust employers. It's just that they know that accidents do happen, that applicants are occasionally called directly, and the service loses out on the service charge it has earned. Just so this can't happen, employment services will re-move your address. If it's at the top of the page, they will block it out in black ink, thereby destroying the beauty of your résumé. If it's at the bottom, it can be easily and neatly removed, and your résumé, which you've spent so much time and effort pre-paring, will still have all its punch and pizzazz.

2. *Your objective* comes next and is the same for both your short and your long résumé. One of the top so-called résumé experts in the country advises job hunters to leave the objective out of the résumé and put it in the cover letter. This tells me that this man has never been in the human resources department of a large company. He would soon see that résumés either get sep-arated from their cover letters or the cover letters get folded to the back so that the résumé is on top and visible. Without your objective right at the top, you're asking potential employers to do a lot of digging and guessing. When they are processing hundreds or thousands of résumés, they have no time for that.

Your résumé, with no objective, may wind up in the nearest wastebasket.

When he picks up the résumé, the employer asks, What is this person applying for? Imagine you were telephoning for the job. You would say in the first few words just what you were after. Do that in writing. Everything else in the résumé must be tied into this objective, to show how you fit the situation you want. Here, and all the way through, avoid putting down extraneous material. Don't say anything about yourself that does not have a direct bearing on your job objective.

In your objective, be both broad and specific. By this I mean that you should broadly define your overall objective, then tailor it to a particular type of position. For example, your objective might read, "Sales, concentrating on national distribution," or "Sales to food wholesalers," or "Sales to architects and engineers." Beyond this, don't say "engineer" when you should be saying "civil engineer" or "hydraulic engineer." Don't say "advertising" when you mean "advertising copywriter" or "advertising art director." Let the reader of your résumé know, immediately and up front, what you want to do.

This may mean preparing résumés with different objectives for different jobs. It may mean highlighting certain work experience to show your credentials for a particular job. For example, a job seeker from California with a background in international banking came to one of our Massachusetts offices to seek a new position. There are few jobs in international banking in western Massachusetts, however, so our Professional Employment Counsellor helped him refocus his résumé toward an objective of financial analyst. Pinpointing this objective, and emphasizing the duties on his last job as they related to financial analysis, got him the position he wanted.

If you pinpoint your goals and experience via a well-phrased objective, the reader can easily evaluate everything in the résumé in terms of your objective. The reader can then decide whether or not you are qualified for the available job. The reader doesn't have to play games, which saves both his time and yours.

3. *Education*, if you are a recent graduate or if you have a special degree or degrees qualifying you for a particular job, comes next. (If your education is not current or not particularly relevant to

the job you are seeking, describe your work experience next and your educational background thereafter.) Start with the highest degree first and then list your other schooling in declining order of importance. In each case, include the name of the institution, the degree, and the date completed. If you don't have a college degree, note any credit hours you have toward a degree as well as any specialized courses you've taken. If you do have a degree, your comprehensive résumé is the place to include major and minor subjects, job-related courses, grade-point average, honors, awards, and activities.

4. *Work Experience*, if you've been out of school for a while, is the heart of your résumé. Here is where you want to, indeed must, put your best foot forward. You want to create the best picture of yourself consistent with the facts. You don't want to clutter the picture by giving irrelevant information undue prominence. But how do you give proper emphasis for this particular job hunt to the position you held four years ago, while minimizing what you've been doing for the last two years?

If you have this problem, you'll want to consider the difference between a chronological résumé and a functional résumé. In a chronological résumé, appropriate for most people, you'll list each position you've held (even if the jobs were within the same firm), starting with the most recent one and working backward. In a functional résumé, list the functions (field of specialization or types of work, such as engineering or sales promotion or personnel management) that are related to your present job objectives; briefly describe (remember, use those action verbs) the work you have done in each of these fields. Choose a chronological résumé if your work experience has built from job to job, with increasing responsibility, toward the job you now want. Choose the functional approach if there are gaps in your work history or if you've held recent jobs that are not on your current career path.

Either way, as you list the jobs you've held, remember these points:

- Start with the company name, if it is highly recognizable and a credit to you, or with the job title, if that has more punch. Always include the location of the facility where you were employed and the name and title of your immediate superior.

• Include months as well as year if it will make your record appear more stable. Noting that you held a job from 1984 to 1986 could mean only fourteen months on the job if you worked from December 1984 to January 1986. It could mean almost three full years on the job if you worked from January 1984 to December 1986. There is, of course, a difference.

• Use action words to describe your duties. We said this before, but we'll say it again. Wherever possible, say that you "directed" or "developed" or "organized" or "sold." See the list below for samples of highly suitable action and self-descriptive words.

• Don't use jargon or gobbledegook. Don't say that you "coordinate the communication program and develop cost structures for high-tension facilities between source and points of distribution, securing easements, completing surveys, aerial and topographical, and calculating specifications." Instead say that you are a transmission engineer and note that you "directed the entire XYZ project, bringing it in three weeks under schedule at a cost saving of $48,000."

Key Words for Résumé and Cover Letter Preparation
ACTION WORDS

achieved	arranged	classified
acquired	assembled	compiled
adapted	assisted	completed
administered	budgeted	conceived
analyzed	built	conducted
anticipated	calculated	coordinated

corresponded

created

delegated

demonstrated

designed

developed

directed

edited

established

estimated

evaluated

expedited

explained

facilitated

formulated

generated

handled

imagined

implemented

improved

increased

initiated

instituted

instructed

intervened

interviewed

invented

launched

located

logged

managed

mastered

mediated

moderated

motivated

negotiated

operated

ordered

organized

participated

persuaded

pinpointed

pioneered

planned

prepared

presented

produced

programmed

proposed

recommended

recruited

reduced

referred

reorganized

represented

researched

revised

saved

scheduled

set up

simplified

sold

solved

streamlined

structured

supervised

supported

taught

trained

translated

updated

wrote

SELF-DESCRIPTIVE WORDS

active	consistent	foresight
adaptable	contributor	idealistic
adventurous	cooperative	imaginative
aggressive	cost-conscious	independent
alert	creative	individualistic
ambitious	decisive	industrious
analytical	deliberate	innovative
articulate	dependable	insightful
artistic	determined	instrumental
assertive	diplomatic	inventive
attentive	disciplined	logical
aware	dynamic	loyal
bold	economical	mature
broad-minded	effective	methodical
businesslike	efficient	meticulous
calm	energetic	natural
capable	enterprising	objective
careful	exceptional	open-minded
challenging	experienced	optimistic
clear thinking	fair	organized
competent	farsighted	original
competitive	firm	patient
confident	flexible	perceptive
conscientious	forceful	persistent

personable	resourceful	tactful
persuasive	responsible	team player
precise	responsive	tenacious
productive	self-confident	thorough
proficient	self-reliant	thoughtful
rational	sensitive	tolerant
realistic	serious	trusting
reasonable	sincere	understanding
reflective	sophisticated	versatile
reliable	systematic	vigorous

5. *Organizations and affiliations* should be listed, along with your activities therein, if they are relevant to the position you are seeking. Don't include religious or social groups unless they contain actual work experience; stick to professional and business associations. Don't abbreviate, even though you may assume the initials are clear in context. AMA, after all, may mean American Medical Association; it also stands for American Management Association. Similarly ABA means the American Bankers Association, the American Bar Association, and the American Booksellers Association. Will the real organization please stand up?

6. *Remarks*, or "Special Skills" or "Miscellaneous," is a heading for relevant information that may not fit under one of the standard résumé headings: languages spoken, articles published, community positions held, relevant hobbies, personal strengths, and so on.

This kind of information on a résumé is sometimes more important than it may seem. One applicant's door-to-door selling experience as a student helped him get a managerial position in a municipal convention and tourist bureau a number of years later because it indicated that he was good at meeting all kinds of people. Another's hobby of designing her own and her friends' clothes led to a position in a department store buying office. An advertising copywriter qualified with a new agency as a weekend boating enthusiast; the agency had taken on a boat manufacturer's account. And a former chain-grocery manager, whose résumé remarks showed that he was a popular speaker at local service clubs, is now a national lecturer on health-food products.

This section is also the place to list your personal qualities, so long as those qualities fit the job you want. List "versatile, creative, imaginative" for that copywriter's job; stick to "experienced, thorough, inquiring" if your chosen field is accounting.

Again, I urge you, toot your own horn. No one else will do it for you. Don't be like the applicant who came in to me and kept pulling his jacket around him until I finally found out what he was hiding—his Phi Beta Kappa key. His mother liked him to wear it, he said, but he felt it looked like bragging! I told him to go ahead and brag. He worked hard for it, and in fact it will show most employers what he can do. Another applicant, a former college football captain, didn't even hint that he had been an athlete until I pulled it out of him. Yet such leadership ability is of great interest to many employers.

These "incidental" sides of you, in short, aren't. They can be very important, but they must for the most part be recent and relevant. Did you hold a class office? Did you earn part of your way through school? Were you on the school paper, the debating society, the crew? Sales companies look for just such backgrounds. Are you on your town's school board? Do you coordinate the local little league? Put it down!

7. *Personal information*, which comes last, can be a tremendous sales tool, if you let it, and if you use your imagination and creativity. Instead of putting "Married, two children" or "Single," both of which are pretty blah, spiff them up a bit. Look at the difference between "Married, two children," and "Happily married eighteen years. Wife active in community affairs. Children: boy, age fourteen, and girl, age twelve." Or try this one; "Married, husband in career position with Bell Telephone (fourteen years), no reason to expect relocation. Two children, both in high school and both with after-school jobs." See the difference? In these examples, you're giving employers what they're looking for: sound, solid people with stability built into their lives; happy family people who would make good, happy employees. Or, if

you're single, instead of simply saying "Single," try "Single, willing to travel and/or relocate."

Then there's the really personal information: your height and weight. If you choose to include these vital statistics at all, do so with some meaning. For example: "6 feet 1 inch and 180 pounds; health nut; jog three miles per day, nonsmoker." Now you're telling the employer that you're a good, healthy, energetic individual. That's what employers want to hear.

But be careful about the personal information you choose to include. It's okay to mention that you're married and have children if that's a plus for you; it's not okay if you're divorced and have preschoolers at home, because the employer might well decide that you won't be reliable. It's illegal for an employer to ask you about your childcare plans, but that doesn't mean that he won't be concerned. So if you can alleviate his concerns without his asking, do so. Similarly an employer won't ask your age, religion, or national origin, and there's no need for you to volunteer the information. Why take the chance that an interviewer might be bigoted when that bigotry could cost you the job?

If you've been head of volunteer activities for your local church, you may find it worthwhile to include the information as an indication of your organizational abilities (especially if it bolsters an otherwise weak résumé). Just be careful and you'll be protecting the employer as well as yourself. No employer wants to be sued for rejecting someone on racial or religious grounds; they would rather not know what race or religion you are, just so that the question never arises. If you want to include the information because you think it will help your application, you may want to include it in the cover letter rather than in the résumé itself. Use your judgment.

8. *Earnings: Yes or No?* Some "experts" suggest that salary requirements don't belong on your résumé. I disagree. The salary that you can expect to earn on your new job is based on what you earned in your last job as well as on what the company pays for that particular position. Keeping your present salary a secret isn't going to help you get more money. You may get more money through skillful salary negotiations, as described later. When it comes to your résumé, however, you should include your current

salary and (especially if it shows an increase) the salary in your last position. Then, if you think you are worth a sizable increase—and if you can back up the request for such an increase with solid skills—say so. Or if you are willing to take a smaller salary in exchange for a new opportunity, point this out. Geography may play a role too, and you may have to be willing to take a cut if you have moved to a part of the country where salaries are generally lower. Whatever information about the salary you are willing to accept or will insist on having when it comes to negotiating an actual job offer should be included on your résumé. Remember, doing so will save a lot of time, money, and wild-goose chases.

Seven Deadly Sins

Now that you know what to put in your résumé, we're going to tell you, based on our years of experience, what not to put. We call these the seven deadly sins of résumé writing.

1. Making résumé too long
2. Putting data in chronological order
3. Not demonstrating your value to a prospective employer
4. Not showing your accomplishments
5. Misplacing emphasis
6. Including "blockers"
7. Being careless of quality

Let's look at these one at a time.

1. *Making résumé too long.* Your comprehensive résumé can run from four to six pages, if your experience warrants, but your concise, hard-hitting, eye-popping, door-opening sales résumé should be limited to one or two pages. Extra length hinders; it doesn't help. Put yourself in the employer's place. With preliminary screening, there may be hundreds or even thousands of résumés to go through. There may be one specific job to fill, or a number of jobs throughout the company. Long-winded ré-

sumés can confuse or, worse yet, irritate the reader. That's not what you want to do. You want to make it as easy as possible for the prospective employer to keep you in the running, to include you in the next level, to call you in for a personal interview. So keep that résumé short!

2. *Putting data in chronological order.* We've already talked about the chronological form for a résumé, starting with your most recent experience and working back. That's a good résumé technique. What you don't want to do is list your history in direct chronological order: "I was born in 1948, held by first job in 1967," and so on. By the time the reader gets to the real meat of the résumé—if he ever does—he is probably asleep. Remember, no one cares what you did five years ago, much less twenty years ago. What are you doing right now? Today? That's what is important. And that's what you want to stress in your résumé, listing your most recent job first and including the most detail about that job.

3. *Not demonstrating your value to a prospective employer.* Employers hire people for the same reasons that they buy a piece of equipment: They want to see a return on their investment. If they invest $30,000 in a person, what will they get in return? This is basic business reasoning. If the company does not make a profit on staff endeavors (including your endeavors), it will not remain in business and you will not have a job. There are all too many examples—just look at Studebaker—to prove the point.

So show value to your prospective employer by demonstrating how you reduced costs or increased sales or improved efficiency of operations for your last employer. Explain, concisely but completely, how you reduced inventory or created a new filing system or developed a computerized mailing list. This demonstration of value is far more important than all the job titles you can list.

4. *Not showing your accomplishments.* Hand in hand with value, these are the items we mentioned earlier, the ones that make you stand out from the crowd: Won top salesperson award two months out of five, wrote an article for *Computer Age* on . . . , president of the student council, work with the handicapped. These are the items that you may feel uncomfortable or awkward in mentioning. But this is not the place for false modesty. You must mention your accomplishments, and you must do so in

specific terms. Don't just say you supervised a department; say how big that department was. Don't just say you increased sales, say by what percentage. These are the facts that make your résumé stand tall, head and shoulders above the competition.

5. *Misplacing emphasis.* We might call this "no emphasis at all," because too many résumés are just a conglomeration of facts (some good, some bad), usually in the wrong sequence.

Why, for instance, must you put your address right smack at the top? As we said earlier, it belongs at the bottom. Education is usually a top-of-the-résumé item, but in many cases it rightfully belongs further down. It's one thing if you're a recent graduate. It's another if you've been on the job for a while. We had to tell one mechanical engineer, technically skilled but not job-search skilled, to reverse education and experience on his résumé. Having a degree from Ohio State was simply less important than working on electromechanical devices and earning $48,000 a year. Once you are heavyweight champ of the world, in short, you can stop bragging about winning the Golden Gloves six years ago.

A trained eye can pick out dozens of places in a typical résumé where emphasis has been misplaced or left out entirely. Some people ramble on in the objective, telling all about the wonderful company they want to join. Heck, the company knows it's wonderful; you don't need to say so. Others wax poetic about all the wonderful things they want to do for the company: "utilize my skills, training, and talent to the fullest," "reach the full potential of my creative and managerial abilities and talents." What such phrases say, if anyone takes the time to read them, is that you haven't made it yet. Still others list sixteen references, many duplicating the supervisors listed under employers. References don't belong on a résumé at all, and they certainly won't get you an interview. And some job seekers go into boring and repetitive detail about the jobs they've held. Does it really make sense to say that as sales manager you supervised sales? That's like saying that as a file clerk you filed papers. Give potential employers some credit for understanding job titles. And don't fall in love with your own history. As the old song goes, "You've got to accentuate the positive, eliminate the negative, and don't mess with Mr. In-Between." Forget about anything in between.

6. *Including "blockers."* In the employment service profession we've identified certain recurring résumé errors that we call blockers, certain to block you from securing the job you want. These include

- No objective. This can't be emphasized enough. The reader of a résumé should know in advance what it is about; then every fact listed should relate back to that objective.

- Old experience. Talk about jobs held ten, fifteen, or twenty years ago and you'll appear older than necessary. Those jobs, moreover, have little bearing on what you can do today.

- References. Don't list them on your résumé. Every employer knows that you will supply references on request.

- Lying. Whether about schooling, dates of employment, salaries, or job titles, this is the worst blocker of all. Employers are wise to misrepresentation; they check the facts, these days, and insist on documentation.

7. *Being careless of quality.* Is it really necessary to say that your résumé should be neatly typed on top-quality paper and professionally duplicated? That you should check and doublecheck your spelling? I recently received a young man's résumé, a nicely prepared, well-laid-out one-pager. He noted that he had graduated a semester early, was thirty-seventh in his class, and had a 3.5 grade point average. But he undid the good impression this made by misspelling no fewer than eleven words. He certainly wasn't ready for responsibility if he couldn't spell it! If you can't spell, use a dictionary. Or use a word processing program that has a built-in dictionary. At the very least, get someone to check your work or hire a professional to do it for you. Your résumé, remember, is selling you.

Résumé Style

Quality is one thing; appearance is another. Whatever you do, you'll do it with quality, using good paper and a neat format and perfect reproduction. But you may also want to produce a résumé with distinctive style.

Most books and articles tell you to keep your résumé low key in style. They tell you to stick to white, cream, or buff paper and to do nothing fancy at all. This advice is okay if you're aiming for the middle management job market these books and articles are addressing. But we see thousands of people from all walks of life, applying for jobs from file clerk to company president, and we know that there is room in the résumé arena for some individuality and some creativity.

Used wisely, color can make your résumé truly eye-catching. Your résumé is, after all, an advertisement for yourself, and color is what sells in ads. We're not suggesting that you run out and print a four-color résumé with a beautiful picture of you, your spouse, and your children, although we do know an applicant who landed a job in just this way. He sent the employer an eight-by-ten color photograph of his family with a note that said, "This is all the incentive I need to do a tremendous job for you." He had eight children. The employer was so impressed that he called him and hired him on the spot!

Unless you have eight children, try using color without the family photograph. When you choose your paper stock, think about the kind of job you're seeking. Buff, white, and cream are fine for managerial jobs or any job at all in a conservative organization. If you're after an advertising agency job, however, or one in the design department of a department store, try using light pastel green or lavender or any color that will make your résumé stand out in a pile.

Borders can also lend a distinctive touch to your résumé. Just look at the Yellow Pages. Which ads jump out at you? Nine times out of ten, the ones with a border. The same is true of a résumé. Why not tie this whole beautiful package together with a nice border around it? Use a bold border, if that's the kind of job you're after, or a thin, elegant line if that's more appropriate. Either way, you'll be presenting a special package to potential employers.

Type comes in different varieties too, but the best advice here is to stick to a clear, readable typeface. Don't use italic or anything so full of curlicues that it's difficult to read and doesn't look businesslike. Use a crisp, clean typeface, and don't be afraid to use bullets, small, filled-in circles, at the beginning of a statement to call attention to important facts:

- Won Employee of the Quarter five times
- Consistently under budget on expenses

Let's face it. A résumé for a secretary and a résumé for a vice president of finance can and probably should be very different in appearance. By the same token, the résumés of a programmer and an advertising copywriter should be different. Sit down and give your résumé some thought. If you're not sure whether, or how, to be creative, then perhaps you should seek out a professional who can help you make your résumé stand out from the crowd.

Résumé Services

With thought and attention to detail, you can create your own winning résumé. Or you can utilize a résumé counseling and writing service. Note that I did not say résumé "preparation." Taking your résumé and making a few cosmetic changes or no changes at all, simply preparing copies, is résumé preparation. If a "service" charges you $15 or $20, all they're going to do is prepare your own résumé for you. Tote it up—they can't afford to give you the service you need to create a winning résumé. Twenty dollars won't cover their time much less rent, phone, advertising, and so on.

You're talking about marketing a commodity—yourself—worth $250,000 to $1 million or more (if you look at your salary and benefits over the next ten years). Don't cut corners on your résumé. If you want to have outside help, get professional outside help. Get the kind of help where the individual interviews you in depth to find out what you have done, what you would like to do, and what you are qualified to do, then writes your résumé for you.

Résumé Samples

Now let's put theory into practice. You're read all about how to write a résumé. Now you can actually read some winners. Let's start, though, with a before-and-after story.

Look at the "Sally Smith" résumés on the next two pages (a real résumé but altered, of course, to protect the innocent). The first, the "before" part of the story, is a clear illustration of how we freeze up when it's time to write about ourselves. Here was an individual who was in the sales and public relations business, had put on trade shows all over the United States, written ads, knew how to do her job, yet when it was time to write up the résumé, it was four pages of dullsville. Just look at it. Why did she have to write "Name" before her name? Or the word "Address" before her address? It's perfectly obvious to the reader that this is her name and address. Then we were immediately into birth date and age. Giving both is repetitive, but giving either compromises the employer. It's also unnecessary at this stage of the game to put the full address of the telephone company, her current employer; the most that's needed now is general location and then only if it's information that might help to sell her to the next employer. And then, worst of all, she's into the "I, I, I" syndrome.

When you look at Sally's "after" résumé you see right away that it is something special because it is the "confidential" résumé of Sally Smith. Furthermore, it's got an objective. This individual is looking for a job in sales and public relations, and everything in the résumé from here on shows abilities and experience in these areas. Look at that simple job, or what we might perceive as a simple job, as customer service rep for the phone company. Look at what she did on that job that she never bothered to tell anyone about, until it was pulled out of her by one of our Professional Employment Counsellors. Look at the difference that action words make—"designed," "implemented," "developed," "coordinated," "handled"—instead of "I am" and "I do."

In its second version Sally Smith's résumé is a beautiful, hard-hitting résumé printed on light yellow stock with a fine green border. It shows just the right touch of pizzazz and a knack for sales promotion.

Before:

RÉSUMÉ

NAME:	Sally S. Smith
ADDRESS:	2222 West Apple, Apt. 4B
	Alameda, CA 33782
PHONE:	924-622-3121
BIRTH DATE:	September 10, 1967
MARITAL STATUS:	Single
AGE:	24
EMPLOYMENT:	

<u>BELL TELEPHONE COMPANY OF CALIFORNIA</u>

1452 W. Bay St.   June 87–Present Employer
Los Angeles, CA
33791
Phone: 924-444-2121

I am currently employed as a customer service representative in the Final Bill Department at the customer billing center. My duties are that of handling the billing accounts for those customers which have delinquent accounts . . . blah blah blah blah (for three more pages in the same cold, boring style)

The next illustration, the résumé of Linda A. Spragins, is the exception that breaks the rule. We said earlier that an individual just out of school should keep his or her résumé to one page. Linda had just graduated, yet she had such excellent information to convey about both her education and her work experience, information directly relevant to her career objective, that her résumé ran to two pages. But it's two solid pages, and we wouldn't suggest cutting it at all.

Our last illustration demonstrates exactly what we mean by the two-résumé approach, the introductory send-ahead résumé and the detailed leave-with-the-interviewer résumé. Look at and analyze the résumés of Alan B. Stoner. The first gets all the vital information on one page: current and previous employers, highlighted responsibilities and accomplishments at each employer, education, memberships and affiliations, personal data. The sec-

After:

CONFIDENTIAL RÉSUMÉ OF		**SALLY S. SMITH**

OBJECTIVE: SALES/PUBLIC RELATIONS

EXPERIENCE: Customer Service Representative   1986–present

Bell Telephone Company
Los Angeles, CA

- Recognized as senior problem solver and troubleshooter

- Designed and implemented all training programs for department

- Train all new customer service personnel

Sales and Public Relations Consultant   1982–1986

International Sheet Music Society
Seattle, WA

- Developed and presented successful trade shows nationwide

- Coordinated all sales between wholesalers, distributors, and retailers

- Handled display, merchandising, advertising, and promotion

rah, rah, rah—for the rest of the page . . .

---

ond, in five pages, spells out all the information in greater detail. Take a close look at both versions of Alan Stoner's résumé, and think about what you might do with your own.

Cover Letters

In just about every instance a cover letter should accompany your résumé when it's sent to a prospective employer. The only exception might be when you go directly to a hiring authority with a hard-hitting, one-page teaser résumé. In this instance you are letting him know you are available. If they can use your skills, they will call; if not, they won't.

The Confidential Résumé of   LINDA A. SPRAGINS

OBJECTIVE: SALES TRAINEE position with a company that offers career pathing and an opportunity to demonstrate my full potential.

EDUCATION: Bachelor of Arts in Business Administration, concentration on marketing, Mt. Vernon College, Washington, D.C.

ACTIVITIES
AND HONORS:

President of Judicial Board
- Conducted all hearings for various offenses.
- Authorized punishment for individuals who violated the offense.
- Researched, wrote, and successfully campaigned for passage of the academic honor code, which had to be persuasively marketed to students, faculty, and the board of trustees.
- Wrote and revised the procedures and constitution for Judicial Board.

Founder and President of American Marketing Association Chapter
- Organized and coordinated the first collegiate chapter at MVC.
- Arranged and provided activities and speakers to enhance the students' knowledge of all aspects in the marketing field.
- Marketed this organization, which developed into the largest association or club on campus.

Student Member of the Board of Trustees
- Directly involved in the decision-making process on issues and problems facing the college.
- Responsible for providing information on students' needs and desires in all areas of the college.
- Provided my perspective into issues to be voted on.

Organizations
     Student Member, Academic Court
     Executive Voting Member, Student Government Association
     Development Committee
     Honorary Degree Committee
     Student Life Committee
     Resident Assistant
     President of Chapel Committee
     Appeals Court
     Character of Excellence Award
     Citizenship Award
     Student Life Award
     Nominated for Outstanding Young Women of America

EXPERIENCE: **Snelling and Snelling Corporate Headquarters, Sarasota, FL**
1983 Summer Internship
Management Training Program
- Training for recruiting and marketing franchises.
- Successfully completed two-week training program for Professional Employ-ment Counsellors and Managers.
- Performed the Job of Professional Employment Counsellor and successfully marketed people by contacting employers, obtaining job orders, interviewing and evaluating applicants, matching applicants to the job specifications, and ar-ranging interviews for those who qualified for the positions.
- Studied budgets and annual reports.
- Input into computer information on payroll, accounts payable, accounts re-ceivable, and overrides.
- Learned how to tap into West Law System through word processor to track down cases.

Baskin and Sears, Washington, D.C.   **April 1982 to Present**
Law Clerk
- Successfully completed and provided research for fifteen attorneys.
- Travel with attorneys to perform research.
- Responsible for gathering information and preparing manuals for the annual American Bar Association meeting.

Snelling and Snelling Corporate Headquarters, Sarasota, FL
Summer Holidays
- Recruiting calls for franchise prospects
- Receptionist

Ellies Bookstore, Sarasota, FL   **1978–1979**
Inventory Controller

Bresler's Ice Cream Store, Sarasota, FL   **1976–1978**
Assistant Manager
- Ran store and supervised staff in manager's absence.

REFERENCES: The finest of business and personal references available upon request.

PERSONAL: Single, excellent health. Willing to relocate and travel.

2100 Foxhall Road N.W., Washington, D.C. 20007 (202) 331-0400

Alan B. Stoner

Objective:	**Senior Analyst** position with the opportunity to advance to upper management in an organization dedicated to high technology and state-of-the-art hardware.
Professional Experience	**Systems Analyst/Data Processing Manager**
	Marker, Inc., Ithaca, New York
	Report to: J. B. Iken, President and CEO
August 1982 to present	Total and direct responsibility for all systems development from inception to completion, utilizing state-of-the-art equipment: IBM 4341, MVS SYSTEM running IMS-DB/DC, and for maintaining entire system-wide data base and interactive processing system.
Accomplishments	Directed and installed major communications network involving over fifty computers nationwide.
	Established cost-effective utilization of time-share terminal room, which reduced on-line storage costs by over $30,000 per month.
Formal Education	M.S. Computer Science, Ohio State University
	B.S. Computer Science, Ohio State University
	B.S. Business Administration, Penn State University
Professional	COBOL, FORTRAN IV, JOVIAL, DEC, Data General IMS, DB/DC, SQL, QBE, dBASE III
Hardware and Software	IBM 4341, OS, MVS, CPCS, CICS, JES2,3, DOS, JCL
	IBM 3033, 370/168, 370/158, AMDAHL 470V/8,7,6
	PDP 11/70, 11/45, UNIX, XED, PASCAL, C, APL
	UNIVAC 9300-DOS, RPGII
Memberships and Affiliations	Data Processing Managers Association
	American Society of Data Processing Managers
	Rotary International, Club President
	Ohio Jaycees, Former State Director
	Jaycees "Speak-Up" Contest Winner
Personal	Happily married (10 years), wife: Mary Jane
	Three children: David 8, Joan 6, Cindy 3
	Excellent shape: 5 feet 11 inches, 165 pounds
	No physical disabilities

121 Howard Street, Ithaca, NY 10457   Home: (112) 372-8431

I The Comprehensive Résumé of   Alan B. Stoner

Objective: **Senior Analyst** position with the opportunity to advance to upper management in an organization dedicated to high technology and state-of-the-art hardware.

Professional Experience

August 1982 to present

Systems Analyst/Data Processing Manager
Marker, Inc.
687 Roger Blvd., Suite 102
Ithaca, New York 10458
Report to: J. B. Iken, President and CEO
Telephone: (112) 783-5410

Promoted to this position ahead of schedule. Total and direct responsibility for all systems development from inception to completion utilizing state-of-the-art equipment: IBM 4341, MVS SYSTEM, running IMS-DB/DC, and for maintaining entire systemwide data base and interactive processing system. Appointed to four-member planning committee, with responsibility to review, evaluate, and develop company strategic planning, procedures, and policies.

Responsibilities
- Liaison between data-processing department and its users, upper management, and outside service bureau users.
- Presently manage an annual budget in excess of $1.5 million and directly supervise staff of fifty, including programmer analysts, computer operators, outside consultants, and data entry clerks.
- Developing and maintaining systems and programming specifications.
- All programming, testing, and debugging.
- All hardware and software conversions.
- Acquiring and developing staff personnel.
- Designing, developing, and instituting all training procedures.

Accomplishments
- Designed, created,and implemented an accepted software and hardware feasibility study that resulted in creating a cost-effective and efficient operating environment.
- Directed and installed major communications network involving over fifty computers nationwide.
- Successfully designed a module of interactive business systems for new services offered by Marker, Inc.
- Established cost-effective utilization of time-share terminal room, which reduced on-line storage costs by over $30,000 per month.
- Solely responsible for implementation of accounts payable and general ledger analysis for company subsidiaries and conversions of their manual accounts payable to computer systems.

Earnings Package

Salary $55,000; benefit package includes major medical, hospital, full life, dental, savings program, four weeks' paid vacation, and profit sharing.

Reason for leaving: Company's no-growth posture limits opportunity for advancement.

2 The Comprehensive Résumé of	**Alan B. Stoner**

September 1976 to July 1982

Systems Representative/Technical Advisor
Burroughs Corporation
One International Plaza
Pittsburgh, Pennsylvania 15319
Report to: Robert L. Lewiston, Senior Systems Administrator
Telephone: (412) 148-4562

Promoted to position of Technical Advisor. Originally hired as System Representative for the Burroughs Regional Group. Charged with total responsibility to oversee the installation of numerous Level 64 user groups. Additionally developed and implemented technical presentations to data-processing professionals. Had direct supervision of all conversion teams throughout the region. Responsible for surveying various needs to accomplish user goals, and direct interface with corporate offices for fact-finding.

Accomplishments

- Directed, installed, and supervised regional communications network.
- Directed successful installation of several Level 4 accounts, which required the design and writing of many interactive inquiries and data-collecting programs.
- Appointed to the Burroughs Regional Software Package Group in charge of all business systems. Performed analysis of users to determine feasibility of prepackaged software.
- Successfully designed new module for regional billing system.
- Initiated the ongoing evaluation of all new system products and created an in-house training program offering over twenty-five different classes in the areas of programming, system design operations, and business.
- Instituted the restructuring of the Customer Service Department to ensure effective user-data center communications and customer support.

Earnings Package

Salary $38,000. Benefits: major medical (including family), hospital, surgical, dental, life ($50,000) AD&D, company car, profit sharing (matching 1:1)

Reason for leaving: Recruited for Marker, Inc., at $40,500.

3 The Comprehensive Résumé of   Alan B. Stoner

January 1973 to July 1976	**Programmer/Analyst**
	West Hill International
	4000 S. Admiral Drive
	Columbus, Ohio 43085
	Report to: Donald R. Jacobs, Senior Programmer
	Telephone: (614) 169-3000

Started as a programmer trainee directly from college internship while attending graduate school at Ohio State University. Advanced swiftly to programmer/analyst. Directly responsible for daily interfacing with users to determine needs of each. Performed analysis and selection of correct software packages to answer users' requirements. Involved in rewriting and modifying selected packages to users' specifications. Performed all programming and JCL creation to bring projects to timely completion and within accepted budget guidelines. Prepared all documentation for all customized features and additions.

Accomplishments
- Successfully monitored project status (costs, manpower utilization) to produce P.E.R.T. Chart for proper reporting to international headquarters.
- Representative to the Project Team Steering Committee.
- Maintained operating systems to proper patch levels to ensure timely and accurate throughput.
- Received company's President's Club Award in 1974 and 1975.

Earnings Package

Salary $22,000 plus major benefit package which was 100 percent company paid.

Reason for leaving: Career advancement opportunity.

Formal Education:

M.S. Computer Science
Ohio State University
3.5 GPA with honors
Past President of DPME, OSU Chapter
Omicron Pi Honor Society
Taught and tutored various math courses

Assisted in teaching DP classes for the department
B.S. Computer Science
B.S. Business Administration (double major)
Penn State University
3.8 GPA, cum laude
Who's Who Among Students in American Universities and Colleges
President's List
Pennsylvania State Scholarship
Junior Computer Science Technical Society Award
Co-Captain, lacrosse team
Intramural boxing
Earned 75 percent of funds needed for education
R.O.T.C.

4 The Comprehensive Résumé of   *Alan B. Stoner*

Professional	COBOL programming FORTRAN IV programming JOVIAL programming DEC, operations and programming Honeywell Transaction System programming and interactive programming Data-base management: IMS DB/DC, SQL, QBE, dBASE III & DBGT Related courses in Advanced Programming Languages, Advanced Data-Base Design, Computer Architecture, and Computer Graphics.
Hardware and Software	IBM 4341, OS, MS, MVS, CPCS, CICS, JES2,3, DOS, JCL IBM 3033, 370/168, 370/158, AMDAHL 470V/8,7,6 PDP 11/70, 11/45, UNIX, XED, PASCAL, C, APL UNIVAC 9300-DOS, RPGII
Memberships and Affiliations	Data Processing Managers Associations American Society of Data Processing Managers American Management Association Rotary International, Club President Chamber of Commerce Community Chest, Board of Directories Ohio Jaycees, Former State Director Jaycees "Speak-Up" Contest Winner Tau Kappa Epsilon, Past President and presently Regional Representative
Military	United States Air Force, 1965–1971 Captain, Supply and Ordnance Developed fiscal policy and administered budget and supply account Supervised staff of 115 (including 75 civilians) Special training: Civilian management courses for supervisors Equal Opportunity and Treatment School (nine weeks, ten hrs/day) Honorable Discharge Decided against reenlistment in order to return to college to study computer science.
Languages	French, speak and write fluently
Travel & Relocation	Willing to travel up to 40 percent and willing to relocate (prefer Sun Belt)
Personal	Articulate, outgoing, friendly but firm, work well with superiors, peers, and subordinates. Hard-working, honest, ethical, and loyal. Happily married (10 years), wife: Mary Jane (Graduate, Boston College, B.S. accounting) Three children: David 8, Joan 6, Cindy 3 Member, First Baptist Church, Ithaca, New York Teacher, Adult Sunday School Vice Chairman, Deacons Wife teaches third grade Sunday School

5 The Comprehensive Résumé of	Alan B. Stoner

Health & Fitness
Annual physical, excellent health
5 feet 11 inches, 165 pounds, no physical disabilities
Blond, blue eyes, excellent professional appearance
Dress conservatively but authoritatively

Activities
Hobbies: Photography, furniture refinishing, reading (history, archeology, business, and motivational books)
Periodical reading lists: *Computer Age, BYTE, U.S. News & World Report, Business Week, Fortune,* and *National Geographic*
Sports: tennis, golf, scuba diving, marathon running, racquetball

121 Howard Street, Ithaca, NY 10457   Home: (112) 372-8431

In every other case, whether you are answering a blind box number ad in a newspaper or sending a targeted mailing to five hundred companies in your field, your résumé should be accompanied by a cover letter. That letter should, whenever possible, be addressed to a specific individual at the hiring company and focus directly on that company's needs. If you are replying to a box number ad, be sure to include the box number and publication at the top of your letter. The company may have placed ads in different publications with different box numbers, and you want them to be clear about which ad you are answering.

If you are writing to fifty hand-picked companies, seeking a job in sales, you might start out by saying, "I believe I can increase your sales and at the same time lower your cost of sales." Now you have their attention. Keep that attention with a next sentence something like this: "That's because I've done it before for Burroughs and Syntex." Now you can continue: "I have a great deal of excellent experience in sales and sales management, and I'd like to tell you directly why I feel I can be a valuable employee for your firm." Then go for the sale: "I'll call on Monday, the fifth, to set up a mutually agreeable time for us to meet." See the sample letter in this section.

There are several important rules for cover letters:

- Always type your letter, as you do your résumé.

- Devote time and attention to your cover letter; never assume that it will be thrown away. Remember that the letter is the first thing the recipient sees, the first sales piece that is read about you.

- Try to address your letter to a specific person. You may find the appropriate name in a business directory; you may even get the name and title by calling the company and asking the switchboard operator.

- Be brief, clear, and businesslike, but state exactly the kind of position you are seeking and why you are applying to this particular firm.

- Give value. Tell the reader, without bragging, what you have to offer and why it will make good business sense to interview you.

- Always conclude by asking for the sale. Don't do it with that weak, limp, "I'll look forward to hearing from you at your convenience." Instead let them know that you will call on such-and-such date to schedule an interview or, if you are writing from another town, that you will be in the area on specific dates and will call for an appointment.

The cover letter from E. Z. Doesit is an example of a cover letter not to write.

This is a flagrant example of a letter writer interested only in himself and his own problems. Why should any employer care that he's unhappy in his present job? That he feels unappreciated? That he wants to move to Florida? An employer wants to know only what you can do for him. Tell him so in a letter that is bright, positive, upbeat, and a sales tool of the highest magnitude. The cover letter from Christine Donnally and A. Goodbone are examples of good cover letters.

If you were looking for a purchasing agent of military-related electronic components, would you want to read A. Goodbone's résumé? You bet you would. You can plainly see that he's a winner, he knows what's important to you, and he's not wasting your time. Did you also notice how he subtly used the old sales

To: Box No. 475
    Wall Street Journal

Dear Mr. Box,

  I know you are not my own company because your ad told me so. Besides your job sounds much better than anything around here.

  I'm sure you would appreciate me, even though my present employer doesn't. They have stuck me out here in the warehouse without even a decent typewriter, as you can plainly see. My supervisor isn't here half the time, he has something going on the side.

  My wife and I would like to move to Florida, can't stand these winters. You might be able to use her too, she's a good typist and can't find any work here.

  My resume is enclosed, I sure hope you will give me a chance at the job, I'm a hard worker.

E. Z. Doesit
P.O. Box 12
Mountain View, PA 34782

take-away routine by saying that he was under consideration elsewhere? That puts a little pressure on this company to move. If that Human Resources department is under pressure to get a purchasing agent in there to replace one who is leaving or has already left, they are going to respond to this applicant quickly. But he's smart in not putting too much pressure on the employer; he lets them know that he's still responding to ads and he's particularly interested in the company because of its upstate New York location. Keep your cover letters simple and hard-hitting, and wind up by asking for the sale.

Ms. Elaine Neilson
Director of Marketing
National Computer Co., Inc.
2611 W. Madison St.
Chicago, IL 60611

Dear Ms. Neilson:

For the last eight years I have been solving marketing problems for companies such as Zenith and Warner Electronic Systems.

I had the good fortune of being trained by these firms in organization, management and strategic business planning, and am now ready to pass this experience and training on to your organization.

Some highlights:
- At Zenith I created and implemented an advertising and sales promotion campaign that resulted in an increase in sales of over $6 million.
- By developing a market research program to determine the feasibility of expanding the market for Warner products, we were able to increase our client base by 15 percent.

As indicated on the enclosed résumé, I can bring to your firm a high level of expertise in marketing and product management experience with Fortune 100 companies.

Thank you for your time. I will call you Wednesday, March 5, to arrange a mutually convenient interview.

Very truly yours,

Christine Donnally

Box 324
New York Times

ATTENTION: Human Resources Department

Having had five years' experience in purchasing military-related electronic components, I believe I can do an outstanding job for you.

During the last year I evaluated and purchased over $5 million worth of noncontract items. I was able to keep the costs well below budget. I also negotiated the purchase of another $10 million of subassemblies under performance contracts that were highly in favor of our firm.

A prompt call would be appreciated as I am presently under consideration by two other firms. Your location in upstate New York is of interest to me since my wife's parents live there.

Very truly yours,

A. Goodbone

6

Using an Employment Service

You can get a job on your own. But in the all-out war of job campaign, you want to enlist all the weapons at your disposal. Some of the most potent weapons in the job seeker's arsenal are professional employment services. We don't mean that you must stick to a Snelling office. But you'll be missing significant opportunities in your job campaign if you fail to utilize employment services that handle the type of position you're seeking. In fact our two eldest daughters were placed by our competitors. One of them was in a city where we have six offices, yet the competition did the job and did it right.

Using an employment service, whether you or the employer pays the fee, still has to be the greatest bargain going. It's one of the last, if not the only, service to operate on a "no ticket, no laundry" basis. Doctors and lawyers charge you for the time their services take, whether or not they are successful. But if the employment service doesn't find you the job, or find the company the right employee, it doesn't get one thin dime. Turn this fact to your advantage by using employment services in your search.

There are many different kinds of employment services, each filling a different role and meeting a different need. These include college placement offices, religious and nonprofit placement services, state employment services, executive counseling firms, computerized job–job seeker matching services, outplacement firms, temporary help services, résumé services, and recruiting services. It's important to understand what each can and can't do for you. Let's concentrate, first, on the employment services that can do you the most good right now.

Professional Employment Services

These private services, by far the most numerous, are professional enterprises designed to bring job seekers and employers together. Usually employment services either find or create jobs for people or fill jobs listed by employers. Most of our Snelling offices do both, and our files are full of examples of jobs being created for job seekers by employment counsellors who were on their toes. In one dramatic example, one of our offices in Massachusetts placed a young woman who was totally deaf and, unsure of anything she could do, looking for a typing job. During one of her interviews—all conducted by notes being passed back and forth because her speech was unintelligible—she indicated that her real interest was in art. Our counsellor picked up on this and persuaded a printing company to hire her to prepare plates for printing.

You can find a job through a job-filling or a job-finding service, but it doesn't take an MBA to see that your chances are greater if you use a service that does both. Those that simply fill jobs may screen you out over the phone or through a short interview, saving both their time and yours if you don't match the available job. Those that not only fill jobs but also try to find or create jobs will want to see you if at all possible. Then, if positions are available, they will tell you about them and arrange interviews. They may also choose to market you to employer-clients who use people with your skills and attributes.

Professional employment services, both those that fill jobs and those that find jobs, must charge for their services. But it's important to remember that there is a charge only when an employee-employer match is satisfactorily made. It's also worth noting that depending on where you are seeking employment, the type of job you accept, and market conditions at the time, the service charge may be paid by the employer. You'll find more details on service charges later in this chapter. Employment services are responsible for millions of successful employer-employee matches each year. They are, says the Better Business Bureau, "more aware of successful job-winning techniques than most people are likely to be."

Although they have been around in one form or another since the 1800s, employment services have had a spurt of growth over the last thirty years. This spurt is due primarily to the influence of franchising firms. (Snelling and Snelling is one of the most prominent and was the first to franchise in 1956. There are over ten thousand employment services in the United States; approximately fifteen hundred of them are franchises, independently owned while using the name, training system, and techniques of the franchisor.)

Due to the continuing shift in our work force, first from farm to factory and now from factory to service, the demand for employment services will continue to grow. Compare this to real estate. Earlier in the century most people pounded a sign in the lawn and sold their own home. Today most homes and commercial properties are sold by real estate professionals. Leading economic analysts are saying that employment services are one of the hottest growth areas of the 1980s and 1990s. This growth will provide challenging employment for hundreds of thousands and help additional millions of people to move ahead in their careers.

Services Provided

Small or large, independent or franchised, employment services can do a lot for you. Since the employment service gets paid only when you are hired and stay hired, it provides a wide range of services to make sure that you do indeed find not only a job but the right job. Here's what you can expect a good employment service to do:

- Interview you and offer a skilled appraisal of your strengths and weaknesses in the job search.

- Advise you on your career outlook and make suggestions for constructive changes.

- Review your résumé and help you target that résumé toward a particular job, in order to get you the interview you want.

- Make constructive suggestions on appearance and conduct to help you make the most of job interviews.

- Give you detailed information about a specific job opening before you go on an interview and provide background information about the hiring company and the interviewer.

- Keep in constant touch with client firms to keep current with their needs and match you with appropriate openings.

- Attempt to find or create jobs for you if none are on file and you meet their criteria for doing so.

- Fully disclose pertinent facts about you to the company prior to arranging an interview to ensure that you qualify and that every interview is a potential job offer.

- Show you how to be interviewed and like it, get the job offer, and then how to negotiate salary and fringe benefits and ultimately keep the job you want.

Employment services, as the Better Business Bureau points out, can be particularly helpful if you are attempting to move to a different location with your next job. Some—especially franchise networks—can be particularly helpful in this area.

Whether you want to move or not, an employment service can help you conduct an efficient and effective job search. You can sit and circle newspaper job listings for days, never knowing whether or not the particular jobs are right for you. A good service will send you on interviews only when the available job is right. Only a small fraction of available jobs, moreover, even make it into the classified ads. Many companies prefer to work with an employment service instead of placing ads, knowing that the service will screen applicants and refer only the most qualified job seekers. The employment service is a source of jobs not found elsewhere.

What to Expect from a Professional Employment Counsellor

A Professional Employment Counsellor is a highly trained individual whose time is extremely valuable. This doesn't mean that you will be rushed in your agency interview. But the counsellor, like any personnel specialist within a large company, will be very efficient, targeting his or her efforts to bring the right people together with the right jobs.

Very often the counsellor's evaluation of the job seeker starts with the initial phone call. How at ease is the individual on the telephone? Is he nervous? Belligerent or antagonistic? Is she decisive, sure of what she wants? Or indecisive and unsure? Does his voice have the ring of authority? Is it bright, cheerful, bubbly, and enthusiastic, or is it shy and whispery? Are answers well thought out and informative, or is each question answered with a terse yes or no? Is the applicant doing a good selling job to the counsellor, and is the applicant prepared to sell himself to an employer?

We don't know all this instinctively, but we can assess the applicant after we ask a series of questions. The first, just to get the conversation going, is simply, "How did you happen to call us?" (Over 40 percent, we find, come to us on referral by another individual.) Our second question is, "What are you doing presently?" This can reveal a lot about the individual. Some will respond, "I'm not doing anything. I just got fired." This reveals their state of mind, telling us that we've got some work to do before we can send this individual out on an interview. Sometimes it's a simple matter of coaching them not to use the word "fired" when, in fact, economic conditions have led to a general layoff. If we can get such applicants past this mental hurdle, past assuming the layoff was personal rejection, we have a much better shot at putting him or her to work in another good job, possibly even a better job than the one just eliminated.

Some applicants, of course, are seeking a new job while still employed. Here some answer "What are you doing presently?" with "I'm an accountant" or "I'm a secretary"—just the kind of clamshell reply that, although it tells us a lot about the person, would be all wrong to give a potential employer who asks the same question. This really is the opportunity for a sales pitch. Instead of saying "I'm an accountant" and then clamming up, why not say, "In my present job as an accountant, I've been actively involved in arranging a merger with the XYZ company" or "I work as a secretary and act as an administrative assistant, arranging my employer's business trips and conferences and training clerical help." This kind of detailed answer shows us— and a prospective employer—what you can do and that you're motivated to extend yourself on a new job as well.

The third and last question in the preliminary telephone interview is, "What would you like to be doing?" This gets all kinds of replies. For some, it opens up the floodgates of dissatisfaction with their jobs and with their lives. For some it triggers a well-thought-out answer about exactly what kind of job they would like: in a large office or a small one, with responsibility or without, with travel or with none. When people do respond to this question, the answers are revealing. Are their dreams pie in the sky? Or are they being realistic about what it is they want to do? Are they trying to make a tremendous career change? Are they expecting us to perform miracles for them?

COUNSELLOR:	What are you doing presently?
JOB SEEKER:	I sell shoes in a mall.
COUNSELLOR:	Oh, what would you like to be doing?
JOB SEEKER:	I'd like to sell parts in the avionics industry and make $50,000 a year.
COUNSELLOR:	I see. And what qualifies you to do that?
JOB SEEKER:	I read a lot of avionics magazines.

Some people don't know what they want to do. They are likely to say, "That's why I'm coming to you, because I need help and advice and guidance." If this is the case, we'll ask, "Why do you want to leave (or have you left) your present company?" Whatever the answer—lack of recognition, inadequate pay, poor morale, no future, etc., etc.—the answers give us clues as to how we must work with the particular individual. After this discussion, we usually invite the caller in for a personal interview.

The Personal Interview

The in-person session is crucial to the employment process. When you come in, the first thing you'll be asked to do is fill out an application. Filling out the application is good training for filling out an employer's application, so take pains to see that you do it right. That means neatly filling in every blank; you should have a detailed résumé with you so that you have the information at hand, but don't refer the reader of the application to your résumé. Make the application stand alone as a well-thought-out, forceful sales document. Companies love their applications, so make that work for you.

Next you'll be greeted personally in the reception area by a Professional Employment Counsellor. We make it a point in our company to have the counsellor go to the reception area to greet each applicant rather than having the receptionist or secretary escort the individual to the counsellor's office. This is so we can learn more about you. When we walk into the reception area and call your name, do you immediately stand up and walk toward us? Do you put out your hand to introduce yourself? Do you look us in the eye, smile, speak up in a friendly manner? Do you stand up straight, carry yourself with confidence? And are you properly dressed for going on a job interview? We want you to come see us, in other words, as if you were going to see a potential employer.

Our interview technique, developed from thousands upon thousands of interviews, is a unique combination of structure and flexibility, allowing us to get the most and best information in the shortest possible time. The task here is threefold: to find out exactly what you have done in the way of work and in the way of educating yourself, to ascertain what you are capable of doing, and to find out what it is you think you want to do. Then, with our professional experience and know-how, we can try to bring a balance between what you want to do and what we see you capable of doing. We don't want you spinning your wheels on the impossible dream or selling yourself short.

Also during the interview we rate your ability to sell yourself to an employer. Do you sit up straight and look us in the eye? Are you calm and self-assured? Or do you fidget, jingle pocket change, tap your fingers on the desk, chew gum? Do you let your eyes wander around the office—including (a cardinal sin) trying to read the papers on the interviewer's desk—or do you concentrate on the interview itself? If you display any of the traits a potential employer would find troublesome, we tell you so that you'll put your best foot forward when you go out on an actual employment interview.

Even more important, do you know how to bring your strong points into the conversation? Do you respond to all questions with pertinent job-related information? For example, we might ask where you live. You might respond with an address. Or you might give the address but then add that you own your own home and have lived there for fifteen years. Such an answer could show stability. But if it might pose an obstacle because you plan to relocate, you could give the address and then point out that although you own your home, the market is good and you know you'll be able to sell quickly if a good job comes up out of town. Anticipating objections and problems shows that you are thinking ahead. But if you're not, we'll help you to be prepared before we send you out on interviews.

There's a lot of information to be gleaned in the face-to-face interview: your educational background plus pertinent extra-curricular activities, and your actual work experience. With some people, gathering this information is like pulling teeth. You might tell your next-door neighbor over the hedge how hard you work, how much you do, and how you are grossly underpaid. Yet when you get into an interview situation, your mind may go blank, and you may forget all the great things you did for your unappreciative employer. Our job is to pull out that information, collate it, and use the pieces of the puzzle to fit together our specific recommendations for you.

Digging out a person's accomplishments may sound easy, but in reality it's a tough job. You may actually have forgotten about the great things you did on the job in your anger and frustration at leaving the job. We'll help you handle that anger and frustration in a positive way (so that your next employer won't worry that you'll go around saying nasty things about him), and we'll help you focus on the positive aspects of your previous job—what you did that was good and that is transferable to a new job. What were your duties and responsibilities? What authority did you have? What were your relationships with superiors, peers, subordinates, suppliers, and customers? This all has a bearing on how you should present yourself for the next job and, more important, what the next job should be. We'll want to know whom you reported to and where that person stood in the corporate hierarchy. We'll ask what committees you served on, whether you chaired any of those committees, what the committees did, and what part the committees—and you—played in the resultant success of your division or company.

We'll also ask about your interests outside the job. When a receptionist came to one of our offices several years ago, discouraged about her poor job skills and lack of opportunity, our Professional Employment Counsellor discovered that her hobby was fashion illustration. She did some good sketches when things were slow at the reception desk. Armed with this information, we got her a trainee position in the art department of a large department store. After three years, this former receptionist was the store's art director!

You may be too close to your own situation to see it clearly. We will be able to see exactly where you've been going and where you might be able to go. We can bring our years of experience to bear in advising you about job openings not only in your own familiar field but, very possibly, in a field you've never considered but that we see as being right for you. This was the case with the waitress who became a customer service representative in a medical manufacturing company, based on our counsellor's assessment of her person-to-person skills. Part of our job at times is convincing applicants that they can do a particular type of work, that they would enjoy it, and that they at least owe it to themselves to investigate it before turning it down out of hand.

Most people look for a job six or seven times in a lifetime. That's the average number of job changes an individual will make. On the other hand, Professional Employment Counsellors are helping people change jobs every day of the week, hundreds of times a week. Their experience level soars in short order. They are dealing with all different types of personalities, backgrounds, and education. Their clients are usually different types of companies, and they are finding out why companies hire certain types of people and why they don't hire other types of people. They are learning the combinations that go together—combinations made up of appearance and manner, deportment and demeanor, education and experience, attitudes and desires. The trained counsellor puts all of this together and more often than not hits the target right on the nose with suggestions of career paths that could be followed and should be considered.

The ability to reach such conclusions in an economical and expeditious manner is not based on gut feelings or on having pleasant chats with people. It is based on a unique program, on an organized technique of handling individuals from telephone contact to the initial meeting in the reception area to the actual interview. The very order of the interview is vital. We can't—and we don't—start right out asking you what type of job you would like to have. That would be premature. Each item of discussion must come in its proper time frame in a proper order to allow the counsellor to assimilate the information and assign it a proper role in the ultimate decision.

As in all instances, the exceptions make the rule. When we are recruiting a particular skill for a client company, we may never see the job seeker in person. In those instances when the employer is half a continent away and the job seeker is a thousand miles in the other direction, all of this will have to be done by mail, fax, and phone. Exceptions also apply to special situations, such as the experience of executives and engineers, which just cannot be condensed on our normal application form, and additional forms may be required. Most applicants fill out an additional form specialized for their background, to aid us in entering them into our national computer system.

Choosing Employment Services

Okay, I've convinced you. You'll enlist employment services in your all-out war to find the right job. But which ones? How can you know where to begin?

Start by asking friends and business associates if they know and can recommend a Professional Employment Counsellor; a satisfied customer is always the very best referral. But there are other possibilities. Check the classified ads and you'll see which employment services are associated with the kind of jobs that appeal to you. Scan the Yellow Pages looking for details about the size of each employment service, the length of time it's been in business, and its occupational or industry areas of specialization. Or contact personnel departments in your chosen field and ask them which employment services they call on to fill their openings.

When you've narrowed your search, ask whether the employment service subscribes to a code of ethics that includes full disclosure of applicable job information to the job seeker, full disclosure of applicable job seeker information to the company, and nondiscrimination on the basis of age, sex, marital status, physical disability, race, national origin, or religion. Ask about the kind of training their counsellors are given. Find out if a multioffice system has some means of referring job openings and job seekers from one office to another. Then talk to several Professional Employment Counsellors to find those who are knowledgeable about your field of work, who understand your skills and goals, and, perhaps most important, who are on the same wavelength and speak the same language. You'll be working very closely together, and it's important to have a good rapport from the start.

We've also prepared the following checklist to help you evaluate the service you receive. Answer yes or no to each question and then move on to the answers.

- Did you meet the Professional Employment Counsellor face-to-face?

- Were you required to fill out a complete application, in depth?
- Did you have a probing interview that covered your experience, qualifications, and desires?
- Were the available positions described to you in detail?
- Did the counsellor phone the prospective employers in your presence and describe your qualifications?
- After the job interview, were you required to return to the employment service for a critique?
- After getting the job, did your counsellor advise you about how to keep it?
- Did the employment service try to keep you exclusively to itself?
- Was the service charge, if any, spelled out clearly in advance?
- Were you or the company given a written guarantee of a refund if you left or lost the job?
- Were you given a copy of the contract if you signed one?

In most circumstances the answer to every question, except the one about the service trying to keep you to itself, should be yes. If you answer many with no, you may be in the wrong place. A professionally operated employment service should provide all of the functions stated above to secure the best possible job for you. Just keep in mind the exceptions previously noted, in some special job-search situations. And note too that when recruiting (to be discussed later), we operate somewhat differently. The material in this section deals with the professional employment services that concentrate just as hard on finding or creating a job for you as on finding an employee for a client company.

Let's examine these functions more closely:

1. *Did you meet the Professional Employment Counsellor face-to-face?* The personal touch is at the heart of effective job counseling. You must meet the Professional Employment Counsellor face-to-face. Attempting to decide your qualifications for an available position over the telephone is self-defeating. If you phone, per-

haps in answer to a newspaper advertisement, are asked your education and experience, and are then told you are not qualified for the job, you can be sure the counsellor is just sitting there trying to fill a job and has no intention of helping you find the right position. There is nothing intrinsically wrong with that; it just means that if you're really serious about your job hunt, you must keep looking for a service that will be too.

When we recruit you, on the other hand, you may be a thousand miles away, and a telephone interview may be essential. Even if you are not qualified for the job at hand, we will keep your file in our computer data base for future opportunities.

No employment service can afford to advertise all of its openings. There may be ten positions available with that counsellor, or with others in the same office, for which you qualify. If you meet their criteria, a Professional Employment Counsellor will search for a position for you, even though one is not available when you first walk through the door. That is why it is important for the counsellor to evaluate you firsthand and determine your qualifications. The counsellor has a multitude of contacts and, many times, after knowing about your skills and desires, can actually create a job because he or she knows best just where such abilities are needed. We've already seen several examples of this resourcefulness. Here's another: One of our New York offices successfully placed a job seeker in a position as a project engineer before the position was officially created. Our counsellor saw the applicant's skills and contacted the client company while plans for the position were still in the works.

2. *Were you required to fill out a complete application, in depth?* If the employment service does not require that you fill out an application in depth, you are being shortchanged. Just sitting and chatting with you or using your résumé to work from is not the sign of the true professional who works in an organized, methodical fashion to dig out the facts. Résumés often leave out vital, important information that may be the key to securing a good job. Who would think, after all, of including on a résumé information about doodling fashion illustrations? Just as most employers insist on their applications being completed, so should the employment counsellor.

3. *Did you have a probing interview that covered your experience,*

qualifications, and desires? Even though you are not an expert at being interviewed, you should have the feeling that your counsellor is going through you and your background with a fine-tooth comb. What are your accomplishments? Why did you resign, or why were you let go? What are your weaknesses? Whom did you report to? How many people did you supervise? What do you really want to do? What are your relocation desires or limitations? When you're sitting with a professional counsellor, he or she is probing every minute, like a doctor, getting a personal inventory that will result in matching you with a fulfilling lifelong career.

If the counsellor just said, as soon as you sat down, "Oh, you're an accountant; I've got a job right here for an accountant," get out of there and go somewhere else, because the counsellor doesn't have the foggiest notion if you're qualified for that particular job or even if it's really what you want to do.

4. *Were the available positions described to you in detail?* Each available position should be described fully to you, and the counsellor should answer any questions about the position to make sure you are both interested and qualified before calling the company to arrange an interview. This is what you are paying for and have every right to expect (whether or not you are actually paying the service charge): to know everything about the job and future opportunities, the company, the person to whom you'll report, any tests that may be given in the employment process, job duties and responsibilities, fringe benefits, and so on. The professional counsellor should provide you with all of this information so you will arrive for your job interview with confidence and enthusiasm. The counsellor may also role-play the interview with you so you'll have a rehearsal before the actual performance. Going in cold, without a knowledge of the company or its requirements, is a good way to lose the job. The Professional Employment Counsellor should do this research for you.

5. *Did the counsellor phone the prospective employer in your presence and describe your qualifications?* After discussing a position that you like and that meets your requirements, the counsellor should immediately call the company in your presence and describe your qualifications to the prospective employer. This gives the employer an opportunity to ask further questions to help determine

whether you are truly a candidate for this job. It can be a great time-saver for all concerned. On some occasions it is not possible, if the employer is out or busy, for the call to be completed in front of you. Nevertheless the call must be placed. It is your guarantee that every interview is a potential job offer and not time-waster.

6. *After the job interview, were you asked to return to the employment service for a critique?* A counsellor who does not ask you to return after the interview, regardless of its outcome, is not performing a professional service. A critique directly after the interview prepares you for the next interview, whether a follow-up session with the same company or an interview with another firm. A good counsellor will always follow through. When a young New Jersey woman went out on three or four interviews with no success, for example, the counsellor in our Morristown office sat her down for some kind, constructive advice on dress and grooming. The next interview, after she took the counsellor's advice, led to a job.

If you are interested in a particular job, the counsellor should help map a concerted campaign to land it for you. That campaign includes a follow-up with you and with the employer, with the counsellor calling the employer immediately after your interview, both for feedback and to push for your hiring. This is where the counsellor really earns his or her keep. So if you're interviewing in the area, be sure to go back to the employment counsellor for a follow-up.

7. *After getting the job, did your counsellor advise you about how to keep it?* After accepting the job, you should receive advice from your counsellor about positive steps to take to make the new position both satisfying and lasting. Most people change jobs about five to seven times during their career. If you haven't changed jobs recently (and perhaps even if you have), there is a great deal you should know about adjusting to a new work environment. This is true whether you are twenty-five or fifty. The counsellor can discuss specific dos and don'ts about dress, office policies, and company idiosyncrasies; the counsellor's knowledge, gained by placing many people over a period of time with the particular company, could take you considerable time to secure on your own.

8. *Did the employment service try to keep you exclusively to itself?* This is the one question, you'll recall, that should receive a negative answer. A Professional Employment Counsellor will not ask you to put all your eggs in one basket. If the counsellor cannot keep you actively involved with appropriate interviews, he or she should encourage you to make use of more than one qualified employment service to aid in your search for a new or better job.

Feel free to approach any employment service and screen it carefully using these guidelines. And be sure to speak up if the second one refers you to a company the first one has already mentioned. You want the employment service to be square with you, and you should be square with it. Furthermore, you don't want to muddy the water and lose out on a good opportunity.

9. *Was the service charge spelled out clearly in advance?* Contracts between you and the employment service are easy to evaluate. The contract should be simple. If it is a page of lawyer's terminology in fine print (except in states that require this), you are usually in the wrong place. The service charge should be spelled out clearly and be easily predetermined. All professional employment services operate on a contingency basis; if you don't take an offered job, you don't owe anything. Because of this, you can feel free to sign a contract whether the service charge is employer-paid or employee-paid. If the service handles both types of jobs, keep your options open. You're the one to make the decision in the final analysis.

There may be no service charge to you or the company when the hire is handled on a "temp to perm" basis. This simply means you will be on the employment service's payroll for approximately sixty working days (three months). If you decide to keep the job and the employer decides to keep you (most jobs are on a ninety-day trial basis), you will go on the company payroll at the end of that period. Companies are hiring accountants, programmers, secretaries, and many other personnel on this basis.

10. *Were you given a written guarantee of a refund if you left or lost the job?* There should be a period of about one hundred days wherein the service charge should be refunded on a pro rata basis (for example, 1 percent per day) if you lose or leave the job for any reason during this period. While nine out of ten job marriages do last because of the thought and research put into

them, some fail for a variety of reasons. In those cases the employment service should adjust the charge accordingly and then go to work to get you another job just as quickly as possible.

11. *Were you given a copy of the contract you signed?* You should always receive a copy of any contract you sign. Keep it, because it spells out both your obligations and the employment service's commitments.

It is important to know, and to remember, that it costs you nothing to register with an employment service; to our way of thinking, no reputable employment service should charge a registration fee in advance. The advice and guidance given by Professional Employment Counsellors, moreover, will make it worth the trip even if they are not able to put you to work at once. If and when they do put you to work, the job will be one you want. At that point, if it is not paid by the employer, the service charge will be due. In most instances, if you paid, you may be able to deduct it on your federal income tax return. In any case, when you consider that the job you get may last five or ten years or even a lifetime, the investment will be the greatest bargain going.

There are exceptions to all of the above guidelines. The employment service may have recruited you, you may be working long distance with the service, all their jobs may be employer paid, and so on. In each case, you must be the judge. Are they helping you? Do they have your best interest at heart? Are they truly professional?

Pros and Cons

I once had someone say to me that all employment services were body shops and should be closed up. This is akin to saying that all doctors are quacks, all lawyers shysters, and all government employees are lazy, good-for-nothing slobs and we should get rid of all of them. Business springs up to serve a need. When that need ceases or other, better ways can be found to accomplish the same end, those businesses fail. Employment services, like doctors and lawyers and government employees, serve a need.

Another complaint is that "employment services are terrible; they work on commission, so they try to push you into a job that you don't want." The commission system can't be all bad. Millions of salespeople work on that basis throughout the United States, selling all kinds of products and services. And the interesting thing here is that basically that complainer is right; if the sales-person doesn't make a sale, he or she does not get paid. That means they're highly motivated to do their job, and that does not mean doing their job wrong. Putting the wrong person in the wrong job is not the way to stay in business if you're working for an employment service. The repeat customer—the employer—is not going to stand for hiring people who leave quickly because the job was wrong for them or who only have to be fired in short order because they can't do the job. Word of mouth plays a large part in the operation of any employment service. As we've noted earlier, fully 40 percent of our applicants come by personal re-ferral, referral by someone else who was happy with the service. So we must be doing something right!

If you ever get the feeling that you're in a "body shop" and that the people there really don't care about you and are not taking a personal interest in you and your problems, then stand up and walk right out the door. For every one you find like that, there are a hundred others who will take a sincere professional interest in you and provide all the help you could want.

Service Charges

All of this service costs money. It's important for you, as a job seeker, to understand the various forms of service charges. These include

1. Employer paid. In three-quarters of all job placements, the employer assumes total responsibility for the fee. But this practice varies widely depending on area, the econ-omy, and, most important, the demand for particular skills. Some areas, such as New York, Chicago, and Los Angeles, are virtually 100 percent employer paid, while others are closer to 50 percent.

2. Job seeker paid. The total fee comes out of your pocket after you are hired, but you pay only if the employment

service does its job right and finds you a job that is completely satisfactory. This is probably the greatest bargain you will ever find.

3. Partial paid. The employer and new employee split the charge on some agreed-upon basis, usually fifty-fifty.

4. Reimbursed. You pay the charge but the employer agrees to reimburse you in whole or in part after a specified period of employment. Because of negative tax implications, this practice has virtually died out, and we no longer recommend it.

5. Advanced. The employer pays the charge at the outset, then deducts it from your pay over a period of time. This too is fading swiftly. If an employer is willing to go this far, he usually will simply pick up the tab. Moreover, the wide use of extended hundred-day guarantees has eliminated the rationale for this method.

6. Temp to perm. No charge to employer or job seeker, as previously covered.

Service charges can range from one-half of your first month's salary to 5, 10, or even 30 percent of the first year's salary. Where the employer pays the fee, this may not concern you. Where you are expected to pay the fee, you can still negotiate with the prospective employer to assume part or all of the charge. But remember, if you do have to pay the charge yourself, you must first be satisfied with the job. Remember too that your commitment to pay a service charge if necessary indicates to a prospective employer that your are highly motivated, ambitious, and willing to work. Consider, how much does it cost you to be out of work for a month or two?

Contracts

The agreement, or contract, should spell out the service charges. It should also spell out your obligations in various situations. You might, for instance, accept a job through the employment service and then lose the job through no fault of your own. You might accept a position, then change your mind before reporting to work. Or you might be referred to a company by an employment service and much later accept a position with that same company. A well-written contract will clearly outline your responsibilities in such situations.

Our own contract, except where state law requires a more complex one, is very simple. It starts out with the words "You are not obligated." This is because anyone who comes to us is under no obligation to go see any of the companies we suggest. If they do go to the company, they are under no obligation to accept the job. If an applicant does accept a job, however, and if the employer is one who does not pay the service charge, then the job seeker is obligated to pay the charge as set out in the contract.

Guarantees

Most of our contracts go on to say in large type that the job is guaranteed for a hundred days at 1 percent of the service charge per day. If you work for ten days and quit or are laid off, in other words, you would get back 90 percent of what you had paid. If you worked fifty days and the company had an unexpected layoff or you and the company just didn't get along and you quit or they let you go, you would get back 50 percent. In such an instance, of course, you would come out ahead because you would have earned much more money than you had paid.

Remember, an employment service places people in jobs and then collects its service charge from either the employee or the employer. What other service is available to you on this basis? Lawyers, doctors, plumbers, and beauticians—all must be paid whether you are satisfied or not. With an employment service the service charge is paid after you have a job and only if you have a job with which you are satisfied.

The United States is the only country in the world that permits a job seeker to engage a Professional Employment Counsellor to find work. In Russia and France an individual needs government approval to change jobs. In Canada and England the law forbids the job hunter to employ anyone to help him better his lot in life. In Germany and Japan an individual cannot hire help to locate employment. But the Supreme Court of the United States has ruled, in part, that "the service rendered in acting as the paid representative of another to find a position in which to earn an honest living is useful, commendable, and in great demand." Our wonderful free-enterprise system, in other words, gives freedom of choice both to individuals and to companies. That in turn allows the cream to rise to the top. That's why we are the most inventive, creative, productive nation on the face of the earth. Good people like you are not stuck in a job because a government bureaucrat thinks that is where you should be. Our Constitution allows you to choose your own career, making the most of your God-given talents.

Other Employment Services

Professional employment services can be of enormous value to you in your job search. Other kinds of services may be helpful too, some more than others. The good news is that every son and his brother want to get in on the act when it comes to finding jobs for people or people for jobs. The bad news is that very few of them are any good at it. It takes skill, time, patience, training, and perseverance. It's a people business. You want a job, or you wouldn't be reading this book. So to fill out the picture, here's a rundown of some of the great variety of employment services.

Recruitment Firms

Sometimes called executive search firms or headhunters, these firms locate qualified individuals to fill specific posts at client firms. In all such cases, the client companies pay for their services.

Some recruiters, depending on the types of assignments they have, will advertise and interview candidates and actively encourage job seekers to call, write, and visit their offices. Others prefer to make their own phone contacts with qualified individuals and do little or no face-to-face interviewing. Specialization is the name of the game, so you must seek out those who handle positions in your area of expertise and then see if they will interview you or accept your résumé. Some areas of specialization:

sales and marketing, accounting, engineering, retailing, banking and finance, aerospace, and pharmaceuticals.

Remember, though, that a recruitment firm's efforts are focused on finding the right employee for their client company. In most cases they do not attempt to find you a position. With the increasing use of computers, however, more and more are accepting résumés from qualified individuals with backgrounds in their specialty. Then, as need arises, they can scan their computer banks for prospects.

What to Do When the Recruiter Calls

Recruiters cover all fields these days. Executive recruiters still work in the $75,000 and up range, but others recruit secretaries, nurses, accountants, engineers, programmers, sales and marketing personnel, lawyers, and a host of other specialties.

A recruiter may get your name from one of a dozen sources; journals, articles, published lists, and so on. In most cases it will be by referral or some good old-fashioned sleuthing.

Since they do not know if you would even consider a new opportunity, most will approach you obliquely, telling you about the search they are on and asking if you know anyone who is qualified. Note: They are not asking if you know of anyone who is looking. Their job is to see if the interest is there.

Recruiters may work for a firm with dozens of recruiters in different specialties or they may be loners working off their dining room table. Don't scoff, some of them make in excess of $250,000 a year. When companies have pressing needs and can't fill them through advertising, word of mouth, employee referral, and the like, they call on employment services (some of which recruit) and recruiters. Many assignments are exclusive, so you won't hear about them any other way. They are part of the hidden job market.

So what should you do when you get such a call? First, don't run tell your boss that someone just tried to recruit you. He's likely to think you are pushing for a raise. He also knows that most good people will get a recruiting call from time to time. One thing is sure, you can't recruit a happy employee. Look at it like an ad that pops out at you from a newspaper or trade journal but is instead coming by phone.

Second, tell the recruiter if you know someone who is qualified and if you are qualified and looking or willing to be looking. Arrange a time for a fuller discussion of the opportunity, then be honest and open about yourself, your background, needs, and desires. No pie in the sky—that happens only in Disney cartoons.

Being in the right place at the right time often means building relationships with good recruiters by recommending others to them, using them to find good staff, and using them to help their own career growth.

Temp to Perm

This is a hybrid service that can be offered by a general or specialized employment service, a recruiter, or a temporary help service. Approximately 85 percent of all temporaries wind up working permanently for some firm. This in turn has led to individuals and companies using this method to try each other out before making a permanent commitment. It is used for accountants, programmers, engineers, nurses, and attorneys as well as office support personnel. If the individual works on the temporary payroll for a specified period of time (usually thirteen to twenty-six weeks), there is normally no charge to them or the company. If the period is shortened at the company's request, it will incur a conversion charge in most cases.

The Temporary Help Industry

As we know it today, the temporary help industry began to develop during the economic prosperity following World War II, with small, local agencies. Today, with large national and international firms as well as small ones, the temporary help industry is a $21.5-billion industry and is the third fastest-growing industry in the nation, behind health care and computers. More than fourteen hundred temporary help companies, through fourteen thousand offices, employ millions of temporaries each year. Approximately 2 percent of the American labor force works on a temporary basis, a figure that is expected to triple in ten years.

Temporary employment services in the United States offer diversified services used by nine out of every ten companies, with temporary work available in a wide range of fields; housework and janitorial services, nurses and lab technicians, clerical and secretarial, computer programming, accounting, engineering, and marketing, to name a few. Word and data processing are exploding into a new field called information management, with temporary help services often providing special training on the latest equipment.

Temporary help was traditionally used solely in emergencies and fill-in situations, by employers replacing ill or vacationing employees. Today temporary workers are viewed as a cost-effective solution for employers facing high labor costs. Temporary workers are now used to staff entire departments, to fill jobs with high turnover or positions created by fluctuating production cycles, to make up special project teams to convert offices from manual to automated procedures, and so on. Some employers use temps virtually year-round, and terms such as "facility planning," "flexible staffing," and "base staffing" are commonly used to describe the integration of temporary employees into client companies' labor-force plans.

If you work for a temporary help firm, you will be employed by that firm. You will be paid by that firm, and the firm will be responsible for withholding taxes from your pay. You will work for a day or a week or a month at a time (sometimes even years) at the facility of the contracting company.

A temporary help firm offers a service that complements that of a professional employment service, and more and more are operating combined services. They can share their customer bases and serve as a joint source of applicants. Temporary work can be a useful way station for the student seeking broad job experience, for the housewife coming back into the job market and wanting to brush up rusty skills, and for the job hunter needing supplemental income while searching. It can also be a permanent way of life for people who want to remain flexible in their commitment to the labor force.

Employee Leasing Firms

Employee leasing firms, like temporary help firms, are also employers. But their employees, unlike temps, work on a permanent basis for the leasing company's clients. Today there are over two hundred leasing firms employing over seventy thousand men and women, with the industry projecting over ten million employees in the next decade.

Leasing's popularity among employers stems from the leasing company's ability, through combining employees, to reduce costs to the employer while increasing benefits for employees. In many cases the entire staff of a small office has been "fired" but has stayed in place, performing the same functions for the same people but employed, after the change, by a leasing company. Leasing just may be the wave of the future for small and midsize companies.

If you work for a leasing firm, you'll reap the rewards of better employee benefits. You'll also have a better chance of moving ahead, because advancement can come in two ways: either within the client company or with another client company of your actual employer, the leasing company.

College Placement Offices

The main function of the college placement office is to help organize on-campus recruiting to bring employers together with graduating seniors. In many instances it also offers placement help to alumni who have been out of school for years or even decades. But the success rate is mixed. We see a lot of recent college graduates in our offices six months or a year after starting the job obtained through a campus recruiter. Some have been let go; others have decided on their own that the job simply isn't right for them. Now that they've had a taste of life in the business world, we are in a much better position to counsel them and help guide them on their next career step. When it comes to placing alumni, most college placement offices have a very poor track record. They simply do not have the facilities, the know-how, or the trained staff to do it.

Religious and Nonprofit Services

Placement services run by churches, the 40-Plus Club, and some government-funded self-help groups have one problem in common: Because there is little continuity in staffing, the knowledge base and contact base are continually being lost. While some of these groups claim excellent placement rates, we have to go back to the truism that anybody can get *a* job. Getting the right job, the best job, now that's another story. If all you want is a job, then you don't need this book or an employment service, nonprofit or otherwise.

Executive Counseling Firms

Many of the same things that professional employment services and résumé services do are also provided by executive counseling firms—providing advice on career management, aiding in self-marketing, helping with résumés and cover letters, and, sometimes, supplying company contacts. But these firms, while charging substantial fees to job seekers for these services, do not carry the guarantee of a job. They do not place people or aid in the placement process, nor do they represent companies in filling their jobs. Think twice before you sign up with one of these firms.

Outplacement Firms

Many of the same services performed by executive counseling firms, for the same kind of substantial fees, are performed by outplacement firms. The difference here is that employers pay the fees on behalf of terminated employees. If you've been fired, you may want to accept the services of an outplacement firm. On the other hand, perhaps you would rather ask for additional severance pay instead and then get out there and conduct your own job search with the aid of people (such as professional employment services) who can really help.

State Employment Services

Every state has a state employment service, established by law and funded by employer-paid tax dollars, to help place the unemployed who have lost their jobs through no fault of their own and cannot find work on their own. Many of the listed jobs are unskilled and close to the minimum wage. Little counseling or direct placement activity is offered. You are unlikely to find the right job through a state employment service.

Job-Listing Firms

For a fee, job-listing firms provide lists of local job openings. The information generally comes from newspaper advertisements or through telephone solicitation. You will probably not find it very useful.

Computer-Matching Firms

Jobs and job seekers are fed into a computer, and the firms purport to put the two together. While more and more employment services use high-speed computers to enhance placement, little takes place without the human interface. Without a highly trained Professional Employment Counsellor able to elicit candidates' skills and interests and available to screen computer listings and provide personal advice, computer listings are virtually meaningless.

In summary, professional career counseling can shorten the time it takes to find a new job. Professional employment services can and do serve a vital and much-needed service in our society today. Whether you're looking for your first job or seeking to make a change, there's little doubt that a professional employment service should be an integral part of your job campaign.

7

Interview Strategies and Salary Negotiations

An effective résumé or an introduction by an employment service may get your foot in the door, but it takes an interview, sometimes more than one interview, to clinch the job. An important part of your job-hunting campaign, therefore, is scheduling interviews. You'll want to go on as many interviews as possible, some (at first) just for practice. And you'll want as many interviews as you can line up, in as short a time frame as possible, in order to secure multiple job offers, weigh the alternatives, and pick the best job offer of all.

But good job interviews don't just happen. You have a lot of preparation to do if you're going to be a successful interviewee, if you're going to get the job offers you want and deserve. Here are the steps to follow—before, during, and after a job interview.

Preinterview Preparation

Interview preparation involves much more than readying your résumé.

Learn as Much as You Can about the Employer

Familiarizing yourself with the company does two things: It impresses the interviewer because it demonstrates your interest in the company and in the job, and it increases your confidence, so that you handle yourself much better during the interview. If you use an employment service, your Professional Employment Counsellor will fill you in on the company. If not, or in addition, try these three ways to gather information about a prospective employer:

Do basic library research. Consult business directories such as *Standard and Poor's Register of Corporations, Thomas Register of American Manufacturers, Dun's Million Dollar Directory, Moody's Industrial Manual,* and others listed previously (ask your research librarian for other source material) for information about the age of the company or organization, the products or services it offers, its current size and anticipated growth, the location of its facilities, and so on. Don't memorize statistics, but get a sense of the company, where it is going, and where you might fit in. Ask a stockbroker for an annual report or a current research paper on the company, and don't forget to check out its major competitors.

Ask around among your friends, colleagues, and relatives. If you can locate people who work for the company, you can glean valuable insight into office atmosphere, the stability of the organization, its rigidity or flexibility, and so on. Visit the company ahead of time if you can, to see the facility and the employees.

One of our counsellors sent an applicant to check out the local Fayva shoe store prior to being interviewed by the district sales manager. The next day the sales manager, who had also been checking out the local store, asked, "Didn't I see you last night?" "Yes," the applicant replied. "I was checking out your company and your products." You know what happened. He was hired.

Use the company itself. Check its promotional material, advertisements, and press releases in your local library. Or call the public relations or marketing department to ask for information. Pay particular attention to details that mesh with your own education, interests, or experience; use such information when you get to the interview. An applicant who is fluent in Spanish, for example, may want to emphasize that point to a company that employs a large number of Spanish-speaking people or does business with Latin America.

All of this research, formidable as it may sound, will not take too long. On one trip to the library you can check out a dozen or more companies. When being interviewed by one company, you can check out other companies in the area. But you will want to keep your facts straight, since you will be interviewing with several companies. I suggest you draw up a separate fact sheet for each company or use a five-by-eight-inch index card. Put the company's name, address, and phone, number at the top, along with the date and place of the interview and name of the interviewer, then list your research notes and the questions you want to ask. After the interview, write down the names and titles of everyone you spoke to, your assessment of the interview, and the follow-up action you will take.

Learn as Much as You Can about the Position

If you are applying for a particular job, you'll be a stronger applicant if you familiarize yourself with that position. Find out as much as you can, through library research and personal contacts, about the nature of the job, the duties and responsibilities, and how the position fits into the overall structure of the organization. Think about your own salary expectations too, and after consulting government studies, newspaper ads, professional associations, and books such as *Jobs: What They Are, Where They Are, What They Pay* (Simon & Schuster, 1992), come up with an acceptable range for this particular position. Your librarian may be able to help here as well.

One cautionary note: It's good to be prepared for an interview for a particular position. But don't be so narrowly focused that you rule yourself out of consideration for other positions. Career consultant Shirley Sloan Fader points to the woman who applied at her local community college to teach evening-session accounting courses. She loaded the interviewer with her in-depth accounting expertise and realized too late that she had thereby missed out on an introduction to business course that she was well-qualified to teach. Familiarize yourself with the company and with the position, but answer the interviewer's questions so that you reveal all your strengths.

Practice, Practice, Practice

Before you walk in the interviewer's door, prepare yourself in practical ways.

Review your comprehensive résumé, your work experience, and your skills. Think about what elements you want to stress in a particular interview. You might even note the highlights on a separate sheet of paper, to jog your memory during the interview, although it would be better to have the pertinent information firmly in your memory.

Prepare the questions you will want to ask the interviewer. You might want to know, for instance, why the position is vacant. Did the last person quit? Why? Or is this a new position, created to fill an expanding company need? If so, just how will this new position fit into the existing company structure? What will you have to do to get ahead on the job? What courses might the company recommend you take? To whom will you report? How long has that person been with the company? Whom does he or she report to? Will you be expected or allowed to train, hire, write manuals, travel, make speeches, attend seminars, and so forth?

Rehearse the interview. Think about the answers you'll give to tough questions (more about this later in the chapter). You don't want to spout memorized replies—that's not the idea at all—but you do want to be able to respond without undue hesitation to questions such as "What do you think you can contribute to this organization?" or "What makes you think this job is right for you?" Think about appropriate answers (they won't necessarily be the same answers in different companies) and practice. Set up a role-playing session and have someone act as your interviewer while you respond. Practice until you answer questions smoothly. Keep in mind that most job seekers change jobs about seven times in a lifetime. So probably the last time you interviewed was three to five years ago. This does not make you an expert inter-viewee by a long shot. Many interviewers do this all day long all year long. They have a leg up on you. So practice, practice, practice!

Dress Properly

If you were selling a product, you would take pains to package it attractively. When you go for a job interview, you are selling yourself. You want to present yourself as an attractive package, well-groomed and neatly dressed. Don't say to yourself that looks aren't important, that all the employer cares about is whether you can do the job. The employer will never find out if you can do the job, much less how well you can do it, if your appearance puts him off from the start. It's not only an emotional reaction, it's a practical one. If you're careless about your personal appearance, the reasoning goes that you may be careless about the work you do. "More jobs are lost by first impression" than by anything else, Max Evans, former fashion director of *Esquire* magazine, stated emphatically in a newspaper interview. "The assumption seems to be that if you don't know how to put yourself together properly, then you may not be too sharp in other areas."

Take the time, in advance, to prepare your interview attire. Consider the company where you're applying for a job. Some companies have actual dress codes; others have unspoken sets of rules, so that a brown suit, for example, is a no-no. Scout your network of contacts for information, or simply hang around the lobby to observe the employees before you go on your interview. If you can't find out for sure (perhaps the company is located in another city), be conservative. Don't wait until the morning of the interview to decide what you're going to wear. Don't choose the day of the interview to try out a spanking new outfit. Take the time to pick out something becoming and businesslike and, very important, comfortable to wear and easy to forget about once you're wearing it. Make sure hems are sewn, buttons are secure, and clothing is pressed. Use a full-length mirror to check your appearance before you leave the house. Once you're seated at the interview, you will have more important things to think about than whether your jacket is restricting motion, your skirt is riding too high when you sit, or your short socks reveal a hairy leg.

For men the appropriate uniform for just about any employment interview is a dark suit with a white long-sleeved shirt (oxford cloth is good; it tends to hold its shape), a striped or small-patterned tie—hold off on the bow tie until you make your mark—in colors that complement your suit (pick up the navy blue of your suit, for example, as the predominant color in your tie), and well-shined black shoes. Hold the aftershave lotion till after 5:00 p.m. and, while we're talking about shaving, how about it? Look at the men at the top or even near the top of the Fortune 500 companies: 90 percent of them have no facial hair at all and fewer than 5 percent have a beard. Stay clean-shaven till you've made it. Then, if you still want to, you can think about growing a beard. We may joke about dressing for success, but dressing for success often leads to success. IBM chief Tom Watson used to line his people up every morning to check their blue suits, white shirts, and conservative striped ties. He even made sure all the men wore long dark socks. Was it important? Well, IBM has sold a lot of computers.

Women have more leeway, but here too the conservative look is best: a dark, skirted suit or jacket and skirt, with appropriate demure blouse (no ruffles, please!), skin-tone stockings and low or midheight pumps (no open toes or spike heels). Use a pocketbook or briefcase, in a neat brown or black leather, but not both; grooming supplies (for touch-up during a long day of interviewing) should fit in your case along with extra copies of your résumé. Be conservative. Stay away from pants (even pantsuits), loud colors, low necklines, tight sweaters, sandals or loafers, and go light on the makeup, jewelry, and perfume. Style your hair in a conservative fashion too. How many women executives do you see with flamboyant hair styles? Remember, Cyndi Lauper is a rock singer, not an executive. Dressing trendily does not project a serious image.

For men and women: Do you have problems with your skin? If so, get some professional help. See a dermatologist, change your diet, get a suntan (but don't overdo your exposure to the sun or a potential employer may think you spend all your time at the beach). Go light on the jewelry. A class ring and a wedding band are okay for men, but don't wear organizational lapel pins at the first interview unless you know for sure that the interviewer belongs to the same organization. Neat earrings are fine for women but don't wear jangly bracelets or neck chains.

You don't have to go all-out and spend a small fortune on your job-hunt wardrobe. But you do, no matter the job, have to be neat. Your clothes should be clean and well pressed, your hair neatly groomed, your shoes shined, your fingernails clean. If you don't fit this description and you come to one of our offices, you won't be sent out on interviews until you shape up. One of our Professional Employment Counsellors in California loaned one woman the money to buy a tailored wool skirt for an interview as a legal secretary. More than one counsellor has directed job seekers into the washroom to tidy up before an interview. And at least one has personally shampooed a job seeker's hair! We know how important appearance can be.

Take-alongs

What should you take with you when you go for an interview? Take a small pad to make notes during the interview; don't rely on your memory. It's important for you to have written notes for your evaluation of the job and to prepare for your second interview. Take a couple of pens, so if one runs out, you'll be able to keep on going. Keep both pad and pens handy, in an outside compartment of your briefcase or handbag, so you won't be fumbling, wasting time, and appearing disorganized. Take a small dictionary, not for use during the interview itself but so that you won't misspell words on application forms and won't have to resort to a See-Jane-run vocabulary.

In addition, take both your résumés. Even though your concise "action" résumé probably secured the interview, the interviewer may ask for another copy. And your comprehensive résumé can serve two purposes: You can use it for your own reference as you fill out the company application form (but be sure to fill out that form completely), and you can leave the résumé with the interviewer. You may even want to circle some points on the résumé, either during or immediately after the interview, and point out to the interviewer the additional qualifications, experiences, and accomplishments that tie in with the position.

There's also an important category of non-take-alongs. This

includes human companions, whether spouses, parents, children, or friends. There are no exceptions to this rule. Even when we placed a young blind woman, her mother escorted her only on the first interview; after that, she made it on her own. It includes inanimate objects: magazines, books, newspapers (keep the classified section, if you need it, in your briefcase), and packages (don't run errands or do your Christmas shopping on your way to an interview; keep your mind on business and you'll look businesslike). And it includes pets. Don't laugh. We once had to bird-sit a woman's parakeet while she went on an interview.

The Interview

Once you've prepared yourself, mentally and physically, you're ready for the interview itself.

Arrival Time

There's a cardinal rule for job seeking; arrive at interviews early, at least half an hour ahead of time. You've been given a set time for your interview; you can assume that the interviewer is a busy person, and you should never ever, if humanly possible, keep the interviewer waiting. Instead, schedule your appointments with enough leeway so that you will arrive at each interview early enough to fill out an application, if requested, with enough time to freshen up in the restroom and review your notes about the company, the position, and the questions you want to ask.

When you are asked to fill out an application, do so completely (and cheerfully) even though you've already given them your résumé. The company knows its own application form and knows where to look for the things that are most important to them. You don't want to wind up a square peg in a round hole, nor do you want a strike against you for not following directions. So fill out the application, in detail; use N/A if a question is not applicable, rather than leaving it blank, and never write "see résumé." Make the most of your good points too, adding the sizzle to the steak. Add your grade point average, if it's good, on the line that asks your education level; tell what percentage of tuition you earned; mention sales records broken, awards obtained, bonuses earned, and so on.

Then you can sit in the reception area, alert and ready, until you are called into the interviewer's office. When you are called—and the interviewer will probably come to get you personally, just to assess your response—stand up briskly, step forward, smile, look the welcomer in the eye, give your name—"Good morning, I'm Sally Jamison"—as you firmly shake hands, and then let the interviewer lead the way. That handshake is important. Ladies, please, no fingertips; the hand is for shaking, not kissing. Gentlemen, please, no bone crushers, just nice and firm. Your handshake should show that you are confident but not aggressive.

Communicate

Effective communication includes listening carefully, speaking clearly, and showing in your expression and your gestures that you are alert and interested. As you answer questions, pause to compose an answer that is concise and thoughtful. Give full answers, not one-word monosyllables. Be sure to stay with important questions until you get your point across, but don't beat a dead horse and don't argue with the interviewer. You may win the argument and lose the job.

While you may wait for the interviewer to start the conversation and set its tone, you'll be making a mistake if you spend the entire interview responding rather than initiating conversation. At a logical point, seize the initiative to raise the questions you want to ask about the company or the job. Ask smart questions that will make you look good, but don't ask questions just to be asking. Be assertive, but don't attempt to control the interview. Flow with the conversation, interspersing your comments, answers, and questions in a firm, confident style without uhs, ahs, and ers. Demonstrate energy, enthusiasm, and competence by leaning forward, gesturing as needed, holding eye contact, speaking at a good pace, and listening intently.

Try to interpret the interviewer's questions so that you can give the answers that are really being sought. "Why do you want to change jobs?" may mean "Are you likely to be a troublemaker here?" "Tell me something about yourself" really means "Convince me that you'll fit into our organization." Be positive and identify yourself with the firm wherever possible. Instead of saying, "If I got this job, would I be expected to . . ." for example, and say instead, "I see, then what you are saying is that in this position you would want me to . . ."

Use the company name in your conversation. A study by Indiana University showed that successful job seekers used the company's name four times as often as the unsuccessful candidate. Use the interviewer's name also. People are proud of their company and of themselves, so try this approach (but always with sincerity): "Mr. Packwood, I'm impressed by your facilities here at Northern Mutual" or "Mrs. Johnson, I've never seen such nice folks as you have here at Randolph Electronics."

Use body language too to convey your enthusiasm and your competence. Don't passively accept a seat tucked up against the wall, for instance; move the chair alongside the interviewer's desk. Don't sit defensively, arms and legs crossed, but lean forward slightly and show your interest. Don't fidget; it's very unnerving for an interviewer to talk to someone who's squirming, playing with keys, jingling coins, drumming fingers on the desk, or checking the time. Start and end the interview with a smile, eye contact, and a firm handshake (please).

Step away from discussion of politics, sports, religion, or anything else outside the subject at hand that could lead you inadvertently into stating an opinion that could differ from the interviewer's. Always remember, people hire people they like. We call this the people principle, and it boils down to hiring advice given by Judge Ziglar, one of the most famous motivational speakers and sales trainers in the country: "If you are not willing to take them home for Sunday dinner with your family, then don't hire them."

In general, just to sum up the message of communication, make statements indicating your cooperation, dependability, sincerity, trustworthiness, and motivation. Try to follow this list of dos and don'ts compiled by the Career Center at Hope College:

DO

Be brief and to the point
Describe your experiences positively
Ask for clarification of vague questions
Be courteous
Support statements with examples
Be active, involved, enthusiastic
Ask questions about the company and the job
Summarize your interest and qualifications
Get a timetable of events: When they will make the decision
and notify candidates

DON'T

Ramble or waffle
Argue with the interviewer
Blame past employers or criticize others
Guess at a meaning or fake a response
Interrupt the interviewer
Expect your résumé to speak for you
Answer just yes or no
Be wooden or passive
Sit on your phone waiting for the job to hatch

Questions You Can Expect

Different interviewers have different interviewing techniques
—you'll find that some interviews are very structured while others
are informal—but there are certain questions you can expect to
be asked in almost any job interview. You'll field them successfully
if you're prepared.

The first three questions are what I call hot potatoes. In one
way or another, they will come up at every job interview. If you
don't answer them correctly, they'll be asked again in a different
way. Rehearse your answers to these three questions and I can
practically guarantee that you will get good job offers.

How can you be of value to us? This question may be asked as
"What is your experience?" "What is your education?" "What do

you know about X, Y, or Z?" It may sound like, "How did you handle this-and-such?" or "Have you ever done thus-and-so?" But the real question underlying all these pseudo-questions is, "How can you be of value to us?"

You may be at a disadvantage because the interviewer hasn't told you just what problems exist on the job or just what you'd be expected to do. Here's where a prebriefing by a good employment service can be invaluable. One way or another, however, you need to be able to act like a politician, to pick up that crumb of a question, turn it around, and give them what they want to hear. For example, when the interviewer says, "Tell us about your education" (a neat, open-ended question if there ever was one), you could say, "I have a BA in trout fly-fishing from Unknown U." Or you could say, "I'm glad you asked that. In my last job I found myself using information and skills I have learned from dozens of the courses I took in college. For instance, we had to get some statistics together for the president and no one in the place knew where to look or how to compile the information. I did, and in short order I had the report on his desk with just the facts and figures he needed to make a vital decision on . . ."

What is it they seem to be looking for? It might be production or sales or cost-cutting ideas. In addition to knowing as much as possible about the company in advance, have your antenna up during the interview and try to determine the best answer. If you're really not sure, use the "backboard" response. When the question is, "Have you ever . . . ?" your response could be, "I'm glad you asked me that. Have I ever . . . ? I'm curious. Could you tell me why that would be important to you?"

People love to talk about themselves and their business. With this response, you've supplied an opening, and as a result, you just might find out what is really on the interviewer's mind. "Well, you see, we have has this problem with turnover in the computer department."

What kind of person are you? Again, this question may come disguised in other forms, from the readily recognizable "Tell me all about yourself" to "What would you say are your strong points?" to "What do you do for relaxation?" What do you think the interviewer wants to hear? Not that you come from Springfield, Massachusetts. Not that you have four lovely children. Not that you enjoy snowmobiling. No, this is not the time to pull out pictures of your children or to enthusiastically describe your favorite leisure-time pursuit. This is the time to present, succinctly, the qualities that suit you for this particular job. Talk about how you've developed strategies to increase sales. Tell the interviewer how you thrive under deadline pressure. Quote a former employer who praised your diligence, your managerial strengths, or whatever. Bear in mind that this question, as open-ended and all encompassing as it sounds, is really highly targeted. The interviewer wants to know what you can do for his company and whether you'll fit in. Keep this "real" question in mind as you answer.

Why are you available? This translates into "Why are you leaving your current job?" If your company has been merged into another or if it's gone out of business, you have a simple, straightforward answer to this question. If it's a closely held business, with no room for you to move ahead, you also have an easy answer. Whatever the circumstances, however—even if you're leaving because your boss is a mean-spirited, authoritarian type—an all-purpose answer is that you are seeking a new and more challenging position, that you've learned all that there is to learn on this job, that opportunities for advancement are limited because the company is too small or it's concentrating on areas outside your field of expertise or whatever. Whatever you say, never criticize your current employer and never put the matter in personal terms. If you have absolutely nothing positive to say about your current position, or if there really is no one reason why you're leaving, just turn the question around and tell the interviewer what you find attractive about the job you're seeking. Indicate too that you think this is the company where you'll stay and build your career.

Thorough preparation, however, will take you beyond these three questions. Here are some of the others you are likely to encounter.

Why do you want this particular job? Your preinterview research will usually help you answer this question, because you know a lot about the job and why you do want it. In some instances, of course, you may have uncovered a brand-new job or run into a company that is willing to create one, and you know little or nothing about it. Either way, instead of responding vaguely with platitudes about how Company X is great to work for, respond convincingly with what you know about the company and the position. "This is a medium-sized firm," one aspiring architect replied, "and I know I'll get varied experience, handling everything from specifications to shop drawings on a wide range of projects. You're not a firm that specializes in just houses or just hospitals, so I'll be exposed to different kinds of architecture while assuming responsibility for different phases of planning and design."

In addition to showing your knowledge of the company, you can and should use your answer to demonstrate what you can do for the company. This is much more important, much more likely to sell you to the employer, than saying what the company can do for you. Never say you want the job because you have an aged mother to care for or a new car to pay for. We all have responsibilities; unless you can use yours to demonstrate your stability, reliability, and character, the employer does not care to hear about them.

Tell me about your current boss. This is a curve ball question that can trap the unwary, because your answer, in the interviewer's eyes, conveys your attitude toward authority, your spirit of cooperation, and your willingness to learn. Never disparage your employer, no matter how awful it has been to work for him or her. Remember, you will be reporting to a boss on your new job, and that boss wants to know that you can get along with people. Find something positive to say, therefore, preferably about the way your current boss has helped you to develop professionally, increase your productivity, or master a complicated technique. Talk about how he delegated work to you, trusted you, or was pleased with your performance. The same logic applies to "Tell me about your co-workers."

How far do you think you can go in this company? or *What are your career objectives?* Don't tell the interviewer that you plan to take over his or her job (if you're being interviewed by the person who will be your supervisor), but do describe your objectives in terms of the overall company. "Company X has an excellent reputation for providing rewards commensurate with performance; I know I can look forward to moving ahead if I contribute to the company's goals as I expect to do."

What are your strong points? Your preinterview research should have told you what this company needs. Knowing their needs, you can respond correctly. If you've managed to find out that the last person who held this job had difficulty getting along with co-workers, this is your opportunity to disclose that you're a team worker, able to get along well with supervisors, subordinates, and peers. If you don't have such specific information about the job, you should still know enough to highlight the personal qualities that will do the most for the employer.

What is your greatest weakness? This is not the time to be brutally honest about a real or imagined failing. Instead simply disclose a "weakness" that is a hidden strength, at least for this particular job. For example: "My husband complains that I won't come home until my work is done, no matter what time it is" or "I'm told it's peculiar, but I really like detail work, the meticulous kind of thing that seems to drive other people crazy" or "I simply have no patience with inefficiency." You might even try a little elaboration: "What bugs me the most is not being able to do those little extra things I want to do. I'm so good at getting my job done ahead of schedule that my supervisors have always had another assignment waiting, and I couldn't get to the pet ideas I've been trying to develop. Tell me, will I have some time here to research and recommend some new money-saving innovations?"

How long do you expect to stay on this job? Turnover costs money, tons of it, so ease the interviewer's mind while at the same time making very clear that you desire to move ahead. "Whatever it takes to master the job and then some. As I mentioned, I'm looking for opportunity to advance. I believe I have what it takes, and I expect a long and mutually fulfilling relationship."

Are you willing to relocate? This is tricky. You want to display enthusiasm and mention your family's adaptability if you are willing to go wherever your employer sends you. But you probably shouldn't rule out a move finally and completely, even if you don't really want to uproot your family, unless you know for an absolute fact that you will never ever be willing to move. An appropriate response in this case might be, "I'd prefer not to move, but would be certainly willing to consider doing so if the right opportunity came along."

What salary do you expect? Don't play games here, especially if the interviewer already knows your current earnings. If this is the case, simply say, "As you know, I'm now earning $29,500, plus I have the use of a company car, and my present employer has a great fringe benefit package. What range has Wilson and Company placed on this job?" Always try to get a salary range from the interviewer before you volunteer your own expectations. Once you know the salary range, you can point out that your qualifications put you in the upper end of that range. (You'll find more detail about salary negotiations later in this chapter.)

The key to answering all questions is to stay firmly on the topic—your suitability for this company and this job. Keep this target in mind, and aim at it in all your answers, and you should hit a bull's-eye in your job search.

Handling Objections

You may run into an interviewer who deliberately puts stumbling blocks in your path, raising objections to what you say. This can be an intentional interviewing technique, as an interviewer tries to see how you handle stress. Show the interviewer how you handle stress. Be calm, be alert, and respond appropriately to objections. Again, being prepared helps. Here are some objections you may encounter:

- "You are too old."
- "You're overqualified."
- "This job is beneath you; why would you take it?"
- "We need someone with at least five years' experience."
- "We hire only college graduates."
- "Who takes care of your children?"

Whatever the specific objection, when you respond,

- Don't become defensive
- Don't become offensive

- Don't invite further response
- Do respond positively
- Do change the subject

Here are some examples that might help in your own interview preparation. When the interviewer says:

"You are too old." If an interviewer does say this—most will be more circumspect, so as not to run afoul of age-discrimination laws—you can reply: "I can see where you might assume that. However, I'm looking for a career opportunity. And I have at least fifteen of my best years left to give your company. Statistics show that most employees don't even last five years in any job. Turnover costs money and I am here to cut your turnover. Now you mentioned that this position reports to the chief accountant. Who, in turn, does he report to?"

You did these things:

- You agreed with your adversary
- You showed him your value
- You changed the subject

"You're overqualified." Try this response: "I can understand how you feel. It is not cost-effective for a company to knowingly hire someone who will only be on the job until something better comes along. But other companies have found that people like me, who have reached a level of top productivity and who don't want to push higher, will produce more, be more stable, and last longer than the inexperienced employees who come and go. Along those lines, I'd like to hear more about your retirement plan."

You did the same three things:

- You showed the interviewer that you understood the objection
- You showed your value
- You changed the subject

"We need someone with at least five years' experience." If you're a recent graduate, try pointing out that your industriousness is demonstrated through the percentage of tuition you earned on your own. Show that the skills you acquired on a summer job, through part-time employment, or in volunteer service can be applied to the job.

Or try what we call the lump-of-clay approach: "I can understand that—it may well be less expensive than training people yourselves. Of course, they may also have to unlearn some of the bad habits they have acquired on other jobs. You wouldn't have that problem with me. I'm ready to be molded into exactly what you need, and I've got the native ability to learn quickly. I don't want to just give this job a try; I want to give it my all. When can I start?"

Now this is hardball. But when you are being turned down for lack of experience, you have very little choice. Sell yourself as hard as you can.

"We hire only college graduates." "I understand that in most cases the more education you have, the better. But it is interesting to find your company still having such a policy. I just read an article saying that many major firms are rethinking that area. It seems they are finding that two years of college six years ago, which I had, is the equivalent of four years today. Also they find that the underdog, so to speak, barks harder, is more appreciative of the job, and outstays many college grads, who feel the world owes them a living. Tell me, since I only have thirty credits to go for a degree, what is your firm's policy on tuition reimbursement?"

If you run into objections, these or others, do the best you can on the spot and then, when you leave, spend some quiet time working out a proper approach. Chances are, in a string of interviews, that you will run into the same two or three objections again and again, so use these three rules:

1. Write out the objection, including any hidden meanings, to be sure you fully understand it. (Interviewers sometimes mask the real objection. The interviewer who asks what kind of personal crises have caused you to be absent from work may really be probing to see if your family situation is well in hand.)

2. Write out your response and the question you'll use to change the subject.

3. Practice, practice, practice until your responses are down pat and you feel confident about responding to any objection that could be raised.

"Who takes care of your children?" Legally you do not have to answer this question. You do not even have to say that you have children or that you are married. Flat refusal to answer, however, won't make a very good impression on a prospective employer. You are looking for a career path, not a three-year lawsuit. So do the best you can, telling the truth, to put yourself in a positive light. "I have a woman who has been with me for years, who takes excellent care of my children. If she is ill, my mother takes over. My last employer can verify the fact that you won't have to worry about my missing work because of my children."

Testing

Intensive questioning is one form of testing your job qualifications. Actual aptitude and honesty tests are another. There are all kinds of tests, ranging from typing and shorthand through overall intelligence, sales ability, and psychological makeup. If you haven't taken tests for many years, you may find test taking difficult. But the more interviews you have, and the more tests you take, the easier you will find them to be. In fact if you don't do well, ask the interviewer for an opportunity to retake the test. If the interviewer agrees, you'll probably be given an alternate form of the test, which will give you additional practice.

Refusing to take a test is tantamount to turning down the job before it has been offered. Don't. Just relax and do the best you can. Most companies don't rely solely on test results in any case but instead weigh those results with everything else they've learned about you through your résumé, the application form, and the interview itself.

Agreed, written lie detector tests do not seem to make sense in some instances; however, if you are asked to take one, don't be resentful. It simply means that the company is trying its best to create a safe, decent place to work. It is trying to eliminate those who are dishonest, who would use or sell drugs, or would be misfits causing internal disruption in the company. As long as you are honest (and we assume that you are!) you should welcome such a test.

When preparing to take a test, any test, get yourself in the right frame of mind. Relax, breathe deeply, empty your mind of extraneous thoughts, pray if you are so inclined, and then concentrate solely on the test. Move right along, don't agonize over individual answers. After all, however you do, it isn't the end of the world. If you don't get this job, there's another one waiting right around the corner. And the more tests you take the better you get.

Team Interviews and Other Idiosyncrasies

We could write a whole book just on the idiosyncrasies of interviewers that we've found over the years. It wouldn't help you much because you'd probably still face a new one or two. But there are a couple of specific areas we will mention.

Team interviewing. One of the most difficult situations you may face is the team interview. Its close cousin, multiple interviewing by different people at different times, is difficult as well, although to a lesser degree. Here's the problem with the group session: Each individual has his or her own idea about how interviews should be conducted; each has his or her own personality. One may appreciate a quick and snappy answer; another may be turned off by it, preferring a more detailed comprehensive response.

There's an old saying in business that committees design things that look like elephants: They have something that resembles a tail at either end. The team interview can have this result. It has its place where technical know-how is being evaluated but really shouldn't be used in assessing qualifications for most other positions. Nonetheless, you may face a team interview. What should you do? Try to ascertain, right at the outset, which member of the interviewing team has the most authority when it comes to hiring. Then play to that person. Be polite to the others, of course, and answer their questions. But answer them in a way that you feel would please the authority in the room, and direct the bulk of your questions back at that person. In the final analysis, this is the person who can override the others if he or she is convinced that you are the right person for the job.

If you are working your way through a series of multiple interviews, treat each one as if he or she were the hiring authority but adapt your response to the individual. If he is analytic and wants a lot of details and facts, concentrate on this. If she is dominant, stand your ground without being offensive. If he is amiable, slow your pace a bit.

Lunch interviews. What do you do when the hiring authority invites you to lunch? Such an invitation is a good sign that you are well on your way to a job offer. But don't sit back and relax, eating and drinking as if this were a social occasion. It is still an interview. Don't smoke, even if your hosts do. Don't order any alcoholic beverages, even if others do. Concentrate on selling yourself, not on eating your meal, but recognize that the employer may be testing your social skills as well as your knowledge for the particular job.

Ask for the job. You've dressed appropriately, arrived on time, filled out applications, answered questions and asked your own, and responded positively to any objections that the interviewer has raised. What more can you do before concluding the interview? You can ask for the job.

If this is a job you really want, if you know you're qualified, ask for it. Now is not the time to be shy or to be afraid of being pushy. Now is not the time to sit back and think, Either they want me or they don't; they'll have to decide. After all, the interviewer may well be sitting back and thinking, I've told this turkey all about our great company and about this terrific job, which is even better than mine, and he hasn't even shown any excitement or emotion. Well, either he wants this job or he doesn't. It's up to him. If you don't show interest at this stage, the interviewer will probably stand up, thank you for coming, and tell you they will get back to you in a few days. If this happens, don't hold your breath waiting for that call. It probably won't come. If you aren't interested enough in the job and the company to say so, then you come across as rejecting them. Think about it. Ask for the job. And, while you may not actually get a job offer then and there, try not to leave without making a specific appointment for another interview or finding out when the interviewer will be making a decision.

There are, of course, exceptions to this rule. If you really don't want the job, don't play games. Thank the interviewer for giving you the time, explain that the job is not right for you, ask if they have any other openings or know of any for which you are qualified, and leave. If, on the other hand, you are interested in the job but see some shortcomings, take a different tack. Explain that salaries have been moving ahead rapidly in your field, if an inadequate salary is the problem, and that the market for your skills carries a higher wage these days. Encourage them to do some checking, to verify that this is so, and that they will have to pay more to get someone with your qualifications. Express your interest in the company and in the job. And ask for a second interview. Decide who can make the decision, the hiring authority or personnel, and then concentrate on convincing that person.

After the Interview

Follow-up is very important. If you don't refresh the interviewer about your special qualifications, you are quickly going to fade into one more face and one more résumé among a crowd of applicants. At Snelling, even though we beat the drums for our referrals, we still expect them to do the following up. You should do the same, and you'll remain in front.

Go Back to See the Company the Next Day

If you haven't been able to schedule a second interview, stop back at the company the very next day. Tell the secretary who you are and that you need only a moment of the interviewer's time. Stick your head in his door, look him in the eye, shake his hand firmly, and say: "I'll only take a minute. I've been thinking about what you said when we talked yesterday, and I'm convinced I'm your man. I realized that I handled a similar situation to yours at West Bend Insurance, where I had fifteen men reporting to me. I was able to cut the budget twenty-three percent, while enhancing productivity. I'm available to see Mr. Wilson this afternoon or tomorrow morning. Which time will best fit his schedule?"

It doesn't matter that they told you they'd be in touch with you. Many companies report to us that they hope against hope that you'll show some initiative, that you'll call them, that you'll say you want the job.

Call the Interviewer the Following Day

Call Human Resources, if that's where your interview took place, to get an interview with the hiring authority. Or call the hiring authority to get the job offer. Either way, say that you'll take only a moment, and then take just a moment, unless the interviewer prolongs the conversation. Thank him for the interview and then, succinctly, supply some fresh information about yourself. If you studied your comprehensive résumé again after the interview, you should have a fresh tidbit to offer. You should be able to say, for example, "I've been thinking about that inventory problem we discussed, and I recalled a comparable situation when I was at Smothers and Willoughby, where I was able to reduce turnover by twenty-six percent. I can bring that same know-how to Mathews and Jamison, Mr. Johnson, and I'd be able to start either tomorrow or Monday. Which would be best for you?"

Write the Interviewer

This letter should be written right after you've made the phone call, because that call provides essential information to build on in the letter. If you are still in the running but haven't yet clinched the job offer, write a short thank-you letter that includes an additional tidbit of information about you.

This postinterview letter is the way to keep you uppermost in the interviewer's mind and to make you stand out as the right person for the job. The letter may be handwritten or typed, but it should be legible, professional in appearance, and enthusiastic in tone. For example:

Thanks again for the opportunity to meet with you and your staff regarding the opening in your Technical Service Department. From our discussion, I am sure that my background in computer applications would fit your needs very nicely. At Ramco I supervised a staff of seven and kept turnover to only one person in three years. I am excited about the opportunity there at Southwestern Electric. When can I start?

If I were to rate these three steps on a scale from one to ninety-nine, along with all the other advice in this book, they would receive a ninety-nine. Everything else is definitely important, but, as any salesperson knows, if you don't keep asking for the sale you are never going to get it. If you want that jump up the ladder, if you want the best job you have ever held in your life, if you don't want opportunity to slip through your fingers, then jot down these three instructions—*visit, call, write*—and put them in your wallet. Read and follow them every time you have completed an interview, and you will be amazed at the number of job offers you get.

If You Didn't Get the Offer

You won't get every job you apply for. You can't and you don't need to. What you want are five job offers so you can select the one that's right for you. If you find yourself being rejected repeatedly, however, it's time to take stock, to sit back and analyze what may be going wrong.

It's not always your fault if you "flunk" an interview. The interviewer may be in a bad mood. Or you may simply not be right for the job. But sometimes there are things that you can do, ways to improve your chances.

One important point is to observe total honesty. You may think you can improve your chances by embroidering, ever so slightly, on your educational or experience credentials. Don't be tempted. It's too easy to check, and prospective employers will check. I've known cases, in fact, where someone who was absolutely perfect for a particular job—and the employer knew it too—lost the opportunity because he fibbed. He could have had the job at forty-one; he didn't have to say he was thirty-six. He could have had the job without a college degree; he shouldn't have claimed one that didn't exist. If you lie on the application, an employer may decide—and who can blame him—that you may not be trustworthy on the job.

Another important thing to remember is that the ability to get along with people is crucial to almost any job. Unless you're going to be alone in a laboratory or in a fire-watch tower, you need to get along with others. Sometimes applicants with all the technical skill that could be desired lose out because they demonstrate that their human-relations skills are below par. I'm thinking of the man who, asked if his family would go along with relocation, set his jaw and said, "They'll do what I tell them to do." That reply, indicating an authoritarian attitude, cost him the job.

When You Do Get the Offer

Once you line up the job offers you want, you'll have to make a decision. There are a number of factors to consider.

Getting the Facts

Some people accept jobs without ever really knowing all the details about the job, its benefits, and its responsibilities. Others lose out on jobs because they try to find out too much prior to getting the offer. Your objective is, first, to get the offer. Then you can ask about salary, fringe benefits, specific duties and responsibilities, and the authority you'll have to get things done. Try to get the company to give you all this information in writing. If they can't, or they won't, then you put it all down on paper so that you'll have it on hand, accurately, for your company-by-company comparison. Set up what Ben Franklin called T-charts, listing the pluses and minuses of each position. Start with salary, then work your way through benefits, location, duties, responsibilities, authority, budgets, opportunity for growth, size of company, and any other factors that concern you.

Be as objective as possible so that you don't make a people-centered decision. While we've stressed throughout this book that people hire people, once you have the job offer, you need to be objective. You need to recognize that, much as you may like the person you'll be working for at the outset, that person could be promoted or hired away tomorrow. So, sure, it's important that you like the people you'll be working with. Just don't let liking those particular people make your job decision.

Factors to Consider

These are some, not necessarily all, of the factors you should consider as you evaluate your job offers. Make up your own list, and be sure you get the details on each of the points listed for each of the jobs offered.

POSITION

Title	Growth potential
Responsibility	Supervisor
Authority	Peers
Budget	Subordinates

EARNINGS

Salary	Incentives
Salary potential	Bonuses
Commissions	Expenses

FRINGE BENEFITS

Life insurance	Tuition reimbursement
Health insurance	Pension and/or profit
Dependent coverage	sharing
Major medical	Company car
Disability income	Low-interest loans
Dental	Seminars and sympo-
Annual physical	siums
Vacation	Club memberships

RELOCATION ASSISTANCE

Moving expenses
Mortgage differential
Mortgage prepayment fees
Closing costs
Bridge loan

Trips to seek new
home
Interim living ex-
penses

NEW LOCATION

Job opportunities for spouse
Schools
Climate
Cultural amenities

Recreational facil-
ities
Cost of living

COMPANY

Reputation in industry
Company size and anticipated
growth

Takeover, acquisi-
tion, or merger
possibilities
Trends in field

Follow up these general questions with specific questions about
your own field of specialization. If you're going into sales, for
instance, you'll want to know about the territory, existing accounts, product acceptance, back-up advertising, market potential, leads supplied, and so on. If you're in production, you'll
need to know about plant and facilities, research and development, and current equipment.

Salary Negotiations

If you have followed our advice and have several offers on the
table, you'll find salary negotiations much easier. Not that you
can or want to play one against the other, but you'll simply have
a much better idea of the value of your particular set of skills.

Some offers, especially below the highest levels, are firm take-
it-or-leave-it situations. Others have a small amount of flexibility.

And some have a good bit of leeway both in salary and in benefit packages. It all depends on your particular skills and on how badly the company wants you as well as on standard company policy. You'll do better if you can find out what that policy is. One way is to be forthright and ask the person who made you the offer: "John, I'm excited about the opportunity here at Miller Chemicals, but, tell me, is there some room to move on that offer you made me?" Most companies will appreciate this approach and give you an honest answer. They may even tell you the upper limit.

Let's face it, all positions have salary ranges. Your job is to find that upper limit. Your job is also to demonstrate your value to the company, in dollars-and-cents terms, so that you'll get that upper limit. For example: "In my last job I was able to save over two hundred thousand dollars in worker's compensation and sales taxes for the company. That was five times my salary. I think I can do the same for you. Now it seems to me that since you don't have to relocate me at great expense to the company, your offer could be increased by two hundred dollars a week. Since Uncle Sam will take a good portion of that if your company keeps it, we're only talking about a little over one hundred dollars a week. Tell me, John, does that make any sense to you?"

Always break the amount down into small weekly or monthly figures. An increase of $200 a week reduced by taxes to $166 a week actual cost to the company sounds a lot better than $10,000 a year in additional salary and a great deal better than $50,000 in annual salary when they were talking about paying $40,000 to start.

If the company's salary is way out of line, see if you can find out why. Ask when they last did a study of going wages in the area. Show them newspaper ads and articles giving salary ranges for people with your background and skills. Try to educate them rather than lose the job if everything else is as you like it.

And don't get locked in because of your past or current earnings. After all, this is a new job, in a new company, and a whole new ball game. You can expect to be paid in terms of the value you represent to this employer in this particular job.

Here are other ways to stretch the dollars, depending on the particular job:

1. If it is a sales job with a base salary plus commission, ask for part of the commission in the base pay and agree to take no commission until you cover the advance. This will be a big help when salary review time comes around.

2. Try to move the salary review date up to ninety days, if it's now six months, and try to get an advance commitment (assuming that everything is going well) for an automatic increase at the end of that period.

3. Weigh the value of your benefits. Make sure you are comparing apples with apples as you evaluate your various job offers. Study the benefit programs in detail, including deductibles and the portion of insurance that you will have to pay. If the benefits are limited, ask if they can be upgraded. It may be easier to get a better benefit package past the accounting department than to get a hefty raise in pay. Such benefits may also be a better bet for you, in tax terms, especially if you're at the upper salary level and have other income.

If you can't budge them, or budge them enough, you may have to resort to the take-away technique:

Bill, you know how excited I am about coming with Armstrong and Associates. I see a real challenge and a career opportunity here. But I want you to know that people with my particular skills are in high demand, and I know why your last person on the job got recruited away. Now, I've got three other job offers and they are all pressing me. We could wrap this up right now and I'd be sitting at that desk tomorrow morning. All it takes is a little flexibility on your part.

Then you go into exactly what it is you want from them in the way of salary and/or benefits, and you wind up by asking for the sale. If you play your cards right, you can still have the job even if you don't get exactly what you want. So long as you're reasonable and don't irritate the employer, you can try to put yourself in a stronger position.

Would You Hire You?

Put yourself in the employer's shoes, as you evaluate yourself for the job.

Do you really meet the job needs? Can you really do what the company is asking you to do? Look at what the job actually requires, not just what the company says it wants in the way of experience and education. Make sure you understand the difference between job specifications that list applicant qualifications (e.g., a bachelor's degree in accounting) and job specifications that tell what the job holder must actually be able to do (e.g., conduct internal audits). And don't fall for a come-on based on your qualifications if those qualifications don't really fit you for the job that must be done.

Are you cooperative and easy to get along with? Or are you the type of person who is late for work, takes long lunch hours, speaks out about company policies to any and all who will listen? Do you frequently lock horns with superiors or fellow workers? Have you antagonized your peers, and do you intimidate your subordinates? Did you quit your last job in a huff and walk off without giving proper notice? Is this the type of person you want working for you?

Are you honest? Can an employer rely on you? Or have you lied about your age, education, prior experience, earnings, sales records, or anything else? Have you padded expense accounts, made misleading statements to customers, claimed someone else's work as your own? Is this the kind of person you want working for you?

Seven Surefire Job Clinchers

I'm interested in your firm because . . .
I can see that you're investing in good people and that is what's most important. I respect the opportunity that you are offering me. When can I start?
I understand your need . . .
And you can see from my record that I'm a problem solver. I have increased sales, lowered costs, cut overhead, increased pro-

duction (whatever is applicable), and, because I understand your need and know that I can fill that need, I'm ready to go to work. When can I start?

I can produce for you because . . .

I know what return on investment is all about. I keep my eye on the budget and on the bottom line, and I can assure you that I will give you 110 percent. When can I start?

I enjoy doing . . .

And that means that I will motivate others around me. I enjoy challenges and I am looking forward to going to work on this one. When can I start?

How can I make myself even more productive for you?

I'm willing to do whatever it takes, whether it is further training, education—you name it and I'll do it. I know that I can do this job for you right now, but I'd like to be even more productive. When can I start?

I will look after your interests . . .

Because I am loyal, that's the way I was brought up, and that's the way I've been in every job I ever held. That will help make this company more successful, and that is going to secure my future and the future of my family. That's why I'm looking forward to being part of your team. When can I start?

I'm a worker, and I want to work for you . . .

I know what it is to work. When I was growing up we all had chores to do. Later I took odd jobs in the neighborhood—cutting lawns, baby-sitting, whatever I could get to keep busy and make some money. I've always given my employers 110 percent, it's the way I'm built. The work ethic is strong in me, and I'm excited about working for Reynolds and Company. When can I start?

Work out your own job clincher that suits you and your personality. Take one of these and work it around to fit you. Then practice it—on your spouse, on your mirror, while you're driving—so that when you find the job that you really want, you'll be able to use this clincher convincingly to land that job. If you package all of these interview techniques into your own personal blend, you'll be able to get the job offer you want for the job that's right for you.

8

Living Happily Ever After

Once you've landed the right job, you'll turn your sights to keeping the job, getting raises, and winning promotions. But you've got to keep your eye on the ball. Don't be like the golf duffer who lands in sand traps because he gets distracted by the others around him. Don't lose sight of your goal.

No matter how excited you are about this bright, new opportunity, you're also a bit apprehensive. This is just a normal fear of the unknown. But with our advice under your belt, you'll have all the self-confidence you need to move ahead and make the most of your job. This chapter will tell you how to get off on the right foot at your new job, how to toot your own horn so that you get the right kind of attention on the job, and how to win recognition in terms of increased responsibility and greater pay.

"Who's on First?"

If you've ever seen the Abbott and Costello routine of "Who's on First?" you'll understand just what you'll face as a new employee. If your company doesn't recognize this and doesn't supply a layout of your surroundings with the name and title of each person in your work group, then you should make up your own chart. Keep a little note pad on you at all times, and as you meet people and find out what they do, jot down the information. Back at your desk, enter full information on each person: name, title, function, and telephone extension. Set up your chart so that you can find people by location (with a diagram of the work area) and by name (with alphabetized listings by both first and last name). At the same time, if you haven't been given a flow chart of the office hierarchy, make up your own list of who reports to whom—and don't forget that real power may have little to do with titles. This will let you see the office pecking order and keep you from inadvertently treading on someone's toes or invading someone's turf.

In these early days on the job it's important to keep your eye on your long-range goal and to avoid distractions. Some of the distractions that can come between you and your goals, if you let them, are the watercooler cool cats, the after-five watering-hole crowd, and the power players.

When it comes to watercooler cool cats, the types who hang around complaining about the company, steer clear. If these people are really dissatisfied, they should get moving and find a job that suits them better. But whether they are truly dissatisfied or just grumbling, you have better things to do. You don't want to be seen keeping company with chronic complainers. And you don't want to have your own positive mental attitude pulled down by their continual harpings.

And how about the lunchtime and after-five drinkers? They may rationalize their behavior by saying they are making contacts, sharpening people skills, and getting ready for the next step up the ladder. In fact they are really wasting both time and money. They would do better to put aside booze money toward opening a business of their own or toward paying their children's college tuition. They would be better off, in terms of time, taking a college course or reading a book or simply being with their family.

Then there are the corporate power players, eager to form alliances to get your support on one issue or another. You may find someone in the company appearing at your desk in the early days, offering to help you out. This may be just as it appears on the surface: a friendly, helpful person. Or it could be someone seeking to add you to their camp, so to speak, attempting to get your loyalty in a power play you know nothing about. Be friendly. Accept information in a gracious way. But take guidance from your boss. Don't play office politics unless you're really sure about what you're doing, and don't play at all when you're new on the job. You have very little to gain and a great deal to lose.

Working with Your Boss

Remember one thing in these first days on the job: Your boss wants to get the very best out of you. He or she is excited about working with you and looking forward to a successful on-the-job relationship. The company has invested a lot just in hiring you, to say nothing of the investment in salary, benefits, rent, phone, equipment, and so on, so it's in their interest for you to be successful.

When your boss offers advice, guidance, or even correction, look at it not as a put-down or unwarranted criticism but as the kind of constructive help you really need if you're going to do your job properly, catch on quickly, and become part of the team. By the same token, don't look elsewhere when you have a question to ask. Go to your superior. But make a note of the answers so that you don't have to ask the same question again. Start your own little manual, even though you may have been given one with your job, adding to it and updating it with the latest things you're being told. Your boss doesn't mind answering your questions—in fact he or she is usually delighted that you ask—but will begin to wonder just how sharp you are when the same question comes up three days in a row.

People occasionally come back to us after two or three days on the job, saying that they just can't take it, the boss is awful, the situation is intolerable, and they are ready to quit. Often, after some discussion, we find that the basic problem is one of communication or, more accurately, failure to communicate. We talk to them, and sometimes we talk to the boss, and we are usually able to overcome the problem. You shouldn't let things get to this state. Ask questions when necessary, be open about your needs, and things will usually be fine.

Getting Ahead: Three Proven Steps for Raises and Promotions

We all know that doing a good job should lead to both raises and promotions. If we've been hired to sell and we go out and set sales records, our company will recognize this. If our job is to do programming and we write programs that work, we'll get a raise. Up to a point, this is true. Most companies do provide slow and steady progress for employees who do their jobs well. But if you're looking for the really big raises, for bonuses, for additional perks and benefits, for rapid promotions, then you're going to have to do more than just do a good job.

Why is it that some people seem to move ahead faster than others? What do they know that the other people don't? What are they doing that others are not doing? It's no secret. Here are three time-tested ways that will help you get ahead on the job.

Performance and Salary Reviews

Most reviews are quick, off-the-cuff affairs, with the boss saying something like, "George, you're doing a fine job and I'm very happy with what you're doing. Here are a few areas that I would like you to work on and where I think you could improve a bit." The employee says, "Yes, you're right. I appreciate your pointing those out to me and thank you so much." If it's a salary review, the boss has also said something to the effect of "Oh, by the way, I'm giving you a six percent increase," and the employee says, "Oh, thank you," and then retreats to his office sulking because he was expecting at least 8 percent. The exact dialogue may be different, but in five minutes, if you're lucky enough not to be interrupted by a ringing telephone and people popping into the office, the whole thing is over. And that's your review for another year.

It doesn't have to be this way. And you shouldn't let it be this way if you want those sizable increases and those meaningful promotions.

Amazingly enough, you can have a great deal of control over your review. If your company doesn't have a formal review program, in which both you and your superior fill out a form that evaluates your performance in many different areas, then you need to put such a system into action on your own behalf. You can keep track of the necessary data, and use it as a springboard for discussion in your salary-performance review. There are three steps to follow:

1. *Keep detailed records of what you have accomplished.* Keep your own notebook of items for review, listing every single thing that has had positive results for the company, the kinds of things that would go on your résumé if you were writing a résumé. Translate each accomplishment into dollars-and-cents benefit to the company whenever possible. For example:

> Wrote a new program that cut clerical time spent preparing invoices by 22 percent, saving the company an estimated $15,000 a year.
>
> Cracked the Wilson account, getting a foot in the door for the company; sales to date have already amounted to $40,000 and should go over $100,000 for the year.
>
> Instituted a new accounting procedure that saved the company over $50,000 a year in state sales tax.
>
> Reorganized the production line to eliminate two jobs, saving the company over $35,000 in salaries and fringe benefits.
>
> Obtained competing bids on printing the new training manuals and saved the company $7,000 over last year's cost.
>
> Recommended the installation of new telephone service, saving the company $2,000 in just three months.
>
> Redesigned purchase order forms, consolidating three forms into one, saving printing costs and clerical time for an estimated savings of $750.
>
> Took a course in employee management; applying the techniques learned has led to more efficient department operation.

In a performance review, you must be the one to toot your own horn. Your boss may know that you've done these things, but he's never seen them all tied together, all listed in one place at one time. He's never devoted as much time to thinking about you as you have. He's never seen exactly what you've saved the company nor understood that you are giving a tremendous return on the company's investment in you. They may be paying you $20,000 or $30,000 or $60,000 a year, but they're getting that back many times over through the work that you do. They are making a profit on you, which is as it should be, but you want them to see that profit so that they can see just how valuable you are and evaluate your pay increase accordingly. The principle applies whether you are a secretary or a vice president. It makes no difference.

2. *Let your boss know how he can get more out of you.* Bosses may think the review is a one-way street, but you want to show them that constructive critiques can, and indeed should, go both ways because you really care about your job and want to do it better.

You may think it's impossible to speak up and tell your boss what he or she might do differently. But it all depends how you put it. At Snelling we encourage our people to tell their supervisors how they can supervise them better and how they can get more out of them. For example, you might say: "Mr. Johnson, wouldn't it make sense to schedule fifteen minutes every other morning for us to get together? I see how busy you are, and I hate to interrupt you when I need answers to urgent problems; scheduling regular time together should help us both."

Or you might even use this opportunity to gently correct your boss: "At the sales meeting a few weeks ago, Mr. Smith, you criticized my performance in front of everyone. That was very embarrassing. I know your criticism was valid, and I accept it and will try to improve my performance, but public criticism damages not only my morale but that of everyone else. If you feel that criticism is warranted again, could we discuss the matter in private?"

Remember, your boss wants productive employees, and employees are more likely to be productive if they are happy on the job. Your boss can't know you're unhappy unless you tell him. This isn't a license for constant complaining. But if you have a legitimate beef, and a constructive suggestion for improving the situation, go directly to your boss to discuss the matter.

3. *Setting goals helps you track your progress.* The third and final part of the performance review will allow you to show your boss what you have accomplished. You must keep track of your on-the-job goals and the progress you're making toward those goals.

Then you can describe what your goals are for the upcoming period and ask your boss to add any additional goals he views as important as well as help you set priorities for the ones that are already on the list.

This involves the boss directly in saying exactly what he expects of you and is one of the most important parts of the review process. When review time rolls around again and the boss has some suggestions about ways you can improve what you've been doing, he will have to acknowledge—once you display your list —that you were given certain tasks and certain priorities and that you did accomplish them. If you didn't accomplish them all, you'll have to talk about the reasons. It may well be that, in the middle of that six-month period, you were handed five new and time-consuming projects.

Bosses have a way of forgetting that you have regular everyday duties and responsibilities when they come along with special projects and new assignments. If it really isn't possible to complete everything you've been handed, it may be time to ask for assistance. Perhaps a temporary or a part-time worker should be hired, maybe someone should be reassigned from another department. At the very least, by conducting this discussion, you'll be showing that you did as well as anyone could possibly have done. At the best, you'll be improving your position and your authority by getting additional help reporting to you.

You don't necessarily want the boss to decide you're overloaded and to remove those tasks. Instead you want to remain in charge of those tasks so that you will become more valuable to your boss. You may have to point out to your boss, subtly of course, that additional help could report to you, instead of to him, so that you can take care of what needs to be done without troubling him with details. This is where you start to build yourself a better job by building your responsibilities to the point of receiving a promotion. Please, please, no empire building. When tough times come, empires and their kings are the first to go.

Offer Value

The second technique for assuring yourself of getting above-average raises and promotions is to show value. One way to do this is simply to ask what it will take, what it is that you have to do or that you can do to make yourself more valuable to the company. Most people ignore this basic step. Yet if you want to know what you have to do to get a raise or promotion, what makes more sense than to ask? Ask your superior. And think about asking, very tactfully, the director of human resources, the personnel manager, or even your superior's superior.

Plan ahead exactly what you will say. You might consider something along these lines: "I know every company has to have both leaders and followers. And I know that plenty of people are satisfied with being followers. But I'm not. I want to move ahead. I'm doing things to improve myself. I'm talking to you now because I'd like you to tell me just what I can do to take another move up. Where is the next opening likely to occur, a step or two up the scale, and what do I have to do to prepare myself so that I'll be considered for the position?"

Whatever your exact words—they'll depend on your position, your company, and, most important, your boss—be careful to phrase your question so that your boss doesn't feel threatened. You do want to know what his chances are of moving ahead, if you might have a shot at his job, but you also want to know what else might be available in the division, in the company as a whole, in a subsidiary. There's an old saying that opportunity is where you find it. This also means that you have to go look for opportunity, because it's not necessarily going to come find you.

Put your request properly, and you may find the personnel director suddenly realizing that you might indeed have the skills for a new opening over at XYZ division. Some companies post all job openings on central bulletin boards; others don't. If your company is one of those that doesn't let employees know (probably on the theory that they'll wind up with disgruntled employees who have been turned down), you may not have known the XYZ position was open, and the personnel director may never have looked to your division to fill the job. Let him know that you're interested, you're available, and you have the right skills, and you may just put yourself in line for a promotion.

Even if a promotion isn't immediately forthcoming, perhaps because a position isn't open, you'll accomplish two things: (1) You'll let people know you're interested in moving ahead, and (2) you'll find out just what you need to do in order to move ahead—take a course, get a degree, or whatever. Once you know what you need to do, you can do it.

Another way of showing value is to make constructive suggestions to increase company productivity. Don't file complaints, but do make suggestions. If you have trouble seeing room for improvement, ask yourself some questions. The following are based on suggestions from Prentice-Hall, publishers of management information: Are we doing this procedure this way solely out of habit? Can the procedure be streamlined, accomplished with fewer steps? Could inspections be simplified without impairing quality? Can space be better utilized, so that work moves more efficiently from desk to desk, workstation to workstation?

Once you have your ideas, be specific, including facts and figures about staffing requirements, budgets, and whatever is required for implementation. Put your recommendation in writing, preferably to more than one person. Start with your immediate superior. Then, if there's no one else logically situated to receive a copy of your proposal, send a copy to the personnel department for your personnel file. Whether or not the suggestion is adopted, the fact that you made it will look good on your record when review time rolls around.

I Care

The third secret to getting raises and promotions is to show that you care, and especially that you care about your boss. It never hurts to stop in sometimes, especially just before closing time, and say, "Boss, you look a little bit harried today. I know things are really heavy, the pressure has been on you, and I just wondered if there is anything I can do to help? Can I stay late tonight and get some work out, or take something home? Just tell me what I can do for you."

When you make these offers, be as specific as possible. For example: "I know you are working on the Johnson project, with the deadline coming up fast. How about if I take it home with me over the weekend and bring it back to you on Monday morning, all wrapped up?" Now, even if he feels you are not qualified to wrap up the Johnson project, he may give you a shot at it over the weekend just to see what you can do. If this happens, you've really got an opportunity to show your stuff.

Whether or not he takes you up on your offer, the boss will recognize that you care and will appreciate your offer to help. Just be sure your offer is sincere. Don't be like the neighbor who stops by when you have the garage all torn apart, ready to paint, and says, "Boy, you really are busy." You say, "I sure am." And he says, as he turns to walk away, "Well, if I can do anything to help you, please let me know." And you holler after him, as he walks faster and faster back across the lawn to his house, "Yeah, sure George, I appreciate the offer, and if I need you, I'll give you a call." When you offer to help, be ready to help. Don't have your coat on, ready to walk out of the office as you speak. Instead have your sleeves rolled up and your scratch pad in hand, so that you're ready to sit down and get to work.

Getting a Raise

Raises usually go along with annual performance reviews. They should certainly go along with promotions. But you may be given increased responsibilities with or without a new title and without a corresponding increase in pay. You may even find a year or more going by without an increase. Now that inflation is down from its record levels, many employers are moving away from regular cost-of-living raises. Instead they are rewarding performance and productivity. What does this mean to you? It means that you have to not only be productive but also demonstrate your productivity. It means that you must let your employer know, in very specific terms, what you are doing and why a salary increase is justified.

You'll be doing this as you go through the steps outlined above. In addition, follow these guidelines:

- Know what your skills are worth on the open job market as well as, if you can, what people with comparable skills are being paid by other employers.

- Consider suggesting additional perks instead of a raise in pay if your boss convinces you that a raise in pay is not forthcoming. Possibilities include a better health or life insurance package, tuition reimbursement, a company car, increased vacation time, a year-end bonus.

- Sharpen your negotiating skills, and rehearse your raise rationale with your spouse or a close friend. Role-playing—you act yourself and the other person acts as your boss, countering your requests for a raise—can help you focus your reasoning and make a clearer case.

Performance and salary reviews are an open door. Marshal your forces and prepare carefully for each one so that you can get the most mileage out of it. In addition, you should continually let your boss know what you are doing for the company. Don't hit him over the head with "Look what I did now," but put constructive suggestions and accomplishments in writing and try to have regular meetings with your supervisor to offer value and to show him that you care.

Your Happiness Quotient

Life on the job is important; that's why we've told you how to make the most of it. But you are more than a worker, you are a human being, and you want to make the most of all your life. To do so, you'll want to (1) keep a balance in your life, and (2) develop your happiness quotient through your attitude toward work.

Keeping a Balance in Your Life

While you're putting your all into your new job, keep your priorities straight. While you're working overtime and bringing work home, in a commendable effort to do the very best job you can and convince your boss that he made the right selection when he hired you, be sure to devote some attention to your family, your physical health, and your spiritual well-being.

If you're a spiritual person and your mode of transportation gets you to the office ten minutes early every morning, take that ten minutes to sit down and just read the Bible. You'll find that it will relax you, give you a feeling of peace and contentment, and prepare you for the day ahead. Resist the temptation to immediately jump into your work and get that ten-minute head start. Your nerves are probably jangled from fighting your way through traffic anyhow. Ten minutes of quiet reading or meditation will give you a better start on the day's work than plunging into phone calls or paperwork can possibly do.

Similarly, when you take work home at night, set your briefcase aside until you've relaxed with your family and perhaps taken a walk before dinner. Always plan on a family meal, then spend some time with your children and your spouse. If you do this, you'll find that you're refreshed and ready to put in another hour or two on the work in that briefcase.

Keeping physically fit will also enable you to get more done, to be more productive on the job. Keep your weight down, get some good, regular cardiovascular exercise, some light weight training to keep muscle tone, and avoid those three pitfalls: alcohol, smoking, and caffeine.

Alcohol and work do not mix. Alcohol at lunchtime is an absolute no-no if you've got a career on your mind. And even if you don't, it could cost you your job through lessened efficiency and productivity in the afternoon. If you feel you must stop on the way home to have a couple of drinks and relax, perhaps you should reevaluate the job you're in. Perhaps the stress level is too high for you, or perhaps you simply need to reassess your priorities. Alcohol is a drug, and alcohol addiction is one of the top problems facing this nation. It also is a major problem facing corporations these days, and they're spending more and more dollars to combat it among their employees. Don't become the target of an antialcoholism campaign.

If you care at all about yourself, smoking is a habit you must break. You know that smoking has been implicated in many serious illnesses. Do you also know that working in a smoke-filled room reduces the oxygen content in your blood and dramatically impairs your ability to think and reason? If the tension of trying to stop smoking and the trauma of a new job are too much to face at one time, then try to set a few basic ground rules for yourself that will help you to stop smoking. For example: Make it a point not to smoke at your desk. Go outside your building when you feel you need to smoke so that you won't contribute to a smoke-filled working environment. You'll help your co-workers, and you'll help yourself as well.

Caffeine, whether in coffee or in cola drinks, is as much a habit as alcohol and tobacco. If you don't believe this, and you're a steady coffee or cola drinker, try doing without either for three days; you'll find out what withdrawal is all about. You'll have headaches, your system will be upset, you'll wonder what's wrong with you. Get past these withdrawal symptoms by kicking the caffeine habit and you'll be more alert, get more work done, and you'll be a better employee.

Your Attitude Toward Work

If you are happy on the job, excited and enthusiastic about the challenges and opportunities it offers, then you are a long way toward bettering your lot in life. Do you get to work rain or shine, or do you take advantage of your sick-leave days and make sure you get every one of them whether you are sick or not? Can you work without continual praise and pats on the back, or do you need constant recognition to keep going? Can you share credit for jobs well done and accept the blame for tasks that fail? Can you admit your mistakes and move on? Do you try to bluff your way through situations you don't understand, or do you have enough confidence in yourself to be able to ask questions when something isn't clear? Taking days off, needing constant praise, unwillingness to admit mistakes, and bluffing your way through are signs of an immature worker. You'll be a much happier worker when you can put these behind you. You'll also be a tremendous asset to your boss and your company.

You will also be much more valuable to your employer when you can be a team player, working closely with other people. Being a loner just won't do. Remember what you thought of the fellow in high school who hogged the basketball and never let anyone else get a shot? Sure, he was a high scorer, but the team more often than not lost. A basketball team can't be a one-man show; neither can companies, divisions, or departments. It takes everyone pulling together to really get the job done.

Are you expecting a job guarantee? Don't. The only security that you really have or need is knowing that you can do a job and, if that job doesn't exist anymore, that you can successfully learn a new job. Keypunch operators may face a decline in jobs, but data processing entry clerks are in demand. Physical education teachers can put their skills to work in health spas and company phys ed programs. Once you know how to do a job and, more important, once you develop a willingness to work, you'll never be without a job. But you must have the confidence in yourself that you can work and learn and change and adapt. You must give everything you can to your current job, while maintaining that all-important balance in your life. And you must be motivated to succeed.

Companies are looking for achievement-oriented people. Achievers know where they are going, they know how to get there, and they know how to keep moving ahead. Your boss is looking for someone who fits this description, someone who knows how to solve problems. Any fool can criticize, complain, and condemn; any fool usually does. The amount of formal education you have is not the measure of how far you can go. "I will" is much more important than "IQ." Are you enthusiastic? Do you have the right attitude? If you do, you will be happy on the job and happy at home. You will have found the right job.

The Job Outlook for Tomorrow

Each year the U.S. Bureau of Labor Statistics looks into its crystal ball and issues a prediction for the future. It develops its projections through a complex series of economic models and surveys, and draws upon information about such diverse factors as defense spending, population trends, immigration, unemployment, and the world's political and economic situation. In an increasingly global economy, the latter pays an important role in the development of the projections. It then feeds all of this information into a computer, and what comes out is a prediction of the job outlook for the next ten years. Here are some highlights of the latest survey for the rest of the 1990s and beyond.

Jobs in the U.S. will increase by twenty-four million over the next ten years. Women in the work force will continue to increase as a larger proportion of them look for jobs and more occupations become available to them.

Services Will Flourish

Nearly four out of five jobs will be in industries that provide services. Opportunities will occur in firms of all sizes in fields as diverse as insurance, banking, financial services, advertising, communications, human services, law enforcement, and ecology. Among the occupations with projected high demand are para-legals, medical assistants, home health aides, data processing equipment repairers, travel agents, auditors, and accountants.

Education services are expected to grow by over two million jobs. Special education teachers will lead the way, followed by bus drivers, counsellors, secondary school teachers, and teacher aides.

As the U.S. population grows grayer, the need for health ser-vices will continue to grow at an accelerated rate. Virtually reces-sion proof, the health care industry will provide jobs for those with all levels of education. By the year 2000 almost seven out of ten of the fastest growing occupations will be in health-related fields. The best prospects will be in nursing, rehabilitation coun-seling, physical and occupational therapy, medical assistants, and home health aides.

Technology will continue to change how work is done. Com-puter technology is growing so fast in almost every field that it will be almost mandatory for workers to have some knowledge of computers. Computer service technicians, systems analysts, and programmers will find a ready market for their skills. The nation's appetite for information has resulted in an unprece-dented explosion in information services. New technologies in print and electronic media will drastically increase the need for communications personnel at all levels.

American businesses depend on marketing and sales to keep their bottom line healthy. Jobs in these fields will grow by about 750,000 by the year 2000. The demand for retail salespersons will account for a substantial portion of available jobs.

Science and Technology

With the continued advances in science and technology, there will be no lack of jobs for engineers. Chemical, mechanical, biomedical, electronic, electrical, and civil engineers will enjoy a seller's market, as will those with special training in robotics, telecommunications, construction, and transportation. This field is wide open for women.

The environment will continue to be a hot topic well into the next century, increasing the need for environmental scientists, toxic and hazardous waste managers, and recycling specialists.

A Bright Future

Keep in mind that these are only predictions. Unforeseen domestic and international economic and political pressures can upset the results of even the most efficient and complex surveys. You should also be aware that new technical advances or popular movements such as concern for the environment may receive extensive media attention and create the impression that many new jobs and opportunities will result. New developments in technology and science, while holding promise for the future, actually result in relatively few new jobs for the present.

In assessing your career choices, keep one thing in mind. Growth of employment is only one source of jobs. Occupations with little or no projected growth can still provide opportunities. Openings can occur for many reasons. People are promoted, transferred, or fired. They die or retire. They move to other cities. They change careers or go back to school. Some open businesses of their own, while others leave the job market to raise families.

All indications point to the fact that as the twenty-first century approaches, opportunities will be unlimited. Just remember that people with the best chances for obtaining the best jobs will be those who have the most education and training and who possess the know-how necessary to look for and find the jobs they want.

9

A Business of Your Own

Throughout this book we've shown you how to find and keep the right job. We've also shown you how to use an entrepreneurial spirit to get ahead on the job. But maybe you don't really want to have a job. Maybe you'd prefer creating your own job, being your own boss, starting a business of your own. If so, you're not alone. Americans throughout history have started businesses of all descriptions. Men and women with the entrepreneurial spirit have started tailor shops and trucking firms, bakeries and banks. Many of the largest corporations we know today started as one person's idea. Many of today's small businesses will be tomorrow's corporations, because the entrepreneurial spirit is very much with us today. According to the most recent available figures from the U.S. Bureau of Economic Analysis, the last five years have witnessed record increases in the number of new business starts.

Do you want to join this number? There are many good reasons for doing so. Here are just a few; check off the ones that apply to you, then add your own:

- To be my own boss, with nobody telling me what to do.
- To use my own imagination, ingenuity, and energy, and reap the rewards of my own hard work.

- To do the type of work I like to do and have always wanted to do.
- No cap on my earnings; instead the harder and smarter I work, the more money I am going to make.
- To live where I've always wanted to live, not where I must live because of the dictates of some job.
- To make more money, a lot of money.
- To work side by side with my spouse and children and have a business that the family can be involved in, one we can pass on to the children.
- Time to be part of my community, to be active in local civic, religious, and business affairs.
- Time for myself and for my family.

Note that these are all positive reasons. There's not a negative one among them. Some people decide to go into business because they think nobody will hire them at their current age; that's nonsense, as we amply demonstrated earlier. Others decide to go into an independent business because they were fired or laid off. That's a reason, all right, but it's not a sound one.

If you really want a business of your own, do so for the right reasons. Don't leave your job because you are unhappy, not until you've laid careful plans for going into business and for being successful. If you've been fired or laid off, in fact, you might do well to take another job, any job, to keep the money coming in while you make the plans and raise the money that you will need to make your new venture a success. In this chapter we'll show you how to get started.

Enthusiasm is essential if your new business is to work. But don't get carried away with enthusiasm in the very beginning. Keep a clear head and be sure to evaluate all the potential disadvantages of a business of your own before you make a decision based on the advantages alone. The downside includes

- The need for sizable amounts of cash to get started and a willingness to live on a bare-bones budget until the business gets established.

- The need to put in enormous amounts of time and energy, working what may be twenty hours a day until you can afford to hire help.

- The risk of failure. A great many small businesses fail, many of them in their first year.

Some people with well-developed business plans and enough start-up capital fail for reasons beyond their control. Most small businesses fail, however, because their owners do not have well-thought-out business plans, adequate capital, or good business sense. Yet our nation needs more small, well-run businesses. They supply, and have always supplied, the majority of the jobs in this nation. In fact in the past decade virtually all job growth came from small businesses—no mean feat, as our work force grew by twenty million people during this time.

Failure need not be a factor in your own business venture. Just use your awareness of the possibility of failure to sharpen your business skills. Follow our guidelines, moreover, and you can greatly increase the odds in your favor.

There are three ways to get started in a business of your own, each with certain advantages and disadvantages: (1) starting a business from scratch, (2) purchasing an existing business, and (3) franchising. We will look at each in some detail.

Starting a New Business

Many people think these are the most economical ways to get into business: start it on a shoestring, start it in the basement, start it part-time. We all hear the success stories of people who have done so—the caterer who started out baking brownies for her own parties, the creator of canvas handbags who started at the kitchen table and now has a nationwide business, the manufacturer of rubber stamps who started with a $1,500 investment and became a $4 million concern.

What we don't hear are the innumerable failures of people who started this way. Why? People don't like to admit these failures. They prefer to bury their mistakes. Why do people start a business from scratch? They rationalize as follows:

- I'm going to make a million dollars (or whatever amount makes you starry-eyed as you read this)
- I can sell anything
- I want my name over the door
- I can pick my own location
- I have a product or service that is unique
- I can start on a shoestring
- I like the challenge

Notice the *I*'s. Your ego, if you let it, can get in the way of sound business decisions.

Why do so many aspiring entrepreneurs fail? There are many, many reasons. Sometimes their timing was wrong. Or their location was wrong. Their idea might have been wrong in the first place. Perhaps they hired the wrong people, failed to promote their product or service properly, or found that the product or service, no matter how well marketed, failed to gain acceptance. There are many reasons why people fail. But usually there are two major reasons: (1) lack of capital and (2) lack of know-how.

If you want to start your own business, you should devote plenty of time and attention right at the outset to sufficient capitalization and to adequate know-how. A business is not a hobby. If you want to succeed, you've got to do your homework.

Your first decision is picking your business, the product or service you will be selling, based on studies of the products and services themselves and of the potential local demand for those products or services. You can't succeed if what you're selling is no good, and you can't succeed if it's good and no one wants it. Do a feasibility study, in which you analyze the product or service itself, the potential customer base, competing businesses, possible locations, and your own expertise. Then prepare yourself further by reading a wide variety of business publications and attending business seminars.

Then you must initiate solid cash planning. And "solid" means just that. Don't just say, "Well, fifty thousand bucks ought to do it." Instead write out a cash-flow projection estimating your potential income and outgo. Estimate your sales volume in view of the market you will serve and the number of competitors sharing that market. You'll find it easier to make a realistic sales estimate if you consult wholesalers and trade associations in your chosen field, your banker and accountant, and statistical sources in your local reference library. Just remember to be realistic. Your sales are likely to grow, but they are equally likely to start small. You'll have expenses at the outset, but you don't want to incur extra expenses by building inventory to overoptimistic levels.

Equally important in your cash planning is an estimate of just what it will cost to get started and to keep your business operating. Start-up costs might include equipment purchases and fixtures, furniture, printing, rent deposits, a phone system, computers, manufacturing and office supplies, license fees, and deposits on rent and utilities. Ongoing expenses include supplies, rent, salaries, and your own living expenses. Again, be realistic, and allow a financial reserve for the unexpected.

Prepare a business plan including at least a one-year projection of marketing and financial goals. Your marketing plan should describe your proposed pricing, distribution, advertising and promotion, employees, and customers. The financial plan should detail operating costs and overhead, cash flow, break-even points, and capital needs.

Finding start-up capital is next on the list. Sources include your own savings, other people (including, but not limited to, relatives, co-workers, former bosses, and friends) who are interested in investing in a new venture, and financial institutions. Before you can tap any sources but your own pocket, however, you will need a formal business plan that includes a cash-flow forecast. This formal plan will help you make a convincing presentation to your funding sources. These sources are described in greater detail later in this chapter.

Whatever your business and wherever it's located, don't be afraid to start small. Consider the following, all legendary American businesses that started small:

- The Bank of America once consisted of a wood-plank counter and a canvas bag holding $80,000.
- Gail Borden worked eighteen hours a day trying to start his condensed milk business in an abandoned mill.
- King C. Gillette sold only 51 razors and 168 blades in his first year.
- Roland Hussey Macy could not make a go of a retail store during the California Gold Rush.
- Willis Carrier was so worried about drawing a crowd for the introduction of his new cooling machine that he scheduled a boxing bout as an added attraction.
- When Paul Galvin was launching Motorola, many states wanted to ban car radios as dangerous diversions.
- William Hewlett and David Packard had $500 in capital when they started a shop in a garage, using an oven in Packard's kitchen to bake paint onto the equipment they made.

Read enough? It's time to fulfill your dream!

Purchasing an Existing Business

Many of the same factors come into play whether you start a new business or buy a going concern. But there are additional advantages and disadvantages to consider, and consider carefully, before you buy a business someone else is running.

On the plus side, buying an existing business can save time and effort and start-up costs while providing you with an established customer base. In addition, a going business can give you

- Immediate cash flow from accounts receivable
- Name and product-service recognition
- Experienced employees
- Facilities and equipment in working order
- Existing suppliers

- Insurance in place
- Ongoing advertising and promotion
- Work in progress
- Goodwill

On the downside, it's also possible to inherit ill will or become stuck with old fixtures and out-of-date merchandise or a location that is going sour. Pitfalls to avoid include

- Overstated profits
- New but unprofitable business (watch out for guarantees made by the old owner, under a contract you must fulfill)
- Worthless accounts receivable
- Insufficient cash flow
- Outmoded equipment or the loss of key employees, making it impossible to compete
- Insufficient training and familiarization by the seller
- Licensing requirements you can't meet or can meet only with great difficulty and cost ("grandfathering" of existing facilities that do not meet code requirements, for example, may not pass to a new owner, and expensive upgrades may be required)
- Problems with location (Is the traffic pattern being changed on the fronting street? Is street parking being eliminated? Will the parking lot next door become the site of a new building? Is a new shopping mall draining business from this part of town?)

Before you purchase a going business, you must carefully evaluate all the potential advantages and disadvantages. You must also, if you're wise, be very careful about specifics:

- Is equipment up-to-date and inventory salable?
- Are refunds due under any contracts with clients and customers?
- Are there outstanding bills that must be paid?

- Will you inherit any pending lawsuits, filed or not, from suppliers, customers, competitors, and so on?
- Will the seller agree to a contractual clause requiring instruction in the business, free of charge and for a specified period of time?
- Will the seller agree to a noncompete clause and refrain from setting up a competing business in the same area for a given period of time?

Due diligence, in which you thoroughly investigate every possible question in advance of the sale, will protect you. So will the use of competent legal and accounting advice. And so, under some circumstances, will the purchase of selected assets rather than an entire business. You might buy customer lists and work in progress, for example, but not buy outdated equipment or inventory or shaky accounts receivable.

Before you buy at all, however, be sure to take a long, hard, cold look at the figures. If they don't work, if the return on investment isn't positive, don't buy. Don't persuade yourself that you can turn a failing business around and make it profitable. All you're likely to do is lose your proverbial (and maybe your actual) shirt.

Business Brokers

A business broker may help you find the existing business that would be right for you. A good business broker can save both time and money in your search, show you how best to structure the deal, and even help you raise the necessary capital. But business brokers come in all sizes and shapes. Some are divisions of major banks or stock brokerage firms handling multimillion-dollar deals. Others are part of realty firms run on either a part-time or full-time basis. Some are solo practices, and some employ a number of specialists.

Some brokers will handle any kind of business at any price, while others specialize in certain types of business. Some represent the seller and some the buyer and some try to represent both. If you think using a business broker will make your search easier, here are some dos and don'ts to consider:

- Do check out the broker, with the chamber of commerce or Better Business Bureau or banks, just as you would any other professional service.
- Do look for a full-time broker who specializes in the type of business you want.
- Do give the broker all the information he requests, holding nothing back, or you will tie his hands and waste both his time and yours.
- Do act promptly on any leads you receive; opportunities to buy good businesses do not last long.
- Do use back-up professional advice, in the form of a business consultant, attorney, or accountant.
- Don't allow the broker to represent both you and the seller; this is as much a conflict of interest as using the same attorney or accountant.
- Don't allow yourself to be high-pressured or rushed into a commitment without doing your homework and without an attorney's advice.

Franchising

With franchising, an individually owned business is operated as an independent part of a larger group of businesses. Franchising has a long and honorable history. King George III franchised companies to set up the American colonies. Cities franchise utilities to provide water service and cable TV, and firms such as Ford, Exxon, and Coca-Cola built their fortunes through networks of franchised dealers. Franchising reaches into every corner of American life, into bookstores and copy centers, flower shops and car washes. Yes, even your favorite football team is a franchise.

Familiar names abound. Here are just a few: Midas Muffler, H & R Block, Kampgrounds of America, Athlete's Foot, Dunkin'

Donuts, Baskin-Robbins, McDonald's, 7-Eleven stores, Holiday
Inn, and not at all least, our own company, Snelling. These are
household names throughout America. These are names that
offer you a chance at a business of your own.

Many small-business owners have been helped to a sound start
by investing in a franchise. You may wish to consider doing the
same. Franchising, as the Small Business Administration points
out, can minimize the risk of going into business. It lets you start
your business under a name and trademark that usually already
have public acceptance. It offers you training and management
assistance from people experienced in your line of business.
Sometimes you can also obtain financial assistance that permits
you to start out with less cash than you would otherwise need.

Specific advantages also include

- Reduced risk of failure, because the "wheel" has been invented and pretested and you know it works

- Ongoing research and development by the parent organization

- Name recognition, registered name and trademarks, often
  leading to instant business and instant income

- Training and a constant flow of information in the form
  of video and audio tapes, manuals, seminars, newsletters,
  and so on

- Motivation provided for both you and your staff via awards,
  diplomas, national recognition

- Site location, if you are opening a new franchise rather
  than buying an existing franchise

- Guidance on legal and tax matters, incorporating, licensing, employee contracts, and so on

- Advertising and public relations, on a national basis, helping your local business to grow

- Group purchasing, which saves you money on supplies,
  equipment, and goods

- The ability to expand a single franchise or acquire additional units

Just as there is a downside to starting a new business or purchasing an existing business, however, there are also some disadvantages to franchising. You will lose a certain amount of control of your business, and you must pay an ongoing royalty to the franchisor.

Nonetheless, franchising is so attractive that it is expected to take in over fifty cents of every retail dollar by the year 2000. According to *Entrepreneur* magazine, three thousand franchise companies in sixty industries are already in place, with more sprouting each year. Its success rate is significantly greater than that of small independent businesses. The SBA estimates that 65 percent of small businesses fail in the first five years, but the Department of Commerce reports that franchises close at under 5 percent. If you are interested in franchising beyond the details presented here, write to the International Franchising Association, Suite 900, 1350 New York Avenue N.W., Washington, DC 20005. You can obtain a copy of the *Franchise Opportunities Handbook* prepared by the U.S. Department of Commerce by contacting the local U.S. Government Book Store (see your telephone directory white pages under "U.S. Government Printing Office") or by writing to Superintendent of Documents, U.S. Government Printing Office, Washington, DC 20402.

Should you consider a franchise? Yes, if you are interested in running a business and making a lot of money. But be careful. Most franchise operations are reputable, but, as in any field, there are a few bad apples in the barrel. To protect yourself, stick with a company whose name and reputation you trust. Evaluate the commitment of time and money that will be required. Assess the backup—in staff, training, manuals, site selection, systems and procedures, and the like—that you will receive from the franchisor. Find out how many franchisees own more than one. They won't buy two or three or more if the deal is no good. With the right franchise, the opportunities can be limitless. You may be content with just one, but you may just want the opportunity to own a dozen. That opportunity should be available.

The Franchise Agreement

Remember, franchising is a system of distribution under which an individually owned business is operated as part of a large chain. You'll benefit from being part of the larger operation, but in turn you must conform to its standards. Otherwise if each individual franchisee went his or her own way, the value of being part of the franchise operation would soon disappear.

You can therefore expect the franchisor to insist on certain things in order to protect the name and system as a whole. Those golden arches, as you might expect, cannot be turned to square green doorways under your operation. But some franchise agreements also set mandatory working hours, permit cancellation of the agreement for certain violations, or impose severe limitations on the right to sell the franchise.

It's important to read the agreement carefully with the help of your lawyer and to understand its provisions. Be particularly careful about:

Limited-term franchises. You probably don't want to work hard for fifteen or twenty years, building your business, and then have the franchisor take it over and run it as a company-operated business. There are some franchises that will last as long as you personally own and operate them. Find out in advance.

Exclusive territories. Do you want the privilege of doing business exclusively in a given area, and the hands-tied feeling that comes with being unable to expand when you've saturated that territory? In many cases, the more franchises in an area the better. More franchises help build name recognition and build your business. Decide what's most important to you, but be sure to study population demographics and market trends before you do.

Capital: Where and How to Get It

Whether you start your own business, buy an existing business, or open a franchise, you will need start-up capital. You've estimated your sales volume and your operating costs, worked up a cash-flow projection, and developed a business plan. Now you're ready to go after the money. Here are some possible sources.

Yourself. Of course, your own savings go on the line first in any new business venture. But don't look only at cash in the bank. Do you have old whole-life insurance policies? Their cash value can be tapped via a low-cost loan. Do you have substantial equity in your home? Similarly that equity can be tapped with either a second mortgage or, perhaps a better bet, one of the new equity access loans that permit you to write checks on a designated amount as you need the cash. This might be the time to sell your home and rent a small apartment near your new business. If you own securities, you can borrow against their value if the time isn't right to sell. If you have a company pension or profit-sharing plan, you may be able to withdraw or borrow money. Explore all the sources of cash at your disposal.

Relatives. Distant or close, from parents and siblings to great-aunts and cousins, relatives with investable money may be persuaded to invest it in you.

Friends. Similarly your friends (co-workers, ex-bosses, neighbors, golf buddies) may see that your projected business is a good investment. With relatives or friends, however, be sure that you draw up a businesslike agreement.

Businessmen. They may be willing to advance venture capital in exchange for a share of your business. If you've packaged your presentation properly, this may be an advantageous source of funds because you may be able to secure business expertise along with capital. Don't worry about giving up a portion of your business, either. Remember, this is only your first business, the one that will give you the capital to open many more.

Partners. You may have always thought of going it completely alone, but a business partner (active or silent) may make a lot of sense, bringing skill or knowledge or experience or contacts that you do not possess on your own. Don't overlook this potential source of both capital and experience.

The Franchisor. If you are taking a franchise, the franchisor may offer capital or leads to sources of capital because it is in the franchisor's best interest to see that you are properly capitalized.

Franchisees. In your own or other businesses, franchisees are often able and willing to diversify in order to increase their own cash flow. They can be an excellent source of capital for a new venture.

Banks. Banks are a resource if you are a worthy credit risk, have a strong financial statement and business plan, and can demonstrate the ability to repay. That last criterion is a stumbling block for many new businesses and may be one for you unless you can show collateral or provide cosigners willing to share the risk. Once you have lined up a banker, keep that banker up-to-date on your business progress; meet with him or her on a regular basis to deliver monthly financial statements and ask advice about major decisions. If you make a friend of your banker, you'll go a long way toward making a success of your business!

Have You Got What It Takes?

"There is plenty of sweat, plenty of fear—and precious little glamour in their stories. These are roll-up-the-sleeves, get-the-job-done sort of people whose enterprise and capacity for toil should cheer those who fret about the demise of the American work ethic."

These are the words with which the *Wall Street Journal* began a special report on small business, describing the characteristics of American entrepreneurs. Those characteristics may surprise you, because they are often not the characteristics that lead to success in the corporate world. "As a group," the *Journal* notes, "the entrepreneurs were less distinguished students, more likely to have been expelled from school, and less likely to have been student leaders or fraternity members than big-business executives. They ran businesses at an earlier age—but have been fired more frequently and have jumped from job to job."

Before you buy a business, start a business from scratch, or purchase a franchise, take a good, hard look at yourself and see if you've got what it takes. You don't have to have dropped out of school or have been fired from several jobs, but you do have to have a degree of stubbornness, determination, and tenacity, along with sizable quantities of self-confidence if you are going to succeed in a venture of your own. You have to be willing to rely on your own resources and able to overcome obstacles in your path. You have to be willing to ignore the possibility of failure and to put up with long hours in the pursuit of your dream.

Scrutinize your own personality. Can you honestly say that you have the willingness and desire to work harder than you ever have before? Are you willing to sacrifice yourself and your family, at least in the early years, while you establish your new venture? Can you forgo the corporate structure and rely on your own abilities?

Are you considered the consummate politician in your present company? It might interest you to know that this is not the mark of an entrepreneur. Do you cover every base, study every move in depth, work out every detail in advance? Sorry, that is not the way successful self-employed people do it. If you are considered a corporate misfit, on the other hand, a troublemaker who won't play corporate politics but who fights instead for what you see as right, then you just might have what it takes.

If you do have what it takes, get moving. Stop daydreaming, stop your wishful thinking, and develop your plan of action. You, and only you, can make your dreams come true.

Suggested Further Reading

Allen, Jeffrey G. *The Perfect Follow-up Method to Win the Job.* New York: John Wiley & Sons, 1991.

Bloomberg, Gern, and Margaret Holden. *The Women's Job Search.* Charlotte, VA: Williamson Publishing, 1992.

Bolles, Richard. *What Color Is Your Parachute?* Berkeley, CA: Ten Speed Press, 1992.

Drake, John D. *The Perfect Interview.* New York: Amacom Books, 1990.

Fowler, Julianne. *How to Get the Job You Want in Tough Times.* Chicago, IL: Passport Books, 1991.

Halloran, James W. *The Entrepreneur's Guide to Starting a Successful Business.* New York: McGraw-Hill, 1992.

Hyatt, Carolyn. *Shifting Gears: How to Master Career Change and Find the Work That's Right for You.* New York: Simon & Schuster, 1990.

Jackson, Tom. *Not Just Another Job: How to Invent a Career That Works for You.* New York: Times Books, 1992.

Kaplan, Robbie Miller. *The Whole Career Sourcebook.* New York: Amacom, 1991.

Kiplinger Books (staff writers). *Take Charge of Your Career.* Washington, DC: Kiplinger Books, 1990.

Krannich, Robert. *Careering and Recareering.* Woodbridge, VA: Impact Publishing, 1991.

Lathrop, Richard. *Who's Hiring Who?* Berkeley, CA: Ten Speed Press, 1989.

Leeds, Dorothy. *Marketing Yourself.* New York: HarperCollins, 1991.

Lott, Catherine S. and Oscar C. *How to Land a Better Job.* Lincolnwood, IL: VGM Career Horizons, 1990.

Naisbitt, John, and Patricia Aburdene. *Megatrends 2000: Ten New Directions for the 1990s.* New York: Wm. Morrow & Co., 1990.

Snelling, Robert O. and Ann M. *Jobs: What They Are, Where They Are, What They Pay.* New York: Simon & Schuster/Fireside, 1992.

U.S. Department of Labor, Department of Labor Statistics. *Occupational Outlook Handbook.* Washington, DC: U.S. Government Printing Office, 1991–92.

Weinberg, Jane. *How to Win the Job You Really Want.* New York: Henry Holt & Co., 1989.

Yate, John Martin. *Knock 'em Dead with Great Answers to Tough Interview Questions.* Holbrook, MA: Bob Adams, 1991.

Yeager, Nell, and Lee Hough. *Power Interviews: Job Winning Tactics from Fortune 500 Recruiters.* New York: John Wiley & Sons, 1991.

Sources of Information

Administration

Administrative Managers
Administrative Management Society, 1101 14th Street N.W., Washington, DC 20005

Personnel and Human Resources Specialists
Society for Human Resources Management, 606 North Washington Street, Alexandria, VA 22314
International Personnel Management Association, 1617 Duke Street, Alexandria, VA 22314

Purchasing Agents
National Association of Purchasing Management, P.O. Box 22160, Tempe, AZ 85285

Secretaries and Stenographers
Professional Secretaries International, 301 East Armour Boulevard, Kansas City, MO 64111
National Association of Legal Secretaries, 2250 East 73rd Street, Tulsa, OK 74136

Telecommunications Specialists
National Telecommunications Association, 55 Broadway, New York, NY 10006

Training and Development Specialists
American Society for Training and Development, 1640 King Street, Alexandria, VA 22313
International Association for Personnel Women, 83 Salem Street, Andover, MA 01810

Typists and Word Processor Operators
Administrative Management Society, 1101 14th Street N.W., Washington, DC 20005

Advertising, Marketing, and Sales Promotion

Copy Writers and Account Executives
American Advertising Federation, 1400 K Street N.W., Washington, DC 20002
American Association of Advertising Agencies, 666 Third Avenue, New York, NY 10017

Graphic Designers
American Institute of Graphic Artists, 1059 Third Avenue, New York, NY 10021

Market Research Analysts
American Marketing Association, 250 South Wacker Drive, Chicago, IL 60606
Marketing Research Association, 111 East Wacker Drive, Chicago, IL 60601

Product Managers
American Advertising Federation, 1400 K Street N.W., Washington, DC 20005
American Marketing Association, 250 South Wacker Drive, Chicago, IL 60606

Architecture and Design

Architects
American Institute of Architects, 1735 New York Avenue N.W., Washington, DC 20006
American Institute of Certified Planners, 1776 Massachusetts Avenue N.W., Washington, DC 20036

Civil Engineers
American Society of Civil Engineers, 345 East 47th Street, New York, NY 10017

Industrial Engineers
Industrial Designers Society of America, 1142-E Walker Road, Glen Falls, VA 22066
Art Institute for Business Designers, Merchandise Mart Plaza, Chicago, IL 60654

Interior Designers
American Society of Interior Designers, 200 Lexington Avenue, New
  York, NY 10016

Communications and Media

Editors and Writers
The Dow Jones Newspaper Fund, P.O. Box 300, Princeton, NJ 08543
American Society of Magazine Editors, 575 Lexington Avenue, New
  York, NY 10022
American Society of Newspaper Editors, P.O. Box 17004, Washington,
  DC 20004

Journalists
American Newspaper Publishers Association Foundation, The News-
  paper Center, Box 17407, Dulles International Airport, Washington,
  DC 20041
The Newspaper Guild, 8611 Second Avenue, Silver Spring, MD 20910
American Society of Journalists and Authors, 1501 Broadway, New
  York, NY 10036
Inernational Association of Business Communicators, 1 Hallidie Plaza,
  San Francisco, CA 94102

Public Relations Specialists
Public Relations Society of America, 33 Irving Place, New York, NY
  10003
O'Dwyers Directory of Public Relations Firms, 271 Madison Avenue,
  New York, NY 10016

Technical Writers
Society for Technical Communications, 815 15th Street N.W., Washington, DC 20005

Television News Assistants, Announcers, and Reporters
National Association of Broadcasters, 1771 N Street N.W., Washington,
  DC 20036

Computers

Computer Engineers
Electronics Industries Association, 2001 I Street N.W., Washington, DC
  20006

Computer Operators
American Federation of Information Processing Societies, 1899 Preston White Drive, Reston, VA 22091

Computer Service Technicians
International Society of Certified Electronics Technicians, 2708 West Berry Street, Fort Worth, TX 76109
Electronic Technicians Association, 604 North Jackson Street, Greencastle, IN 46135

Programmers
Institute for the Certification of Computer Professionals, 2200 East Devon Avenue, Des Plaines, IL 60018

Systems Analysts
Association for Systems Management, 24587 Bagley Road, Cleveland OH 44138

Counseling

Employment Counsellors
National Association of Personnel Consultants, 3133 Mt. Vernon Avenue, Alexandria, VA 22305

Psychologists
American Psychological Association, Educational Affairs Office, 1200 17th Street N.W., Washington, DC 20036
National Board for Certified Counselors, 5999 Stevenson Avenue, Alexandria, VA 22304

Rehabilitation Counselors
National Council on Rehabilitation, Emporia State University, 1200 Commercial, VH-334, Emporia, KS 66801
American Rehabilitation Counseling Association, 633 South Washington Street, Alexandria, VA 22314

Social Workers
National Association of Social Workers, 7981 Eastern Avenue, Silver Spring, MD 20910

Education

Librarians
American Library Association, 50 East Huron Street, Chicago, IL 60611
American Society for Information Science, 8720 Georgia Avenue, Silver Spring, MD 20910

Teachers and Teacher Aides
National Education Association, 1201 16th Street N.W., Washington,
 DC 20063
American Federation of Teachers, 555 New Jersey Avenue N.W., Wash-
 ington, DC 20001

Engineering

Aerospace Engineers
American Institute of Aeronautics and Astronautics, The Aero Space
 Center, 370 L'Enfant Promenade S.W., Washington, DC 20024

Biomedical Engineers
Biomedical Engineering Society, P.O. Box 2399, Culver City, CA 90230

Ceramic Engineers
The American Ceramic Society, 757 Brooksedge Plaza Drive, Wester-
 ville, OH 43801

Chemical Engineers
American Institute of Chemical Engineers, 345 East 47th Street, New
 York, NY 10017
American Chemical Society, 1155 16th Street N.W., Washington, DC
 20036

Electrical and Electronic Engineers
Institute of Electrical and Electronic Engineers, 345 East 47th Street,
 New York, NY 10017
Electronic Industries Association, 2001 Pennsylvania Avenue, Wash-
 ington, DC 20006

Engineering Technicians
Electronic Technicians Association, 604 North Jackson Street, Greencastle, IN 46135

Industrial Engineers
American Institute of Industrial Engineers, 25 Technology Park, Nor-
 cross, GA 30092

Mechanical Engineers
The American Society of Mechanical Engineers, 345 East 47th Street,
 New York, NY 10017

Nuclear Engineers
American Nuclear Society, 555 North Kensington Avenue, La Grange
 Park, IL 60525
Junior Engineering Technical Society, 1420 King Street, Alexandria,
 VA 22314

Petroleum Engineers
Society of Petroleum Engineers, P.O. Box 833836, Richardson, TX 75083

Robotic Engineers
American Association of Artificial Intelligence, 445 Burgess Drive, Menlo Park, CA 94025

Finance

Accountants and Auditors
American Institute of Certified Public Accountants, 1211 Avenue of the Americas, New York, NY 10036
National Association of Accountants, P.O. Box 433, 10 Paragon Drive, Montvale, NJ 07645

Bank Clerks and Tellers
National Bankers Association, 122 C Street N.W., Washington, DC 20001

Bank Officers
American Bankers Association, Bank Personnel Division, 1120 Connecticut Avenue N.W., Washington, DC 20036
National Association of Bank Women, 500 North Michigan Avenue, Chicago, IL 60611

Economists
National Association of Business Economists, 28349 Chagrin Boulevard, Cleveland, OH 44122
American Economic Association, 2014 Broadway, Nashville, TN 37203

Financial Analysts
Finance Executives Institute, 10 Madison Avenue, Morristown, NJ 07960

Securities Brokers
Securities Industry Association, 120 Broadway, New York, NY 10271

Health Care Specialists

Dental Assistants and Hygienists
American Dental Assistants Association, 919 N. Michigan Avenue, Chicago, IL 60611
American Dental Hygienists Association, 444 North Michigan Avenue, Chicago, IL 60611

Dietitians

The American Dietetic Association, 216 West Jackson Boulevard, Chicago, IL 60606

Medical Office Assistants

American Association of Medical Assistants, 20 North Wacker Drive, Chicago, IL 60606

Medical Records Administrators

American Medical Records Association, John Hancock Center, 875 North Michigan Avenue, Chicago, IL 60611

Nurses

National League for Nursing, Career Information Services, 350 Hudson Street, New York, NY 10014

National Federation of Licensed Practical Nurses, P.O. Box 18088, Raleigh, NC 27619

American Nurses Association, 2420 Pershing Road, Kansas City, MO 64108

Occupational Therapists

American Occupational Therapy Association, 1833 Piccard Drive, Bethesda, MD 20850

Pharmacists

American Council on Pharmaceutical Education, 311 W. Superior, Chicago, IL 60610

American Society for Pharmacology, 9650 Rockville Pike, Bethesda, MD 20814

Physical Therapists

American Physical Therapy Association, 1111 North Fairfax Street, Alexandria, VA 22314

Physician Assistants

American Academy of Physicians Assistants, 950 N. Washington Street, Alexandria, VA 22314

Speech Pathologists and Audiologists

American Speech-Language-Hearing Association, 10801 Rockville Pike, Rockville, MD 20852

Health Technology

Biomedical Equipment Technicians

Association for the Advancement of Medical Instrumentation, Washington Boulevard, Arlington, VA 22201

Dental Laboratory Technicians
National Association of Dental Laboratories, 3801 Mount Vernon Avenue, Alexandria, VA 22305

Diagnostic Medical Sonographers
Society of Diagnostic Medical Sonographers, 12225 Greenville Street, Dallas, TX 75231

Electrocardiograph Technicians
National Society for Cardiovascular Technology, 1101 14th Street N.W., Washington, DC 20005

Medical Laboratory Technicians
American Society for Medical Technology, 2021 L Street N.W., Washington, DC 20036

Surgical Technologists
Association of Surgical Technologists, 8307 Shaffer Parkway, Littleton, CO 80127

X-Ray Technologists
American Society of Radiologic Technologists, 15000 Central Avenue S.E., Albuquerque, NM 87123

Insurance

Actuaries
American Society of Pension Actuaries, 2029 K Street N.W., Washington, DC 20006
American Academy of Actuaries, 1720 I Street N.W., Washington, DC 20006

Claims Adjusters
National Association of Public Adjusters, 300 Water Street, Baltimore, MD 21202

Underwriters
American Council of Life Insurance, 1001 Pennsylvania Avenue N.W., Washington, DC 20004
Insurance Information Institute, 110 William Street, New York, NY 10038

Law

Attorneys
American Bar Association, 750 North Lake Shore Drive, Chicago, IL 60611

National Association for Law Placement, 1666 Connecticut Avenue N.W., Washington, DC 20001

Paralegal Assistants
National Association of Legal Assistants, 1601 South Main Street, Tulsa, OK 74119

National Paralegal Association, P.O. Box 406, Solebury, PA 18963

Shorthand Reporters
National Shorthand Reporters Association, 118 Park Street S.E., Vienna, VA 22180

Retailing

Buyers
National Retail Merchants Association, 100 West 31st Street, New York, NY 10001

Merchandisers
National Retail Federation, 100 West 31st Street, New York, NY 10001

Sales

Advertising Sales Representatives
Television Bureau of Advertising, 477 Madison Avenue, New York, 10022

Newspaper Advertising Bureau, 1180 Avenue of the Americas, New York, NY 10036

General Sales Representatives
Sales and Marketing Executives International, Statler Office Tower, Cleveland, OH 44115

Insurance Agents and Brokers
National Association of Life Underwriters, 1922 F Street N.W., Washington, DC 20006

National Association of Professional Insurance Agents, 400 North Washington Street, Alexandria, VA 22314

Real Estate Agents and Brokers
National Association of Realtors, 430 North Michigan Avenue, Chicago, IL 60611

Retail Salespeople
National Retail Federation, 100 West 31st Street, New York, NY 10001

Sales Managers
Sales and Marketing Executives International, Statler Office Tower, Cleveland, OH 44115

Science and Technology

Chemists
American Chemical Society, 1155 16th Street N.W., Washington, DC 20036

Geologists
American Geological Institute, 4220 King Street, Alexandria, VA 22302

Meteorologists
American Meteorological Society, 45 Beacon Street, Boston, MA 02108
National Weather Service, Personnel, 1-RAS/DC 23, Rockville, MD 20782

Microbiologists
American Society for Microbiology, 1325 Massachusetts Avenue N.W., Washington, DC 20005

Physicists
American Institute of Physics, 335 East 45th Street, New York, NY 10017

Travel and Tourism

Airline Ticket Agents and Reservationists
Airline Employees Association, 5600 South Central Avenue, Chicago, IL 60638
Air Transport Association of America, 1709 New York Avenue N.W., Washington, DC 20006

Flight Attendants
Air Transport Association of America, 1709 New York Avenue N.W., Washington, DC 20006
Future Aviation Professionals of America, 4959 Massachusetts Boulevard, Atlanta, GA 30337

Hotel and Motel Managers and Assistants
American Hotel and Motel Association, 1201 New York Avenue, Washington, DC 20005

Travel Agents
American Society of Travel Agents, 1101 King Street, Alexandria, VA 22314

Index

accountants, 31
achievement-oriented people, 205
action words, 104, 108–11
adaptive skills, 64
ads, job, 79–82, 86–87, 90–93, 96–97
alcohol, 203
American Academy of Achievement, 47
appearance, personal, 165–67
Apple Computer, 14, 81
applications, employment, 140, 144–46, 168–69
aptitude tests, 64–65
attitude, 58–59
automation, 3–5

benefits, fringe, 158, 185, 186, 188, 189
Better Business Bureau, 136, 137, 217
"bit-company burial grounds," 13–14
Bill of Rights, 12
blind ads, 86–87
"blockers," 117
body language, 141, 170
bosses, 194–95, 197, 198, 199, 200, 201
brainstorming, 45
business brokers, 216–17
businesses:
    franchise, 14, 15, 217–220
    purchase of, 214–16
    small, 14, 15, 211
    U.S. Bureau of Economic Analysis, 209

capital
    acquisition of, 213, 220–22

start-up, 213, 220–222
careers:
    decisions on, 3, 43–44, 52–53
    goals for, 15–17, 144, 174–75
cash-flow projections, 213
Cetron, Marvin, 5–6
checkups, physical, 60–61
child-care, 19, 179
Chrysler Corporation, 13
clerical supervisors, 1
Coca-Cola, 31
college placement offices, 158
community activities, 68, 69
computer maintenance and repair, 20, 85
computer-matching firms, 160
computer programmers, 2, 16
Conference Board, 57
cost-of-living raises, 201
cover letters, 87, 88, 122, 130–33
credit, financial, 220–22

Dawkins, Peter M., 34, 46
decision making, 43–44
Dictionary of Occupational Titles, 8
diet, 59–61
direct-mail campaigns, 87–89
directories, business, 87–89, 162
Directory of Directories, 89
discrimination, 10, 18–19
divorce rate, 18
Dun and Bradstreet, 4–5
Dun's Million Dollar Directory, 89

education, 6, 10, 66–67, 102, 103, 106–
107, 178
Employee Leasing Firms (ELCs), 158
employment history, 102, 107
employment services, 82, 86, 105, 134–
160
  advances required by, 152–53
  application forms for, 140, 143, 145
  charges for, 134, 145, 149, 151–52
  code of ethics for, 144
  commission-basis of, 151
  competition among, 144
  contracts of, 149, 150, 152–53
  employers charged by, 151–52
  employment counselors in, 32, 60, 67,
    85, 142, 150
  evaluations by, 138, 144–45
  interviews by, 135–36, 137, 140–43
  jobs filled and found by, 135–36
  partial payment to, 152
  professional, 135–54
  pros and cons of, 150–51
  referrals by, 145, 146–47
  refunds guaranteed by, 149–50, 152,
    153–54
  reputation of, 150
  research by, 162–63
  retainment of, 148
  selection of, 144–54
  services provided by, 136–38, 144–45
  types of, 134–36, 145, 146, 154–60
  use of, 134–60
entrepreneurs, 6, 209, 212, 222, 223
equity access loans, 220–21
Evans, Max, 165
executive counseling firms, 168
executives, 30–32
executive search firms, 154
experience, work, 9, 10, 102–3, 106–8,
  116–17

Fader, Shirley Sloan, 163
family history, 103
family relationships, 41–45, 52, 54–55
Fayva, 162
Figler, Howard, 67–68
financial industries, 6
Ford Motor Company, 13
Fortune, 81
Franchise Opportunities Handbook, 219
franchises, 217–20

Entrepreneur magazine, 219
Franklin, Benjamin, 185

Garfield, Charles, 49
goals:
  career, 16, 144
  personal, 29–30, 32, 197–98
Goodrich & Sherwood Co., 41
government jobs, 82

"happiness quotient," 202–4
headhunters, 164–65
health, 59–61, 202–4
Heller-Roper Small Business Barometer,
  15
Hope College Career Center, 104, 170–
  171
Houseman, John, 35
Huntsman, Jon M., 50, 51

Iacocca, Lee, 13–14
IBM, 43
inflation, 201
interests, personal, 62–63
International Franchising Association,
  219
interpersonal skills, 52, 61–62
interviews, 61–62, 71–72, 161–85
  appointments for, 168–69
  asking for job in, 181–82
  background research for, 162–64
  body language in, 170
  "clinches" for, 190–91
  communication in, 169–71
  dos and don'ts of, 171
  dressing for, 165–67
  by employment services, 136–38, 140–
    143
  follow-up of, 148, 182–84
  honesty in, 179–80
  lunch, 181
  multiple, 180–81
  objections encountered in, 176–79
  practice for, 164–65
  pre-, 89–92
  preparation for, 92, 161–68
  procedure for, 168–82
  questions asked in, 164, 165, 169–76
  role-playing in, 147
  scheduling of, 89–92
  second, 182–83
  strategies for, 161–85

successful, 185–87
take-alongs for, 167–68
team, 180–81
telephone as tool for, 89–92, 138–40
testing and, 179–80
unsuccessful, 184–85
Ivester, Douglas, 31

James, William, 70
job hunting:
expense of, 92, 98
myths about, 3–12
personal plan for, 76–77
preparation for, 49–70, 72–74
research and, 68, 87, 88, 162–64
sequence for, 76–77
strategies for, 30, 71–99, 148
telephone as tool in, 89
times for, 77–78
job-listing firms, 160
job market:
competition in, 3–4, 77–78
dynamics of, 1–28
employer needs and, 12–15
expectations of, 11–12
hidden, 84–85
opportunities in, 1–12
reentry into, 3
women in, 17–20
job outlook:
bright future, 207
science and technology, 207
services, 5
U.S. Bureau of Labor Statistics, 205
jobs:
ads for, 79–82, 86–87, 90–93
age and, 177
categories of, 2, 6–7, 87
change of, 23–25, 55–56, 142–43
creation of, 12–13, 85–86, 135–36
entry-level, 4–5
facts about, 185–87
high-pressure, 29, 30–32
part-time, 75–76
qualifications for, 177
quitting of, 55–56, 75
security of, 204–5
simultaneous offers for, 71–72
temporary, 156–57

leasing firms, 158
letters, postinterview, 183–84

libraries, 67, 68, 86–87, 162–63
lie detector tests, 179–80
living standards, 4–5, 18–20
loans, 220–22

Magowan, Peter A., 53–54
Managerial Woman, The, 6
managers, 41, 53–54
Mary Kay Cosmetics, 4
mental preparation, 53–54, 56–58
military service, 102
motivation, 45–48

negotiating skills, 202
Networking, 83–84
newspaper ads, 79–81

office politics, 195–96
outplacement firms, 160
overqualified applicants, 177
overtime, 202

"people, data, and things" test, 37–38
people principle, 170
performance, job, 192–94
reviews of, 195–98
perks, 202
physical preparation, 59–61
pigeonholing, 16
"Plan for All Seasons, A" (Huntsman), 50
population growth, 4–5
Porter, Rufus, 73
positive thinking, 49
potential, personal, 69–70
"power players," 193, 194
productivity, 34, 38, 197, 200, 201, 203
Professional Employment Counsellors,
19, 32, 60, 67, 85, 138–40, 144, 145,
146, 149, 150
promotions, 195–201

raises, 33, 35, 195–96, 201–2
Reader's Digest, 47
reading, 68
recruitment firms, 154–55
references, 117
religious placement services, 159
relocation, 11, 15–17, 42–43, 55–56,
113, 136–38, 175–76, 187
résumés, 52, 71, 92
accomplishments listed in, 115
addresses on, 104–5, 116, 120

résumés (*cont.*)
  chronological vs. functional, 107–8, 114–15
  color of, 118
  comprehensive, 101, 164, 167
  contents of, 101–117
  counseling and writing services for, 119
  cover letters for, 86–87, 122, 130–33
  data for, 102–3, 114–15
  emphasis in, 116–17
  extraneous material in, 106
  grammar in, 104
  introductory, 101, 168–69
  key words for, 108–11
  length of, 101, 114–21
  names on, 104
  objectives stated in, 104–6, 120
  organizations listed in, 111
  paper for, 117, 124
  personal information in, 112–13
  photographs for, 118
  preparation of, 103–22
  quality of, 124
  samples of, 121–30
  "seven deadly sins" of, 114–17
  special information in, 111
  spelling in, 124
  style of, 103–4, 108, 117–19
  type for, 103
  writing of, 100–33

salaries, 3, 13, 20–21, 34–35, 113–14, 176
  negotiations of, 176, 186, 187–89
  reviews of, 194–95, 201–2
  of women, 18–20
sales managers, 6, 86, 189
Scientific American, 73
Sears, Richard W., 81
self-confidence, 59, 67
self-descriptive words, 104
self-employment, 223
self-evaluation, 190
self-tests, 36–37
Simon, Julian L., 4
Simon, Sidney, 36
skills:
  evaluation of, 49, 201
  types of, 63, 64, 65

Small Business Administration, 14, 218, 219
small businesses, 4, 5, 14, 15, 209, 211, 218–19
smokestack industries, 4
smoking, 203–4
Snelling, 9, 11, 32, 58, 71, 85, 134, 135, 136, 182, 197, 218
Standard and Poor's, 88
state employment services, 160
stenographers, 2

Taber, Carol, 6
tax breaks, 67, 98, 150
T-charts, 185
telephone:
  in interviews, 90–93, 138, 139
  in job hunting, 89, 92–93
telephone operators, 2, 7
temporary help firms, 156, 157
Thomas' Register, 89
travel, 42, 46, 92
Treacher, Arthur, 29–30
tuition reimbursement programs, 67
typists, 2

unemployment, 75
unemployment rate, 2, 5

value, personal, 198–99
"Values Journal," 36

The Wall Street Journal, 31, 42, 80, 222
Ward's Business Directory of U.S. Public and Private Companies, 89
"water-cooler cool cats," 193
Watson, Thomas J., Jr., 166
Welch, Mary Scott, 84
women:
  discrimination against, 10, 19
  in job market, 17–20
  occupations of, 18, 19
  older, 10
  proper attire for, 166
  salaries of, 18, 19
  training of, 67
work content skills, 64
Working Woman, 6
Workmen's Compensation, 188

FOR THE BEST IN PAPERBACKS, LOOK FOR THE

In every corner of the world, on every subject under the sun, Penguin represents quality and variety—the very best in publishing today.

For complete information about books available from Penguin—including Pelicans, Puffins, Peregrines, and Penguin Classics—and how to order them, write to us at the appropriate address below. Please note that for copyright reasons the selection of books varies from country to country.

In the United Kingdom: For a complete list of books available from Penguin in the U.K., please write to *Dept E.P., Penguin Books Ltd, Harmondsworth, Middlesex, UB7 0DA.*

In the United States: For a complete list of books available from Penguin in the U.S., please write to *Dept BA, Penguin*, Box 120, Bergenfield, New Jersey 07621-0120.

In Canada: For a complete list of books available from Penguin in Canada, please write to *Penguin Books Canada Ltd, 10 Alcorn Avenue, Suite 300, Toronto, Ontario, Canada M4V 3B2.*

In Australia: For a complete list of books available from Penguin in Australia, please write to the *Marketing Department, Penguin Books Ltd, P.O. Box 257, Ringwood, Victoria 3134.*

In New Zealand: For a complete list of books available from Penguin in New Zealand, please write to the *Marketing Department, Penguin Books (NZ) Ltd, Private Bag, Takapuna, Auckland 9.*

In India: For a complete list of books available from Penguin, please write to *Penguin Overseas Ltd, 706 Eros Apartments, 56 Nehru Place, New Delhi, 110019.*

In Holland: For a complete list of books available from Penguin in Holland, please write to *Penguin Books Nederland B.V., Postbus 195, NL-1380AD Weesp, Netherlands.*

In Germany: For a complete list of books available from Penguin, please write to *Penguin Books Ltd, Friedrichstrasse 10-12, D-6000 Frankfurt Main 1, Federal Republic of Germany.*

In Spain: For a complete list of books available from Penguin in Spain, please write to *Longman, Penguin España, Calle San Nicolas 15, E-28013 Madrid, Spain.*

In Japan: For a complete list of books available from Penguin in Japan, please write to *Longman Penguin Japan Co Ltd, Yamaguchi Building, 2-12-9 Kanda Jimbocho, Chiyoda-Ku, Tokyo 101, Japan.*